Current Topics in Early Childhood Education

Childhood Education

Volume V

Current Topics in Early Childhood Education

Volume V

Editor
LILIAN G. KATZ

Associate Editors
Paula J. Wagemaker and Karen Steiner

ERIC *Clearinghouse on Elementary and Early Childhood Education,
University of Illinois at Urbana-Champaign*

ABLEX PUBLISHING CORPORATION
Norwood, New Jersey 07648

Printed in the United States of America

This publication was prepared with funding from the National Institute of Education, U.S. Department of Education, under contract number 400-78-0008. Contractors undertaking such projects under government sponsorship are encouraged to express freely their judgment in professional and technical matters. The opinions expressed in this volume do not necessarily reflect the positions or policies of NIE or the Department of Education.

ISBN 0-89391-248-4(C)
ISBN 0-89391-249-2(P)   ISSN 0363-8332

Ablex Publishing Corporation
355 Chestnut Street
Norwood, New Jersey 07648

Contents

Preface

Each of the chapters included in this fifth volume of *Current Topics in Early Childhood Education* addresses an issue of concern to those who work with young children, their families and caregivers, as well as to those involved in related policy making and implementation. The topics addressed in this volume fall into three broad groups.

The first four chapters are addressed to current and emerging topics related to curriculum and teaching strategies. Almy and her colleagues examine the most recent evidence concerning the educative functions of play and suggest some ways that teachers can assist others in understanding this important subject. Fischer and his coauthors synthesize a rich body of recent literature on social role acquisition and social cognition, both of which are areas of rapid learning during the preschool period. Evans, writing about the development of aesthetic sensibilities and reporting on the implications of methodological problems involved in research about aesthetics, reminds us to consider a topic frequently overlooked in the hurly-burly of everyday life with children. Spencer and Baskin present a review of recent research concerning a new curriculum topic in the field: the uses of computers in early and elementary education settings.

The next three chapters address a range of issues concerning the lives of children outside the early childhood educational setting. Powell presents an analysis of the assumptions underlying parent education programs, describing some relationships between these assumptions and speculating on their effects on programs. Long and Long synthesize available research findings concerning the increasing number of children left alone to care for themselves or for their siblings. The effects of this self-care arrangement, popularly called "latchkey," are not simple, these authors argue. They also suggest a number of alternative courses of action parents and community agencies might consider to help families cope with problems of after-school care and the supervision of young children. Finally, Friedman's chapter provides a review of what is now known about the operation and problems of employer-supported child care, discussing the relationship of such care to the needs of employed parents.

Each of the volume's last two chapters takes up issues with indirect, though considerable, effects on children. Goodnow and Burns recount the vicissitudes of influencing governmental bodies to act for the benefit of children, specifically describing internal dissention within the field of early childhood education and care within Australia, as well as detailing relationships between social issues and specific program policies shared by many other countries. In the last chapter, Katz reviews some current concerns in the preparation and training of teachers and caregivers who work with young children, indicating some recent insights into these issues.

Thus, some of the topics included here are of perennial interest and are likely to be readdressed in future volumes in the *Current Topics* series. Others reflect concerns that are clearly new; only time will tell whether these subjects will become of permanent concern to those involved in the development and education of young children. Whether the topics are traditional or new, permanent or fleeting, we hope that readers will find these chapters helpful and stimulating, and that interest in the series will continue to be reflected in suggestions for future volumes.

Lilian G. Katz, Ph.D.
*Director, ERIC Clearinghouse on Elementary
and Early Childhood Education*

1

Recent Research on Play: The Teacher's Perspective

Millie Almy, Patricia Monighan, Barbara Scales, and Judith Van Hoorn

University of California, Berkeley

Teachers of 2- to 6-year-olds must often justify the curriculum they provide. As critics express concern about low levels of academic achievement in elementary and secondary schools, questions trickle down to programs in kindergartens, preschools, and day care centers. One of the most persistent questions has to do with play. How can the generation that will come of age in the twenty-first century cope with its problems if they spend too much time "just playing," rather than acquiring basic skills?

Current scepticism about play is not new. It originated in the Puritan ethic that dichotomized work and play. While play is no longer seen as sinful, neither is it believed to be very worthwhile. The definition of play, and not merely the belief that play is not worthwhile, involves reference to certain intangibles—a fact that goes against the grain of the behaviorist tradition that has dominated education and psychology. Only recently has play become an area of interest to many researchers. For example, in 1970, *Carmichael's Manual of Child Psychology* (Mussen, 1970), a reference work widely used by researchers, had no chapter on play. Mention of play, doll play, playfulness, and games was limited to two dozen of its 2400 pages. In contrast, the 4th edition of the manual (Mussen & Heatherington, 1983) includes a chapter on play with some 450 references, about 60% of them referring to work completed since 1970. A dozen or more books, intended for the general reader as well as the researcher, have also appeared.

The beleaguered teacher who studies this literature will find few certain answers and may have some fond assumptions challenged. While teachers share researchers' concerns for the effect of play on the child's development, their perspectives differ. The evidence that teachers observe bears little resemblance to the data that most researchers collect. Teachers, when planning for or reflecting on children's play, may differentiate social from cognitive behavior, or constructive play from dramatic play, or focus on an individual child to the exclusion of the other children in the group. More typically, however, their focus is on the "whole child" and on that child as a member of a group. Nevertheless, teachers are in a strategic position to see how the play of both individuals and groups relates to their "non-play" and how it changes over time. We think that teachers have important information and insight to offer researchers, while research can broaden teachers' understanding of play.

Teachers have a different perspective on certain theoretical issues than researchers. They have questions that they would like the researchers to address. They also have a unique opportunity and responsibility for answering their own questions about how children play. In doing so, they will more effectively support the play and the learning of the children in their groups and perhaps contribute to the growing body of knowledge about play.

In the material that follows, we briefly review the theories that inform recent research and discuss the features of play as seen by researchers. This is followed by a description of the development of play and some of the issues teachers need to consider as they assess the play of the children in their groups. A related issue is the consideration of individual differences in play. We then examine the ways teachers may facilitate children's play. Finally, we consider the teacher's role in explaining to parents and administrators the importance of play for the developing child.

THEORIES OF PLAY

Since the days of Froebel (1898), most teachers have seen play as an essential ingredient in the early childhood curriculum. Teachers' ideas about the nature of that ingredient, its long-term importance, and their own responsibility for it have varied considerably depending on the theories or ideologies that they follow. Play often represents those aspects of the curriculum that enable children to follow their own inclinations, as opposed to those aspects involving instruction or routines. Ideas about what play does for children may reflect theories that are now regarded as classic. Thus, the notion that "play gives the active child an acceptable outlet" comes from the "surplus energy theory," while the concept that you should "balance the academics with active play" reflects "recreation theory." "They learn through their play" represents "practice theory." "Play reflects the culture" has its roots in "recapitulation theory."

A more direct influence on teachers' thinking about play probably originates in twentieth-century theories associated with psychoanalysis

(Erikson, 1950; A. Freud, 1964; Isaacs, 1930, 1966). The guiding ideas here may be "children work out emotional conflicts in play" and "in play, children develop mastery." (Piaget (1962) also contributed to current ideas of play. These may include "play is involved in cognitive development," "play develops in stages," and possibly, "play is assimilative and serves to incorporate or consolidate the child's experience."

The views of several other theorists have begun to appear in the literature of early childhood. Bruner (1972, 1976) sees play as "serious business," an important factor in evolution and development. Lieberman (1977) describes "playfulness" as a personality trait, a component of imagination and creativity. Singer (1973) finds in make-believe play a process which "if it is gently fostered as a human skill can make life infinitely richer and more exciting" (p. 259). Sutton-Smith (1971a, b, 1979), who has served as a synthesizer of psychological and anthropological approaches to play, also describes play as "performance." Vygotsky (1967) sees play as an aspect of the preschool child's living in which he or she advances beyond the ordinary accomplishments of the age period and anticipates development in thinking that will only become characteristic later on. As Vygotsky puts it, in play the preschool child is "always above his average age, above his daily behavior." Accordingly, "play creates the zone of proximal development of the child" (p. 16).

The views of the anthropologist Gregory Bateson influenced other theorists and researchers. Bateson (cited in Schwartzman, 1978, p. 219) in addition to examining the significance of the message "this is play," shows how the child in play learns that "there is such a thing as a role" and also that "the choice of style or role is related to the frame and context of behavior." Following these lines, Schwartzman (1978) examines play as communication.

In general, the theories that are available are not comprehensive but consider only selected elements in the play of young children. None of them, with the possible early exception of Isaacs (1930, 1966), addresses the issue of play in the education of young children. However, some authors (Biber & Franklin, 1967; Forman & Hill, 1980; Kamii & DeVries, 1980) have recently attempted to provide bridges from selected theories to practice in the classroom.

THE DISTINGUISHING FEATURES OF PLAY

The available theories are in considerable agreement about certain features that distinguish play from other behaviors (Rubin, Fein, & Vandenberg, 1983). These agreements in definition enable researchers to compare results from study to study. Teachers, although their purposes differ from those of the researcher, also need to agree on the nature of play. They may consider whether knowledge of the following features can help them to clarify what is going on when, for example, they watch a child intently making her way through an obstacle course, or see another child laughing as he assembles a collage.

Intrinsic Motivation

This feature cannot be directly observed but may only be inferred. The child's interest in an activity may reveal itself in expressions of happiness or pleasure, but it may also be reflected in a serious demeanor and insistence on continuing. While intrinsic motivation is clear in a self-initiated activity such as pretending to be Wonder Woman, it may also arise in the desire to continue an activity that may have been initiated by the teacher, such as a lotto game or a construction project.

Activities that intrinsically motivate are likely to be those that permit the child to resolve discrepancies between the novel and the familiar (Berlyne, 1960; Bruner, 1972; White, 1959). Not only play with objects (Forman & Hill, 1980) but also pretense play (Vygotsky, 1967), such as that occurring when a child plays with baby dolls following the birth of a sibling, provide examples of motivation for play precipitated by novel experiences.

Attention to Means and Not Ends

Although intrinsic motivation is an essential feature of play, it alone is not sufficient to mark an activity as play. According to Piaget (1962), in play, "assimilation," the incorporation of new information into existing mental structures (concepts or beliefs), takes precedence over "accommodation," the modification of those structures to fit the demands of the environment. In play, children are less concerned with a particular goal than they are with various means of reaching it. Since the goals are self-imposed, they too may vary as the play proceeds. The child who knows how to solve a puzzle stacks the pieces in new arrangements or uses them as props in pretense play. For example, Martin, while involved in house play, rubbed a toy iron over the top of a plastic cauliflower, saying, "I need to iron mine to bake it." After carefully running the iron over all the surfaces of the cauliflower, he returned to what appeared to have been the original goal. He said, "OK, we can eat now."

Trying out patterns of action and thought previously acquired and combining them in new ways within a play situation appears to contribute flexibility to the child's thinking and problem solving (Dansky & Silverman, 1973, 1975; Smith & Dutton, 1979; Sutton-Smith, 1968; Vandenberg, 1980). The new combinations may be accompanied by a sense of discovery and exhilaration. Miller (1973) borrows the term "galumphing" from Lewis Carrol's poem, "Jabberwacky" to describe this feature of children's play. The child who becomes an airplane while enroute to a destination is "galumphing'' as was the child who ironed the cauliflower. ''Galumphing'' with ideas lacks the smoothness and efficiency that characterizes enjoyable work or goal specific activity, but it is experimentation that may enhance creative thinking. ''Galumphing'' is a feature that is lacking from curricula that are programmed to have the child arrive at only ''correct'' responses.

Nonliteral Behavior

This feature, limited to pretense play, begins as early as the first year of life (Fein, 1981) and is a predominant feature of preschool play. For example, Danny, playing in the sandbox, made ''cream of mosquito'' soup. He added small pebbles to several scoops of sand, saying that the rocks were mosquitoes. After he ''cooked'' the soup, he gave several children pebbles to use as ''money'' to buy the soup he was selling. The child's ability to transfer objects and situations to ''as if'' frames of reference enables him or her to transcend physical reality.

The exercise of ''make-believe'' is thought to contribute to the child's later skill with hypothetical reasoning (Fagen, 1976) and abstract symbols (Fein, 1981; Pellegrini, 1980) and to the understanding of logical transformations (Golumb & Cornelius, 1977; Saltz, Dixon, & Johnson, 1977).

Freedom From External Rules

This feature is often cited to differentiate play from games with rules, but it presents somewhat of a paradox. Although there are no *externally* imposed rules in the play of preschool children, play has implicit rules in at least two senses. In the first place, as Vygotsky (1967) shows in describing sisters who play at being sisters, the imaginary situation already contains rules of behavior. A more recent illustration comes from our observation of a group of children playing veterinarian. The behaviors of the girl playing the role of veterinarian and of the boy playing a German Shepherd dog with a wounded paw revealed their understanding of the rules pertaining to the doctor/patient relationship.

Second, observational studies viewing children's play as communication (Garvey, 1977; Schwartzman, 1978) have revealed the rules that children generate as they try to enter the play situation and establish and pursue a plot and their roles in it. An example that we observed showed how negotiation through understanding of the rules occurs. Two boys wanted to play the role of father. The first boy said: ''I'm the father.'' The second boy countered: ''No, I am.'' The first retorted: ''I want to be the father.'' The second submitted, saying: ''OK, you could be the father and I'll be the grandfather. Then we can both be fathers.''

Following ''rules'' and taking roles in play is a pleasurable, intrinsically motivated experience for the child; in it children learn to understand not only their own roles and the rules that define them, but also the roles and rules of others. Coordinating several roles in a dramatic theme may prepare the child to engage in simple games with collective rules as he or she approaches the primary grades. Such behavior engages children in a beginning understanding of the rules and roles of society at large (Mead, 1934).

Self Rather Than Object

Just as the teacher needs to be sensitive to the child's use and understanding of play rules and roles, it is important to distinguish between child's play and exploration. In exploration, the child confronts an object that has not previously been in the foreground of attention. Exploration of an object is guided by the question, "What is this object and what can it do?" In play, the question is self-referenced, "What can I do with this object?" and the answer is, "Anything I wish" (Hutt, 1971; Weisler & McCall, 1976). Exploration, in Piaget's terms, is accommodative, and play is assimilative. The distinction is an important one not only in assessing the child's behavior but also in planning curricula. For the teacher, the question is, "What is the appropriate balance between experiences that encourage exploration and those that encourage playing?"

Traditional elementary education appears to have relied heavily on accommodation (mainly of a verbal sort), making minimal provision for the children to play with the concepts they were acquiring. In contrast, traditional early childhood education, as represented in, for example, the early English nursery school directed by Susan Isaacs or the Bank Street nursery school, provided for both exploration and play. More recently, some preschools have seemed overcommitted to novelty (in the form of a new activity or new materials nearly every day), without allowing much time for either spontaneous exploration or play. Other preschools remain committed to play but make little provision for the novel or its exploration. There is some evidence (Hutt, 1971) that play with an object before it has been fully explored may limit the child's discovery of its specific properties. For example, the teachers in one center noted that the children never used certain hand puppets except in the way that the teachers had prescribed when the puppets were new. They noted a similar lack of exploration of the properties and possibilities of a roll-away game that had been introduced with specific instructions as to how the game was to be played. The balance of exploration and play, or the novel and the familiar, may be an important issue for early childhood education.

Active Engagement

The zest that preschool children bring to their play is evident in their overt action and verbalization and in their unwillingness to be distracted. As children grow older, and play becomes interiorized in daydreaming, the engagement of the child's attention is not as readily identified by the adult observer.

The question of how actively preschool children are attending to their play is an important issue for their teachers. The teacher, surveying the classroom and its activities, needs to ask how many children are deeply involved in their play and how many are engaged in desultory activities that may reflect little more than boredom. Children, like adults, have "low" days. However, the intellectual withdrawal of too many children on too many days should be cause for teacher concern.

This brief sketch of current theories of play and the aspects on which they appear to agree can only suggest the wealth of material that has potential implications for the teacher's study of play. If our description of the features of play enables the teacher to distinguish more surely when children are at play and when they are not, it still provides less than the teacher needs to know when setting expectations for children's play.

THE DEVELOPMENT OF PLAY

Teachers have long recognized that the play of 2-year-olds differs from that of 3-year-olds, and that they in turn play differently from 4-, 5-. and 6-year-olds. A 2-year-old sets the table in the playhouse with toy plates and silverware and plastic food. These actions indicate that he or she is copying what has been seen in reality. A 3-year-old in the same situation shows less concern for the realistic nature of the props. A block serves for a cup and a leggo becomes the bottle for the doll in his lap. He or she talks with the "baby," producing crying noises or demands in a high-pitched voice.

Four- or 5-year-olds can imagine the dishes and silverware, and can take the roles of family members and weave a plot around them. A telephone call from Grandma at the bus station is readily incorporated into the household activities. For these older children, the focus is on the drama played out among the roles in the context of the playhouse. Reality is extended and elaborated rather than reproduced directly. Plots often carry over from one day to the next and may be elaborated and extended over months.

Researchers, studying the play of children systematically, have made fine-grained analyses of the increasing social and cognitive complexity of children's play in the years before age 6. Early studies were mainly descriptive, but recent research has more often been guided by theory. Drawing particularly on the ideas of Piaget and Vygotsky, researchers have studied infants and toddlers to see when and how pretense play begins (Fein, 1981). A substantial number of studies have been conducted in preschools and day care centers (Rubin, et al., 1983). Some have looked at the cognitive aspects of children's play, some at the social aspects. Others have attempted to combine the social and cognitive elements. A fourth focus has been on children's communication during their play.

In this section we present some of the findings from this research. These findings may assist teachers in assessing the play of children in groups and in setting expectations for the development of play as children grow older. The section is organized around the sequence of development of play described by Piaget (1962).

The bulk of the available research relates to dramatic play. It covers only sketchily sensorimotor play, constructive play, and games with rules during the years from 2 to 6. Much, if not most, of the research has been conducted in middle-class settings and may not apply universally. The studies of early pretense play extend below the ages of major concern in this article, but we have included some reference to them since the teacher of older children may find some children whose play has not yet moved beyond the sensorimotor period.

According to the theory of Piaget, the play of the infant progresses from sensorimotor activity to pretense or symbolic play at around 15 to 18 months. Symbolic play predominates throughout the period under consideration here until around the age of 6 or 7 years, when games with rules begin to assume greater importance. Within this framework several kinds of play can be considered.

Sensorimotor Play

Sensorimotor play, sometimes labelled "practice play" or "functional play," begins in early infancy. The baby, having acquired some pattern of action (such as grasping or looking), repeats the pattern or "schema" just for the sake of grasping or looking. As Piaget (1962) notes, whether a particular schema is used playfully or otherwise depends on the context. As the infant grows older the schemata are coordinated and applied to an increasing array of objects. The objects serve as "an opportunity for activity" or for play "that is a happy display of known actions" (p. 93).

The infants' sensorimotor encounters with the environment are, of course, not limited to physical objects but include their caretakers as well. Some of these encounters become ritualized just as do other combinations of sensorimotor actions, like those involved in bathing or getting ready for sleep. Such rituals signal the child's beginning awareness of his or her own actions and the imminent emergence of symbolic play.

Sensorimotor play does not disappear with the advent of symbolic play. Teachers recognize it when they see chidren running for the sake of running, jumping up and down exuberantly, clapping one block against another, or repeating nonsense phrases over and over. Play of this sort, according to studies reported by Rubin et al. (1983), drops from 53% of all free activity between 14 and 30 months to 44% or less between 3 and 4 years and to 33% or less from 4 to 5 years. By the time children are 6 to 7 years old, such functional play may comprise less than 14% of all play. The elaborate "space chase" games, derived from television, that children play outdoors combine elements of sensorimotor and dramatic play. The joy that comes from running, leaping, and crouching is enhanced with the excitement of an imagined flight with Darth Vadar or Wonder Woman.

Sensorimotor play is always present in the behavioral repertoire of both children and adults. The adult who jogs, dances, plays tennis, or doodles with a pencil is engaged in sensorimotor play. Such play declines with development only in its frequency relative to symbolic play.

Sensorimotor play beyond the infancy period seems to have received somewhat cursory attention from researchers. Most preschool teachers have experienced sensorimotor play at group or circle time. One child begins snapping her fingers, or clicking her tongue, and the activity quickly becomes a group phenomenon. Teachers would like to know more about the factors that precipitate sensorimotor play and about the circumstances under which it becomes contagious. Does the child see it as different from other kinds of play? To what extent is it an ingredient in rough and tumble play or in movement play, or even in dramatic play? Such information would enable the teacher to understand better both group and individual behavior in the classroom.

Symbolic Play

Symbolic play, from early forms in infancy through the preschool period, has been much studied in recent years. Researchers have hypothesized that make-believe is related to a variety of cognitive and social skills. Looking at the manifestations of pretense in the infant, they observe characteristics that are also found in the thoughts of mature individuals.

Characteristics.   The earliest pretend gestures of the infant, appearing at 12 or 13 months of age (Fein, 1981; Nicolich, 1977; Rubin et al., 1983), are seen as *decontextualized*; the pretense behaviors, resembling behaviors associated with eating, sleeping, or some other familiar experience, are detached from the circumstances usually surrounding them. The baby initiates sleeping behaviors when it is not bedtime, or replicates drinking behaviors when there is no liquid in the cup. From the cognitive perspective, it is "as if" the gestures have begun to stand for or symbolize the situations of sleeping or drinking. From the standpoint of social development, the child seems to have abstracted, in a rudimentary fashion, the rules that pertain to the situations, such as where and how one sleeps, what one drinks and in what utensils, and so on.

Self-other Relations.   Pretense play during the second year shifts from self-referenced behavior (the child drinks from the cup) to other-referenced behavior (the child has the mother or a doll drink from the cup). Initially, the child takes an active role, and the doll serves as a passive recipient of the child's actions (Overton & Jackson, 1973; Werner & Kaplan, 1964). Later, however, the child treats the doll as though the doll were the active agent (Fein & Robertson, 1974). These shifts in pretense behavior appear to form a developmental sequence (Watson & Fisher, 1980). From 12 to 30 months of age, children show a steady increase in the tendency to have the doll act as a separate individual.

Examples of the child's developing ability to sustain the identity of a doll, or even an imagined companion, are many. Four-year-old Barbara brings her Mickey Mouse doll to preschool. Mickey "interrupts" Barbara's conversations with adults and other children. Speaking in a high-pitched voice, he demands a drink of water or asks a question. Three-year-old Susan brings an imaginary rabbit to the center each day. She consults with the rabbit before engaging in the activities provided.

The ability to act as if one were another person is a prerequisite to later role taking. Here, the child must coordinate his or her own self-identity with the role of another (Gould, 1972) and then extend this into sequences of familiar activities (Fenson & Ramsay, 1980). Role taking, in its turn, appears to be related to the more complex taking of the perspective of the other that is inherent in successful social relations and probably also in the solution of a variety of intellectual problems (Mead, 1934). Although these relationships have not been firmly established in empirical research, the child's role taking does provide the teacher with clues as to the progress the child is making in both social and cognitive development.

Object Substitutiion.   The child's ability to substitute one object for another (for example, a shell for a cup) has been of considerable theoretical interest (Piaget, 1962; Vygotsky, 1962, 1967; Winnicott, 1971) and has been studied extensively (Fein, 1981; Rubin et al., 1983). A study by Fein (1975) concerns single and double substitutions. At 24 months, nearly all of the children studied pretended to feed a toy horse with a cup. When the horse was replaced with an abstract wire form or when the cup was replaced by a shell, 70% of the children also accepted the pretense. But only 23% were able to maintain the pretense in the double substitution, when the wire form was presented as the horse together with the shell as a cup. Follow-up studies have examined how the nature of the substitute objects affects the children's pretense. Such objects may resemble the realistic object in form, as a shell resembles a cup, or in function, as a bottle resembles the cup, or in neither form nor function, as would be the case of a toy car, for example. As object with an ambiguous function, such as a block, is easier for the child to substitute than is an object with a conflicting function, such as the toy car (Elder & Peterson, 1978; Golomb, 1977).

Although young preschoolers (ages 2 and 3) may prefer highly proto-typical objects in pretend situations, this preference shifts as they grow older (Fein, 1979; Pulaski, 1970). By age 5, nonrealistic objects evoke richer and more varied fantasy themes. Children at this age indicate preferences for objects that allow them to exercise pretend schemes with a minimum of conflicting perceptual cues and a maximum of leeway for successive trans-formations with the same object.

Findings such as these open up many questions of interest to the teacher. For example, does the provision of realistic objects inhibit the play of older children? Might such replicas serve to facilitate the play of an older child who seems less imaginative than most?

The ways children use, or don't use, props in their play may provide interesting clues to their development. Does the child require a prop to ini-tiate play? How flexible is the child in transforming an object into a prop? Do the transformations appear to be planned or spontaneous? Are props really needed, or is the presence of objects only in the "mind's eye" suffi-cient? In the latter case, what about the actions of the child? Are they con-sistent with the object represented? Questions such as these may supplement the questions that teachers have traditionally asked about children's sym-bolic play and what it may represent in emotional as well as intellectual and social terms. (For a discussion of the latter question, see Gould, 1972).

Some Problems in Definition.   When one child announces, "I'm the Daddy" and another says, "I'm the Mommy," we anticipate a bit of drama symbolizing something from home or television. Shift the scene to the block corner. Two girls are silently stacking blocks, one atop another. Do the blocks represent some building they have seen? Or is the play symbolic? With only this much evidence, we do not know. At a table nearby, a 4-year-old looks up from his crayon drawing and says, "See my house!" We know that he has been engaged in symbolic behavior, but is it play? We use these instances to indicate that the lines between symbolic and other types of play are not always clear.

Most of the research attempting to establish the incidence and kinds of symbolic play children engage in when they are in preschool settings uses predefined categories. These categories may be applied directly to the on-going behavior of the children, viewed one by one, or applied later to de-scriptive protocols of that behavior. Under these circumstances some of the symbolic transformations and their significance may elude the researcher. Some problems arise because, as Schwartzman (1978) and others have shown, the text of the play always depends on its context.

Teachers, who are often privy to what has preceded a particular play episode, may be better able to make sense of it than researchers who are bound by a category system and the constraints of the time for observation.

When 3½-year-old Jane sits whining in the playhouse chair, hitting its arms repeatedly, the uninformed observer may classify Jane's behavior as unimaginative, repetitive, and immature. In contrast, Jane's teacher recalls the more typical play of several weeks ago, in which Jane enacted a dramatic rescue from a fire truck. Jane has just had a new baby brother and her preschool play is appropriate to assimilating the dramatic change in her life at home. While teachers may have particular insight into children's play behaviors, their responsibilities for the guidance and care of groups of children may limit their perspectives also.

From the teacher's viewpoint, the most common type of symbolic play is that labelled "dramatic play," usually occurring in areas set up with props to assist the children in depicting certain themes from their own experiences. Such play is not, however, limited to those areas but may occur in conjunction with constructive play in the block area, or when the child is painting, using play dough or clay, or riding a tricycle.

Dramatic Play.   Pretense play may be solitary, but from the age of 3 years it is more likely to involve more than one child. For example, Johnson and Ershler (1981) conducted a longitudinal study of children who were 3-year-olds at the beginning of their observations. They found a steady increase in both the amount of children's dramatic play and the maturity of their social interaction.

The social characteristics of dramatic play change as children grow older. Early childhood teachers may recall from their textbooks that the play of 2- and 3-year-olds is often described as solitary and parallel, while that of 4- and 5-year-olds is described as associative and cooperative. As Hartup (1983) points out, this is an oversimplification. The *frequency* of solitary play among 5-year-olds does not differ greatly from that of cooperative play at that age (Parten, 1932; Barnes, 1971). The incidence of parallel play is also similar to that for associative and cooperative play. The important changes in dramatic play during the preschool years are not quantitative but qualitative, as represented in the older children's abilities to sustain increasingly complex social interaction. Such interaction also reflects increasing cognitive maturity.

One researcher (Smilansky, 1968) uses the term "sociodramatic play" to describe play that is cognitively advanced. In such play, "the child's efforts are aimed at reproducing, as exactly as possible, the world as he observes it, as he understands it and insofar as he remembers it" (p. 71). The highest level of sociodramatic play includes six "evaluative factors": imitative role play, make-believe in regard to objects, make-believe in regard to actions and situations, persistence (in a play episode for at least 10 minutes), interaction with at least two players involved, and verbal communication. Smilansky's criteria have been adapted for use in several other studies, including some in which categories of social participation from Parten (1932) were nested in Smilansky's cognitive categories (Rubin et al., 1983).

Perhaps the main value Smilansky's criteria have for teachers is that they enable them to think of the variety of transformations and interactions that can go on in a play episode with two or more child actors. However, it may be possible to penetrate the intellectual meaning of the play episode more deeply.

Bateson (cited by Schwartzman, 1978) suggests that children are not only learning how to play roles, but are also learning that there are rules about roles. In a similar vein, Schwartzman comments that

> Play. . .enables the child to learn (and also to comment on) *rules for relationships.* It is not primarily an activity that teaches the *content* of specific roles because it focuses on relationship forms. This is the significance of the example of sisters "playing sisters," where the girls are playing with the *idea* of "a relationship" and the *idea* of "context." (p.274)

Further light on the complexities of dramatic play comes from studies of the ways children communicate in it. Garvey (1974), from observations of dyads of previously acquainted nursery school children, notes five types of action, both gestural and verbal, that children use to communicate "this is pretend." She also notes how they organize play episodes and types of roles they most frequently assume. The underlying competencies she describes are, first, the ability to differentiate play from non-play and to understand with the partner(s) when a play state is evident. Second, the children must abstract organizing rules for interaction and see them as mutually binding. Third, the players must be able to identify a theme, contribute to it, and agree on its modification. Such analyses of children's dramatic play seem to be potentially useful for teachers who want to understand and support it as effectively as possible.

Constructive Play.   Researchers and teachers would have little disagreement in identifying dramatic play, but these groups may disagree among themselves as well as with each other when it comes to constructive play. The problem is suggested by Piaget (1962) who writes, "Making a house with plasticene or bricks involves both sensorimotor skill and symbolic representation." He adds, however, that "drawing a house (construction) is a move away from play, in the strict sense, toward work" (p.110).

From their examination of recent research in preschool and kindergarten classes, Rubin et al. (1983) report that "constructive play is the most common form of activity, ranging from 40% of all activity at 3 1/2 years to approximately 51% at 4, 5 and 6 years" (p. 79). Tizard, Philps, and Plewis (1976), in a study of English preschool centers, suggest that the high proportion of constructive play may be an outcome of an environment that emphasizes the manipulation of objects, presumably including opportunities for construction.

That constructive or manipulative activity need not preclude imaginative activity is evident in a recent observation in a preschool. Kevin had built a three-tiered structure from play dough and had placed smaller pieces of dough around it, like stepping stones. He walked a cookie cutter shaped like a man around the structure, chanting "I'm walking on the sidewalk! I'm walking on the sidewalk!" Then he hopped the cutter up and down in front of the structure. In a low gruff voice he said, "Little pig, little pig, let me come in. I'll huff and I'll puff and I'll come in." Then he changed to a high voice, "Not by the hair of my chinny chin chin!" In a normal voice, he said, "Whoa! B-r-ck!" and crushed the play dough structure with the cutter. Clearly, both constructive and imaginative activity is present in the child's play. Nevertheless, Tizard et al. (1976) have proposed that manipulative activity may inhibit symbolic activity. In contrast, Forman and Hill (1980) see the "open-ended playing around with the alternative ways of doing something" as "constructive play" that "by definition builds on itself to increase the competence of the child" (p. 2).

What seems to be needed on the part of both researchers and teachers is greater attention to what children do with the variety of objects they encounter in a preschool. Are their activities merely manipulative (that is, is the play at a sensorimotor level), or are they constructive in the sense of using the objects to create new objects or new effects, or is dramatic activity also involved? When it is subjected to sufficient scrutiny, constructive play may be seen to have a place in the curriculum overlapping with dramatic play, and it may be perceived to be equally important.

Games With Rules. In Piaget's (1962) theory, constructive play evolves toward work and dramatic play toward games with rules. In the years from 4 to 7, children begin to be able to participate in games with rules. Such games arise out of sensorimotor combinations (races, ball games) or intellectual combinations (cards, chess) and are regulated either by a code that has been handed down or by mutual agreement. According to Piaget, these games are also competitive. More recent cross-cultural work suggests that competition is defined differently in different cultures and that some cultures place more emphasis on collaboration and cooperation than on competition (Schwartzmann, 1978)[1].

Games with rules differ from pretense play in that the rules have been established in advance and determine how the play is to go. Any alterations in the rules must be agreed upon by the players beforehand. These predeter-

---

[1] For a consideration of competition from Piaget's view, see Kamii and DeVries (1980).

mined structures contrast with the ad hoc negotiation and flexibility of dramatic play.

The literature related to games is voluminous, but we have found little that describes the ways young children under the age of 6 begin to acquire skills in and gain understanding of games. Two exceptions are Piaget's (1965) early investigation of games with rules, which includes several 5-year-olds, and Kamii and DeVries's *Group Games* (1980), a book that reports on the ways these two authors introduced such games in the preschool.

Some Issues in the Development of Play

Three issues related to the development of play deserve further comment. The first has to do with solitary play. We have noted that solitary play maintains its position relative to group play throughout the preschool years. What appears to change with development is its symbolic complexity and its availability as a choice in varying social contexts. There is accordingly little reason to assume that it is qualitatively inferior to other kinds of symbolic play, and there may be good reason to make provision for it in the curriculum. One of the present authors (Monighan) concludes from systematic observation of solitary play in her preschool that facilitation of solitary play may encourage the young child's sense of mastery of the environment. Such a sense of mastery and well established schemes for one's own activity appear to provide a solid base for the cooperative play, sharing of ideas, and social dialogue that are expected from school-age children. Consolidation of cognitive schemes in a solitary context may also contribute to the development of problem-solving skills and reliance on an inner locus of control in educational settings (Moore, Evertson, & Brophy, 1974; Singer, 1973; Strom, 1976).

A second issue has to do with parallel play, which like solitary play remains at rather high levels throughout the preschool years (Hartup, 1983). Closer attention from both researchers and teachers may reveal that parallel play involves coordination of gestural, if not verbal, behaviors. Thus, it may sometimes represent greater social maturity than is implied in the usual definition of "play beside but not with" another child.

A third and related issue has to do with the cognitive categories that have been imposed on children's play, sometimes in conjunction with categories of social participation. The question is whether these categories adequately represent the processes involved in play, particularly from the viewpoint of the child in a particular context. As discussed above, the evidence now shows that the social participation categories are not hierarchical, although the cognitive categories may be so. Better assessments of children's development in play may come from studying play episodes in their interactive entirety, rather than by attempting to pinpoint them on dimensions whose relationships are not yet understood.

ASSESSMENT: INDIVIDUAL DIFFERENCES

Whether the children in a classroom come from similar or diverse socioeconomic backgrounds, individual children, even of the same age, will differ from one another in the ways they play. Some of these differences seem to be matters of personality, and some seem to depend on the sex of the child. Others are attributed to cultural and social class differences in childrearing, including time spent watching television. Research related to all these factors tends to be inconclusive and, especially in the case of sex, cultural background, and socioeconomic status, controversial.

Personality

Teachers can often identify children in their groups who seem particularly playful or imaginative. These traits have also interested researchers. For example, Lieberman (1977) found that kindergarten teachers could make reasonably reliable ratings on personality attributes associated with playfulness. More recently, Jenkins (1982) found that preschool teachers had difficulty making such ratings. Younger children and children from different cultrual groups may manifest playfulness in different ways. Perhaps, also, preschool teachers are less experienced in making ratings than are kindergarten teachers. A similar problem is attached to the identification of imaginativeness, a personality factor that has been studied extensively by J. L. Singer and D. C. Singer and their colleagues (see for example Singer, 1973; Singer & Singer, 1976). They found that children vary widely in both the frequency and the consistency of their make-believe.

The possibility that children differ from an early age in the style of their symbolic activity is also being explored. Wolf and Gardner (1979) have identified one group of children as "patterners" on the basis of their interest in the physical properties and arrangements of objects, and another group "dramatists" because of their interest in people. Like most of the other personality variables, style is intriguing, but its long-term significance, if any, is as yet unknown.

Handicap

As mainstreaming has brought more children with mental, physical, or emotional handicaps into preschools and centers, teachers have become concerned with appropriately providing for their play. Consideration of the research related to this issue goes beyond the scope of this discussion. Rubin et al. (1983) include a rather detailed survey of recent studies, and the research continues to grow. Rubin et al. underline the importance of finding ways to make play possible for handicapped children so that they, like other children, can enjoy its features and reap its benefits.

Sex

The old adage that boys will be boys, conforming to sexual stereotypes, is confirmed in research showing that boys prefer fictional super-hero roles while girls are more likely to take familial roles. Boys are also more likely to engage in rough-and-tumble play (Rubin et al., 1983). According to both recent studies and studies dating back to 1927 (Fein, 1981), boys also prefer blocks and transportation toys to dolls and house toys. However, as Fein points out, and as teachers can readily observe, the important question is not where children play or with what but rather what they do in their play.

Teachers of preschoolers report that the introduction of more feminine role models in the media and children's literature may be affecting children's play. Girls playing the role of the film *Star Wars'* Princess Leah have been observed using Barbie dolls as catapults, missiles, or hand-held weapons. Preschool boys have also taken to *Star Wars* "figures" (the manufacturer's term for what are essentially dolls) and are happily dressing and feeding them in much the same ways as girls play with their dolls. As popular culture changes, both boys and girls may have more permission to expand their play into domains traditionally reserved for the opposite sex.

Childrearing Influences

Early research on pretense play, stimulated by psychoanalytic and social learning theories, focused on the ways the content of children's play reflected family dynamics. More recent research has turned to the ways parents encourage or discourage pretense and related behaviors. An important element in parental childrearing which affects play is the amount and kind of television viewing permitted. Children who watch a great deal of television play less imaginatively than those who watch less (Fein, 1981; Singer & Singer, 1976).

Research on the effects of television viewing on children's play is limited. Concern has shifted from the content of children's television to the process involved in the viewing experience (Winn, 1977). Singer and Singer (1976) report that highly imaginative children choose to watch very little television. On the other hand, Singer (1973) points out that some exposure to television, particularly if mediated by an adult coviewer, may stimulate ideas for imaginative play. The research does not specify the optimal amount

of viewing time for young children. It does suggest that without adult media-
tion, the passive nature of viewing, with its limited opportunity for dialogue
and symbolic construction, may restrict the child's imaginative behavior. In
addition, children's viewing is always meshed with other factors that may
influence the kind and amount of play.

Several recent studies (Feitelson & Ross, 1973; Griffing, 1980; Rosen,
1974; Smilansky, 1968; Smith & Dodsworth, 1978) have found that children
from lower- and working-class homes display less imaginative play, at least
in the preschool, than children from middle-class homes. These findings are
criticized on several grounds, including the ethnocentrism of the researchers,
the methods used to assess the play, and the fact that children from similar
backgrounds in other circumstances do reveal imaginative play (Eifermann,
1971; Fein & Stork, 1981; Freyberg, 1973).

The array of toys and other materials children from lower socioeconomic homes find in the typical middle-class preschool, and the encouragement they receive to play with them, may contrast sharply with the home
setting and the attitudes of the parents. Thus, the preschool may seem a
"strange situation" to the child from an economically disadvantaged home.
He or she, as Fein and Stork (1981) and Tizard et al. (1976) show, is more
likely to reveal competence in settings offering more freedom of movement
than the typical classroom.

Sutton-Smith and Heath (1981), drawing on the work of Schwartzman
and other anthropologists and linguists, state that many play researchers
have taken an unduly narrow view of play, discussing it as if it were a solitary affair between a player and the players's toys or imaginings. This view
reflects the literary, schooling tradition of middle-class culture and contrasts with the oral tradition of other cultures. Sutton-Smith and Heath provide several examples to show that the difference between children brought
up in the oral tradition and those brought up in the literary tradition is not
imagination but the way in which it is expressed.

All of this points to the importance of the teacher's knowledge of and
sensitivity to the cultural traditions that may influence the ways children
play. Teachers, if they are open to communication with parents, are often in
a better position to acquire such knowledge than is the researcher who observes specific bevaviors for a relatively short period of time. The teacher's
knowledge is important both to the assessment of play and also to the provisions that are made for it.

HOW TEACHERS CAN FACILITATE CHILDREN'S PLAY

Two recent studies from England underscore the importance of the teacher's
grasp of theory, as well as ability to recognize the distinguishing features of
play, to understand the nature of play's development, and to be able to

assess the play of children in their groups. All of these are essential to the facilitation of children's play.

In an observational study of preschool centers, Tizard et al. (1976) found little evidence of complex, advanced level dramatic play. Centers that had well trained teachers did not differ significantly from centers where the teachers had not had such training. The study led Tizard (1977) to question whether play is indeed "the child's way of learning." She describes how some English nursery school teachers, drawing on the theories of Isaacs, Gesell, and Piaget, have evolved an ideology of play that says that teachers must not initiate or take a major role in play lest they interfere with the child's creative impulses. Such an ideology seems a travesty of the views of education held by Isaacs, Gesell, and Piaget. It demonstrates that the proponents of a theory, through failure to come to terms with all of its implications, sometimes become the theory's worst enemies.

A second study (Sylva, Roy, & Pointer, 1980) took a different tack from the Tizard study in that it drew on the experience of preschool teachers to establish criteria for the evaluation of play as rich (complex and imaginative) or simple (ordinary and dull). This study, like the study of Tizard, found a preponderance of simple play. This suggests again that teachers may pay lip service to play without really understanding it or knowing how to add to its complexity and imaginativeness or how to promote its fullest development.

Teachers influence the play of children by providing a physical and social environment that is conducive to play and by responding to and participating in the play. Phyfe-Perkins (1980) reviewed more than 100 studies concerning the effects of the physical environment on children's behavior in preschool settings. She concludes that if a setting is to provide and support developmentally appropriate activity for all the children involved, teachers must engage in systematic observation of the children at play.

Some of the questions that such observations might address have been discussed earlier. These include the proportion of novel to familiar objects, the proportion of replicas and structured materials to unstructured objects and materials in relation to the ages and maturity of the children, the availability of sex-typed toys to both sexes, the provision of toys to match differing styles of play, and the adequacy and availability of outdoor play areas.

After organizing or reorganizing the physical environment, teachers need to observe the effects of such changes on the children. For example, do the changes result in larger or smaller groups of children in particular areas? More or less verbal interaction? More cross-aged or cross-sexed groups? More aggression or more cooperation? Is there more sensorimotor, constructive, or dramatic play? Are the play episodes sustained longer? Studies show that the space and the resources available affect the behavior of both children and teachers (Phyfe-Perkins, 1980; Kritchevsky, 1972). Other important variables are not only the number of children but their sex, ages, cultural background, and capabilities. The play of mixed-aged groups must differ from that of single-age groups, but the literature provides little evidence about such differences. Hartup (1983) notes that 90% of the literature on child/child interaction is limited to interaction among age-mates.

The findings in studies on the effects of environmental variables on the play of children often seem to be specific to the particular preschool setting, underlining the importance of the teacher's systematic observation. For example, one of the present authors, Scales, and the staff of her center, focused their observation of children's communication in two different areas where tables were available and discovered that the two settings elicited quite different kinds of communication. These findings enabled them to modify arrangements in order to facilitate different kinds of play.

Assuming that teachers have given attention to the physical and social environment of a center and that their assessment of the play of an individual child or of the group shows that it is limited in scope, quality, or quantity, what is their further responsibility? Recent research includes a number of play training and tutoring studies (Burns & Brainerd, 1979; Freyberg, 1973; Rosen, 1974; Saltz et al., 1977; Smilansky, 1968). However, the results are not conclusive (Rubin et al., 1983). Nevertheless, teachers who know the techniques used in the play training studies may see possibilities for involvement that will go beyond that of a passive observer without depriving the children of the spontaneity and autonomy that are the essence of play.

INFORMING PARENTS ON THE EFFECTS OF PLAY

The teacher's convictions about the importance of play do not necessarily correspond to the views of parents. Few parents believe that preschool Jacks and Jills should abstain from play, but they do question whether the preschool puts sufficient emphasis on children's work. In this they reflect the concern of some researchers. Tizard (1977), for example, questions whether teachers who are afraid to interfere with the children's play might not contribute more to the children's learning by being more instructive—for example, by working with them on constructive projects and teaching them games with rules.

The dichotomy posed by the old saying "All work and no play makes Jack a dull boy" is a false one. The issue is not play versus work, nor play versus instruction, but an appropriate balance between play and work or instruction. Nevertheless, the teacher needs to be able to justify that balance, drawing on both theory and research. Unfortunately, the research that attempts to show what children learn through their play, or how their playing affects their later development, is not yet able to answer many questions.

Teachers need to reply mainly on their own knowledge of theory and observations of the way the theory manifests itself in the play of the children in their groups. And researchers need the information and insight that teachers can provide in order to give direction to a rapidly expanding area of child development research.

Current research on the outcomes of play falls roughly into three categories: experimental studies designed to reveal the effects of play on problem solving, studies focused on role taking and its effects on other social and cognitive functions, and studies correlating children's play behavior with their achievement in schools. The research related to problem solving suggests that the flexibility developed through play with objects contributes to success in tasks requiring multiple solutions (Sylva, Bruner, & Genova, 1976). The effects of play on problems with a single solution are less clear cut (Rubin et al., 1983).

Studies have related role taking as a feature of training to a variety of outcomes. These include creativity, the ability to conserve quantity, and to shift mentally from one's own orientation in space to the orientation of another person. The studies have also examined the effects on social participation and cooperation and on the ability to assume the perspective of another person who is experiencing strong affect. It must be noted, however, that these studies have not produced consistent results. (Rubin et al., 1983).

A recent study of kindergarteners' play (Pelligrini, 1980) using Piagetian categories, shows that the level of children's play is a good predictor of achievement in prereading, or reading readiness activity, language, and writing. A study such as this must be viewed with caution since it provides no direct evidence that it is the provision of opportunities for play *in school* that is the crucial factor in the prediction. On the other hand, the author does describe the apparent continuity between the symbolic skills and processes involved in play and those required in reading and writing.

The teacher's understanding of this continuum may be a powerful argument for the justification of play in the early childhood curriculum. It is, however, an argument that must be used judiciously, otherwise the teacher may seem to be promoting play as "cognitive child labor" (Sutton-Smith, 1971a) by failing to take sufficient account of the unique features of play. Thus, any allusion to possible resemblances between preschool play and later academic skills ought not to be divorced from the notion of play as a context in which the child functions "a jump above himself" (Vygotsky, 1967). In this play context children have opportunities for mastery, self-confidence, and self-regulation, as well as for becoming socially responsive and cooperative. The play context provides opportunities for developing the flexibility and creativity that may share importance with present day "basic skills" as we enter the twenty-first century.

CONCLUSION

In reviewing the recent research on play from the perspective of the teacher we have noted the abundance of material that has potential interest for teachers of 2- to 6-year-olds. At the same time, we have suggested that the available theory is not always clear. The different kinds of play are not-always well defined. The functions they serve and the relationships among them are sometimes ambiguous. On the other hand, the research provides many clues for teachers to use in assessing the play of children in their groups and in providing a physical and social environment conducive to rich, complex play. Furthermore, as teachers systematically observe children's play, becoming, in effect, researchers of classroom practice, their insights may help to clarify some of the confusions and ambiguities in current research.

Teachers who, drawing on recent research and their own classroom research, justify an important place for play in the early childhood curriculum will not lose sight of their responsibilities as instructors. They will take account of the allure of play but will also recognize children's needs to acquire information and skills in a variety of ways. Bearing in mind Piaget's view of play as assimilation, they will not neglect the accommodative aspects of learning. Preschool children, at their own level, need to encounter the physical and the social worlds in ways that help them to clarify and understand. Teachers have responsibility in these areas as well as for providing the play opportunities in which children can consolidate and make personally meaningful the experiences they have had.

REFERENCES

Barnes, K. E. Preschool play norms: A replication. *Developmental Psychology,* 1971, *5,* 99–103.

Berlyne, D. E. *Conflict, arousal and curiosity.* New York: McGraw-Hill Book Company, 1960.

Biber, B., & Franklin, M. The relevance of developmental and psychodynamic concepts to the education of the preschool child. *Journal of the American Academy of Child Psychiatry,* 1967, *6,* 5–24.

Bruner, J. S. The nature and uses of immaturity. *American Psychologist,* 1972, *27,* 687–708.

Bruner, J. S., Jolly, A., & Sylva, K. *Play: Its role in development and evolution.* New York: Basic Books, 1976.

Burns, S. M., & Brainerd, C. J. Effects of constructive and dramatic play on perspective taking in very young children. *Developmental Psychology,* 1979, *15*(5), 512–521.

Dansky, J. L., & Silverman, W. I. The effects of play on associative fluency in preschool-aged children. *Developmental Psychology,* 1973, *9,* 38–43.

Dansky, J. L., & Silverman, W. I. Play: A general facilitator of associative fluency. *Developmental Psychology,* 1975, *11,* 104.

Eiferman, R. R. Social play in childhood. In R. E. Herron & B. Sutton-Smith (Eds.), *Child's Play.* New York: John Wiley & Sons, 1971.

Elder, J., & Peterson, D. Preschool children's use of objects in symbolic play. *Child Development,* 1978, *49,* 500–504.

Erikson, E. H. *Childhood and society.* New York: W. W. Norton & Company, 1950

Fagen, R. M. Modeling: How and why it works. In J. S. Bruner, A. Jolly, & K. Sylva (Eds.), *Play: Its role in development and evolution.* New York: Basic Books, 1976.

Fein, G. A transformational analysis of pretending. *Developmental Psychology,* 1975, *11,* 291–296.

Fein, G. Pretend play in childhood: An integrative review. *Child Development,* 1981, *52,* 1095–1118.

*Fein, G. Play and the acquisition of symbols. In L. Katz, M. Glockner, C. Watkins, & M. Spencer (Eds.), *Current topics in early childhood education* (Vol. 2). Norwood, NJ: Ablex Publishing Corporation, 1979. (ERIC Document Reproduction Service No. ED 152 431).

*Fein, G., & Robertson, A. R. Cognitive and social dimensions of pretending in two-year olds, 1974 (ERIC Document Reproduction Service No. ED 119 806).

Fein, G., & Stork, L. Sociodramatic play: Social effects in integrated preschool classrooms. *Journal of Applied Developmental Psychology,* 1981, *2,* 267–291.

Feitelson, D., & Ross, G. S. The neglected factor—play. *Human Development,* 1973, *16,* 202–223.

Fenson, L., & Ramsay, D. Decentration and integration of child's play in the second year. *Child Development,* 1980, *51,* 171–178.

Forman, G. E., & Hill, F. *Constructive play: Applying Piaget in the preschool.* Monterey, CA: Brooks/Cole Publishing Co., 1980.

Freud, A. *Psychoanalytic treatment of children.* (trans. N. Proctor-Gregg) New York: Schocken Books, 1964.

Freyberg, J. Increasing the imaginative play of urban disadvantaged children through systematic training. In J. L. Singer (Eds.), *The child's world of make-believe.* New York: Academic Press, 1973.

Froebel, F. *The education of man.* (trans. W. N. Hailmann). New York: D. Appleton & Co. 1898.

Garvey, C. Some properties of social play. *Merrill-Palmer Quarterly,* 1974, *20,* 163–180.

Garvey, C. *Play.* Cambridge, MA: Harvard University Press, 1977.

Golomb, C. Symbolic play: The role of substitutions in pretense and puzzle games. *British Journal of Educational Psychology,* 1977, *47,* 175–186.

Golomb, C., & Cornelius, C. B. Symbolic play and its cognitive significance. *Developmental Psychology,* 1977, *13,* 246–252.

Gould, R. *Child studies through fantasy: Cognitive-affective patterns in development.* New York: Quadrangle Books, 1972.

Griffing, P. The relationship between socioeconomic status and sociodramatic play among black kindergarten children. *Genetic Psychology Monographs,* 1980, *101,* 3–34.

Hartup, W. W. The peer system. In P. H. Mussen & E. M. Hetherington (Eds.), *Carmichael's manual of child psychology: Social development.* Vol. 4 New York: John Wiley & Sons, 1983.

Hutt, C. Exploration and play in children. In R. E. Herron & B. Sutton-Smith (Eds.), *Child's play.* New York: John Wiley & Sons, 1971.

Isaacs, S. *Social development in young children.* London: Routledge & Kegan, Paul 1930.

Isaacs, S. *Intellectual growth in young children.* New York: Schocken Books, 1966.

Jenkins, Y. The relationship of playfulness and play style context to divergent thinking. Unpublished doctoral dissertation, University of California, Berkeley, 1982.

Johnson, J. E., & Ershler, J. Developmental trends in preschool play as a function of classroom play and child gender. *Child Development,* 1981, *52,* 995–1004.

Kamii, C., & DeVries, R. *Group games in early education: Implications of Piaget's theory.* Washington, DC: National Association for the Education of Young Children, 1980.

Kritchevsky, S. Physical settings in day care centers. In E. Prescott & E. Jones (Eds.), *Day care as a child-rearing environment*. Washington, DC: National Association for the Education of Young Children, 1972.

Lieberman, J. N. *Playfulness: Its relationship to imagination and creativity*. New York: Academic Press, 1977.

Mead, G. H. *Mind, self and society*. Chicago: University of Chicago Press, 1934.

Moore, N. V., Evertson, C. M., & Brophy, J. E. Solitary Play: Some functional reconsiderations. *Developmental Psychology, 1974, 10,* 830–834.

Mussen, P. H. (Ed.). *Carmichael's manual of child psychology* (Vol. 1 & 2), (3rd ed.). New York: John Wiley & Sons, 1970.

Mussen, P. H. & Heatherington, E. M. *Carmichael's manual of child psychology* (4th ed.) Vol. 4. New York: John Wiley & Sons, 1983.

Nicolich, L. M. Beyond sensorimotor intelligence: Assessment of symbolic maturity throughn analysis of pretend play. *Merrill-Palmer Quarterly, 1977, 23,* 89–99.

Overton, W. F., & Jackson, J. P. The representation of imagined objects in action sequences: A developmental study. *Child Development, 1973, 44,* 309–314.

Parten, M. B. Social participation among preschool children. *Journal of Abnormal Psychology, 1932, 27,* 243–269.

Pellegrini, A. D. The relationship between kindergartener's play and achievement in prereading, language, and writing. *Psychology in the Schools, 1980, 17,* 530–535.

*Phyfe-Perkins, E. Children's behavior in preschool settings: A review of research concerning the influence of the physical environment. In L. G. Katz, C. H. Watkins, M. Quest, & M. Spencer (Eds.), *Current topics in early childhood education* (Vol. 3). Norwood, NJ: Ablex Publishing Corporation, 1980. (ERIC Document Reproduction Service No. ED 168 722).

Piaget, J. *Play, dreams and imitation in childhood*. (trans. G. Gattegno & F. M. Hodgsom) New York: W. W. Norton & Company, 1962.

Piaget, J. *The moral judgement of the child*. (trans. M. Gabain) New York: The Free Press, 1965.

Pulaski, M. Play as a function of toy structure and fantasy predisposition. *Child Development, 1970, 41,* 531–537.

Rosen, C. E. The effects of sociodramatic play on problem-solving behavior among culturally disadvantaged children. *Child Development, 1974, 45,* 920–927.

Rubin, K., Fein, G., & Vandenberg, B. Play. In P. H. Mussen & E. M. Hetherington (Eds.), *Carmichael's manual of child psychology: Social development*. Vol.4 New York: John Wiley & Sons, 1983.

Saltz, E., Dixon, D., & Johnson, J. Training disadvantaged preschoolers on various fantasy activities: Effects on cognitive functioning and impulse control. *Child Development, 1977, 48,* 367–380.

Schwartzman, H. B. *Transformations: The anthropology of children's play*. New York: Plenum Publishing Corp., 1978.

Singer, J. *The child's world of make-believe*. New York: Academic Press, 1973.

Singer, J., & Singer D. Imaginative play and pretending in early childhood: Some experimental approaches. In A. Davids (Ed.), *Child personality and psychopathology: Current topics* (Vol. 3.). New York: John Wiley & Sons, 1976.

Smilansky, S. *The effects of sociodramatic play on disadvantaged preschool children*. New York: John Wiley & Sons, 1968.

Smith, P. K., & Dutton, S. Play and training in direct and innovative problem solving. *Child Development, 1979, 50,* 830–836.

Smith, P. K., & Dodsworth, C. Social class differences in the fantasy play of preschool children. *Journal of Genetic Psychology, 1978, 133,* 183–190.

Strom, R. The merits of solitary play. *Childhood Education,* 1976, *52*(3), 149–152.

Sutton-Smith, B. Novel responses to toys. *Merrill-Palmer Quarterly,* 1968, *14,* 151–158.

Sutton-Smith, B. The playful modes of knowing. In N. E. Curry (Ed.), *Play: The child strives toward self-realization.* Washington, DC: National Association for the Education of Young Children, 1971a.

Sutton-Smith, B. A syntax for play and games. In R. E. Herron & B. Sutton-Smith (Eds.), *Child's play.* New York: John Wiley & Sons, 1971b.

Sutton-Smith, B. (Ed.). *Play and learning.* New York: Gardner Press, 1979.

Sutton-Smith, B., & Heath, S. B. Paradigms of pretense. *The Quarterly Newsletter of the Laboratory of Comparative Human Cognition,* 1981, *3* (3), 41–45.

Sylva, K., Bruner, J., & Genova, S. The role of play in the problem-solving of children 3–5 years old. In J. Bruner, A. Jolly, & S. Sylva (Eds.), *Play: Its role in development and evolution.* New York: Basic Books, 1976.

Sylva, K., Roy, C., & Pointer, M. *Child watching at play group and nursery school* (Oxford Preschool Research Project, Vol. 2) Ypsilanti, MI: High/Scope Press, 1980.

Tizard, B. Play, a child's way of learning? In B. Tizard & D. Harvey (Eds.), *Biology of play.* London: William Heinemann, 1977.

Tizard, B., Philps, J., & Plewis, I. Play in preschool centres II: Effects on play of the child's social class and of the educational orientation of the centre. *Journal of Child Psychology and Psychiatry,* 1976, *17,* 265–274.

Vandenberg, B. Play, problem solving and creativity. In K. H. Rubin (Ed.), *Children's play.* San Francisco: Jossey-Bass *New Directions for Child Development (No. 9),* 1980.

Vygotsky, L. S. *Thought and language.* Cambridge, MA: The MIT Press, 1962.

Vygotsky, L. S. Play and its role in the mental development of the child. *Soviet Psychology,* 1967, *12,* 62–76.

Watson, M. W., & Fischer, K. W. Development of social roles in elicited and spontaneous behavior during the preschool years. *Developmental Psychology,* 1980, *16,* 483–494.

Weisler, A., & McCall, R. Exploration and play. *American Psychologist,* 1976, *31,* 492–508.

Werner, H., & Kaplan, B. *Symbol formation.* New York: John Wiley & Sons, 1964.

White, R. W. Motivation reconsidered: The concept of competence. *Psychological Review,* 1959, *66,* 297–323.

Winn, M. *The plug-in drug.* New York: The Viking Press, 1977.

Winnicott, D. W. *Playing and reality.* New York: Basic Books, 1971.

Wolf, D., & Gardner, H. Style and sequence in symbolic play. In M. Franklin & N. Smith (Eds.), *Symbolic functioning in childhood.* Hillsdale, NJ: Lawrence Erlbaum Associates, 1979.

2

Putting the Child Into Socialization: The Development of Social Categories in Preschool Children*

Kurt W. Fischer and Helen H. Hand

University of Denver

Malcolm W. Watson

Brandeis University

Martha M. Van Parys

University of Denver

James L. Tucker

Denver, Colorado

Every child is born into a specific society and must learn the categories and rules prescribed by that society. Children must understand, for example, what boys and girls are, what children and adults are, what doctors and patients (or their society's equivalents) are, and how people in each of these categories are supposed to act. Without an understanding of these social categories and rules, children cannot act competently as members of their society.

The processes by which a society teaches children these categories, as well as numerous other social rules, are collectively called *socialization*. Analysis of the processes of socialization has been one of the central focuses of developmental theory and research, and there has been substantial progress toward explaining how a society affects its children (*e.g.*, Hartup, 1970; Maccoby, 1980). Virtually all existing theories of socialization have tended to suffer from a single shortcoming, however: They have focused

* Preparation of this chapter was supported by a grant from the Carnegie Corporation of New York. The statements made and views expressed are solely the responsibility of the authors. The authors would like to thank the following individuals for their contribution to various aspects of the chapter: Michael Bender, Paul Corbitt, Susan Harter, Howard Leventhal, Marilyn Pelot, Sandra Pipp, Ralph J. Roberts, Jr., Sheryl Kenny, and Phil Shaver.

almost entirely on the impingement of the society on children and have neglected the role that the developing child plays in his or her own socialization (see Lerner & Busch-Rossnagel, 1981).

A full understanding of the processes of socialization in childhood requires taking into account how children understand what is demanded of them and how that understanding changes with development. In socialization, as in all other types of learning, children are not merely passive recipients of pressures to behave in a certain way. They strive to understand what is demanded of them, and they behave in terms of that understanding (Fischer, 1980; Kohlberg, 1966).

The classic cognitive-developmental approach, however, has not provided much help in analyzing the development of social categories in preschool children. Piaget's (1924/1928, 1946/1951) general argument was that the child did not really understand social roles and other social categories until the elementary school years, when he or she entered the concrete-operational period, and other research in the Piagetian tradition has mostly supported his argument (Bigner, 1974; Marcus & Overton, 1978). Nevertheless, anyone who has worked with preschool children realizes that there is something seriously wrong with the Piagetian claim. Indeed, preschool children seem often to be obsessed with social categories and rules.

Recent research and theory has corrected Piaget's mistaken portrait. A number of studies have shown that the cognitive capacities of the preschool child are much richer than were portrayed by Piaget (Case & Khanna, 1981; Fischer, 1980; Gelman, 1978). The development of social cognition—knowledge about people and interactions with them—seems to be especially notable during this period. By age 2, most preschoolers know that other people are independent agents, and they quickly put this knowledge to use to build categories for making sense of people's actions. By the age of 3, they seem to have mastered a number of these categories, and then, over the next few years, they proceed to gradually decipher the relations and complexities of social categories. With the beginning of elementary school, they have become highly competent at functioning in their society.

PHASES OF DEVELOPMENT AND PHASES OF SOCIALIZATION

There is so much for children to learn about their societies. Although the preschool period seems to be an especially important time for social learning, much is also learned in infancy, elementary school, adolescence, and even adulthood. An understanding of the nature and limitations of preschool development requires placing the events of the preschool period in the broader context of social-cognitive development throughout the lifespan.

Social-cognitive development seems to proceed through three general phases. In infancy, babies learn the basic skills of social interaction. In childhood, they learn concrete social categories and the rules associated with them. In adolescence and adulthood, they learn about social systems and networks, and how to operate within them.

Infancy: Learning How to Interact

Infants are born enmeshed in a family and a society, and they are of course affected by that society at many different levels. But in the first two years of life, the major focus of what they learn is the fundamentals of social interaction—how to take turns, how to talk to someone, how to get someone to do what you want. Most of this learning occurs in the family.

The development of turn-taking has been described in some detail by Kaye (1982), Sander (1975), and others. Shortly after birth, most infants take part in their first turn-taking as they nurse at breast or bottle. The mother establishes an interaction in which baby and mother take turns. The baby sucks for a while, and when he or she happens to pause, the mother jiggles him for a moment and pauses. Sucking then resumes until the baby pauses again, the mother jiggles again, and so forth. In this very early form of turn-taking, the baby need hardly contribute anything at all, since the mother can establish the back-and-forth rhythm by herself. It is enough for the baby to suck periodically to "participate" in turn-taking.

Within a few months, however, infants begin to anticipate the back-and-forth rhythm of feeding, and by the end of the first year, they have established turn-taking as a basic type of social interaction, even generalizing it to include situations that their parents did not initiate. For instance, mother feeds 1-year-old Joey some cereal, and then Joey wants to feed her some.

In language development, too, fundamental sensorimotor patterns of social interaction are laid down in infancy. By about 1 year of age, for example, most children regularly produce what is called "expressive jargon" (Fischer & Corrigan, 1981): They use the intonation contour of a sentence without actually saying any words. A caregiver can even hold a "conversation" in expressive jargon with a skilled infant, alternating with the child in producing "sentences without words."

Besides turn-taking and expressive jargon, 1-year-olds have also learned many procedures for influencing others to do what they want—not only by crying or whining, but also by calling out for "Mama," pointing to a desired object, extending outstretched hands so as to be picked up, and so forth (Kaye, 1982; Tronick, 1982).

With their sensorimotor intelligence, infants have already mastered many of the fundamental rules of social interaction by the second year of life. Sensorimotor intelligence is limited, however, to connecting sensations or perceptions with responses (Fischer, 1980; Piaget, 1936/1952). Consequently, the rules of social interaction are defined by and manifested in the actions of the infant and do not take the form of general concepts. It is not until the next period of childhood that true concepts concerning social interactions emerge. Clearly, the social-interaction skills of infancy are merely a beginning, since social interactions will become more complicated as the child comes to understand social categories and social systems.

Childhood: Learning Social Categories

At about the age of 2 years, toddlers develop a radically new mental capability called "representation," which allows them to move beyond the sensorimotor intelligence of infancy (Corrigan, 1983; Fischer, 1980; Piaget, 1946/1951). One of the first results of this new capability is that the toddler can represent other people as independent agents, who act on their own independently of the child's action (Fischer & Jennings, 1981; Rubin, Fein, & Vandenberg, 1983; Watson & Fischer, 1977).

The capability of representing other people as independent agents gradually leads to the ability to categorize other people's actions in the ways that they are defined by society. With this ability comes the first blossoming of social categories. Here is how boys act, here is how men act, here is how girls act, and so forth. The development of these social categories into roles and other social relations comprises the heart of this article and so will be described in detail later.

Notably, all these categories involve concrete behaviors and characteristics. As late as age 10 or 11, there is still no understanding of social systems or networks. Children do not understand social categories the way a sociologist or political scientist thinks of them, in terms of their relation to a set of social roles and norms in a social system. Instead, they conceptualize social categories in concrete, personal terms (Adelson, 1975; Rosenberg, 1979). The role of President of the United States, for example, is typically understood by children as the position that allows an individual to tell anyone what to do—in other words, the "big boss."

Adolescence and Adulthood: Learning Social Systems and Networks

Just as the capability of representation ushers in a new phase in social development at 2 years of age, so the capability of "abstraction" brings another new phase at 10 to 12 years. The young adolescent gains the ability to go beyond the concrete characteristics of real people in social categories to understand those categories in more general, less tangible terms (Adelson, 1975; Rosenberg, 1979; Selman, 1980). To the child at this age, the President does more than order people around; he or she is the head of state and commander in chief, responsible for making the government carry out its many functions effectively and honestly.

This kind of understanding requires that social categories be considered not just in the concrete terms of how real people interact with each other, but in the abstract terms of how social systems and networks operate and how people fill niches in these systems. Only the first glimmering of understanding of social systems and networks appears by 12 years of age, of course. Development continues beyond that age, probably at least until the mid-20s (Broughton, 1978; Fischer, Hand, & Russell, 1983; Kitchener & King, 1981).

The topic of this chapter is the development of social categories during the preschool years, not the development of understanding social systems and networks. It is important, however, to place preschool development in the context of the entire lifespan. In a significant sense, the concrete social categories developed during the childhood years merely lay the foundation for the more sophisticated understandings that eventually make the adult a fully participating member of society.

THE DEVELOPMENT OF SOCIAL CATEGORIES

Progress in children's understanding of social categories is slow and gradual, with important developments appearing as early as 1 year of age and as late as the elementary school years. The course of development between 1 and 7 years is systematic but complex. On the one hand, children show systematic developments of social-cognitive abilities at certain ages, but on the other hand, the age of development of an ability varies enormously depending upon the particular task and the context in which it is assessed.

Traditionally, there have been two opposing approaches to studying social development. Socialization approaches, which are based on learning theory, have emphasized how different tasks and contexts produce variations in social development. Cognitive-developmental approaches, based on theories such as Piaget's (1924/1928; 1946/1951), have emphasized how children's social understandings change systematically with age. The contradiction between these two types of approaches is more apparent than real, however. There can be both systematic change with age and variation across tasks and contexts at the same time (Fischer & Bullock, 1981; Hand, 1981-b).

Both Child and Environment

Both the child and the environment obviously contribute to any particular behavior, and a full explanation of developing behavior therefore requires consideration of both. The traditional emphasis on either changes in the child or influences of the environment will not suffice.

Since environmental factors are always contributing to performance, it is misleading to attribute to a child of a particular age a general capacity for understanding some type of social category. For example, a child does not develop a single general capacity to understand the social role of doctor; instead, the ability it demonstrates varies widely across tasks and contexts. This unevenness in performance is what Piaget (1941) called *"décalage horizontal."*

Because there is no single age at which an ability is seen in all situations, it is not possible to attribute one age to each step in the development of social categories. What can be done, however, is to describe the age of first development of an ability, when most children demonstrate it on the simplest task that can be devised to assess that ability. With this task as an anchor point, researchers can then proceed to describe how the child gradually becomes able to demonstrate the ability on more complex tasks and in a wider range of contexts (Bertenthal, 1981).

In the case of social categories, the simplest tasks that we have been able to devise generally involve imitative pretend play. The individual child is shown a pretend story in which dolls behave according to certain social categories; for example, a doctor-doll examines a patient-doll who is sick. The child is then asked to act out a similar story. Using a general cognitive-developmental approach known as skill theory (Fischer, 1980), we have been able to predict the developmental sequences in which children can act out such stories and the ages at which various steps in the sequences develop. We have also begun to pin down some of the factors that lead to unevenness in performance with changes in context, as will be explained later.

Skill theory is designed to integrate the insights of traditional cognitive-developmental approaches, such as Piaget's, with the insights of environmentally oriented approaches, such as behaviorism. It analyzes development in terms of a series of developmental levels and a set of transformation rules specifying how children can construct more complex skills and thus gradually move from level to level. The processes embodied in the transformations are various forms of combination and differentiation of skills. The theory is constructed in such a way that every skill is defined for an individual child performing a particular task in a specific context. Its constructs combine the contributions of the child with the influences of the environment. According to skill theory, these constructs can be used to predict developmental sequences for any child acting in any domain. These processes of development are elaborated in several published explications of skill theory (Fischer, 1980; Fischer & Corrigan, 1981; Fischer & Pipp, in press-b).

Development of Social Roles

One of the fundamental types of social category is the social role, a cluster of behaviors and characteristics prescribed for a particular category of people, such as doctors or mothers. Despite the importance of roles in all human societies (Edwards & Whiting, 1980; Linton, 1942; Mead, 1934), there has been relatively little research on the development of roles, except for those relating to gender.

In our research, we used skill theory to predict a general developmental sequence of role understanding from infancy to adolescence, as shown in Table 1. We tested the sequence in a series of studies of two types of roles—those relating to a medical doctor and those occurring within the nuclear family (Watson, 1981; Watson & Amgott-Kwan, 1983; Watson & Fischer, 1977, 1980; Westerman, 1980). In general, the strong-scalogram method was used—a separate task was devised to test each step, so that performance could be independently assessed on every step in the sequence (Fischer, Pipp, & Bullock, in press). Because one session did not provide enough time to administer the tasks for all steps, each study tested a subset of the steps in the sequence.

In most of the studies, all the tasks employed the imitative pretending technique. For each step, the child was shown a story that embodied the skill predicted for that step and was asked to act out a similar story. In one of the studies, children answered questions concerning the role relationships of realistic cardboard dolls embodying every major family role (Watson & Amgott-Kwan, 1983). Subjects ranged from 1 to 7 1/2 years of age and were from middle-class families in the Denver and Boston areas.

Because each step was assessed separately, it was possible to test the predicted sequence for every individual child by examining the pattern of "passes" for the set of tasks. To support the predicted sequence, children had to pass all tasks up to some point in the sequence and fail all tasks after that point; that is, their performance had to fit a Guttman (1944) scale. More than 200 children were tested in the several studies, and over 90% of them fit the predicted sequence perfectly. This percentage is virtually as high as could be obtained, given the degree of measurement error in the tasks.

In addition to the strong-scalogram assessment, most of the studies also tested behavior under one or more spontaneous conditions, in which the child made up his or her own stories. Behavior under the several conditions was then compared.

It is important to realize that in everyday behavior, individual children will not necessarily demonstrate all the steps in the sequence in Table 1. Children will show these steps only when they are exposed to contexts that elicit the requisite behaviors. Also, in certain contexts children will show additional steps besides the ones that we have assessed. According to skill theory, no fixed number of developmental steps exists in any content domain; instead, the number of steps varies across children and contexts. However, the sequence tested is intended to reflect typical steps in the development of social roles for middle-class American children.

TABLE 1 A Sequence of Social Role Development

| | | | Examples [b] | |
| | | | | |
Level	Approximate Age of Emergence [a]	Step	Skill	Doctor Role Studies	Family Role Studies
I: Single Social Categories	2–3 years	1	*Self as agent:* A child pretends to carry out one or more behaviors, not necessarily fitting a social role.	Child pretends to drink from a cup or wash himself or herself.	
		2	*Passive other agent:* A child pretends to make a person carry out one or more behaviors, not necessarily fitting a social role.	Child makes a doll drink from a cup or washes the doll, without the doll acting.	
		3	*Passive substitute agent:* A child pretends to make an object act as a passive agent, as in Step 2.	Child makes a block drink from a cup or washes the block, without the block acting.	
		4	*Active other agent:* A person performs one or more behaviors, not necessarily fitting a social role.	Child has a doll drink from a cup or wash itself as if it were carrying out the action itself.	
		5	*Active substitute agent:* An object behaves as an active agent, as in Step 4.	Child has a block drink from a cup or wash itself as if it were carrying out the action itself.	Child labels and describes one or more activities of a doll.

continued

TABLE 1 (cont.)

Level	Approximate Age of Emergence [a]	Step	Skill	Examples [b] Doctor Role Studies	Examples [b] Family Role Studies
		6	*Behavioral role:* A person performs several behaviors fitting a social role, such as doctor.	Child has a doll, as a doctor, use a thermometer and an otolaryngoscope.	Child describes a father in terms of his typical behaviors.
		7	*Shifting behavioral roles:* One person performs one behavioral role, as in Step 6, and then a second person performs a different behavioral role. For instance, the first person acts as a doctor, then the second acts independently as a patient.	Child has a doll, as a doctor, use a thermometer and an otolaryngoscope. Child then has another doll, as a patient, say it is sick and go to bed.	
II: Relations between Social Categories	4–5 years	8	*Social role:* One person behaving according to one role, such as doctor, relates to a second agent behaving according to a complementary role, such as patient.	Child has a doctor-doll examine a patient-doll and respond appropriately to the patient's complaints.	Child describes a father in terms of the father having children and taking care of his children.

continued

TABLE 1 (cont.)

Level	Approximate Age of Emergence [a]	Step	Skill	Examples [b] Doctor Role Studies	Family Role Studies
		9	*Shifting social roles with one common agent:* Two people perform a social role, as in Step 8, and then one of them performs a different social role with a third person. For instance, the first two people act as doctor/patient, then the second two act independently as patient/nurse.	Child has a doctor-doll examine a patient-doll and respond appropriately to the patient's complaints. Child then has the patient-doll interact appropriately with a nurse-doll.	Child describes how a father has children and then how he can change to a grandfather when he has grandchildren.
		10	*Social role with three agents:* One person in one role, such as doctor, relates simultaneously to two other people in complementary roles, such as nurse and patient.	Child has a doctor-doll relate to a patient-doll with the aid of a nurse-doll. All dolls respond appropriately to each other.	
		11	*Shifting roles for the same agents:* Two people perform a social role, as in Step 8, and then they perform a different social role, such as father relating to child. For instance, they first act as doctor/patient, then act as father/child.	Child has a doctor-doll relate appropriately to a patient-doll and then has an adult-doll act as a father to his child.	

continued

TABLE 1 (cont.)

Level	Approximate Age of Emergence [a]	Step	Skill	Examples [b]	
				Doctor Role Studies	Family Role Studies
III: Systems of Social Categories	6–9 years	12	*Role intersection:* Two agent-complement role relations are coordinated so that one person can be in two roles simultaneously, such as doctor and father, and relate to both complementary roles, such as patient and daughter.	Child has a doctor-doll examine a patient-doll and also act simultaneously as father to the patient, who responds as both his patient and his daughter.	Child describes how a father can be simultaneously both a father to his children and a grandfather to his grandchildren.
		13	*Shifting role interactions with one common agent:* Two agent-complement role relations are coordinated, as in Step 12, and then one of those people performs a different pair of agent-complement role relations with a third person. For instance, the first two people act as doctor-father/patient-nurse, then the second two act independently as doctor-husband/patient's mother-wife.	Child has a doctor-doll examine a patient-doll and also act as father to the patient, as in Step 12. Child then has the doctor doll interact as doctor and husband with a woman-doll, who acts as both mother of patient and wife.	

continued

TABLE 1 (cont.)

Level	Approximate Age of Emergence [a]	Step	Skill	Examples [b]	
				Doctor Role Studies	Family Role Studies
		14	*Role intersection with three agents:* Three agent-complement role relations are coordinated so that one person can be in three roles simultaneously, such as doctor, father, and husband, and relate to the complementary roles, such as patient and daughter for a second person and patient's mother and wife for a third person.	Child has one doll behave as a doctor and father to a second doll and as a doctor and husband to a third doll. The second doll interacts as the patient and daughter, and the third doll interacts as the patient's mother and the doctor's wife.	Child describes how a father can be simultaneously a son, father, and grandfather in terms of the complementary roles.
IV: Abstractions about Social Categories	10 years and older	15	*Simple role network:* At least two role intersections are intercoordinated and compared to form a definition of a complex role system, such as that relating two generations within a family.		Child compares family role relations across two generations and recognizes a family in terms of intersecting spousal and parental roles.
		16	*Expanded role network:* At least three role intersections, as in Step 15, are intercoordinated and compared, such as three generations within a family.		Child compares family role relations across three generations including a future generation.

continued

38

TABLE 1 (cont.)

Level	Approximate Age of Emergence [a]	Step	Skill	Examples [b]	
				Doctor Role Studies	Family Role Studies
		17	*Comparison of role networks:* At least two role networks, such as a traditional family unit and a family unit with only one parent, are intercoordinated so that the similiarities and differences between them can be recognized.		Child compares a family with both spousal and parental roles (a traditional family) with one that has only one of those roles—the spousal role in childless couples or the parental role in single parent families.
		18	*Reciprocal role networks:* Both the similarities and differences of role networks are simultaneously considered, and one general network system, such as that relating to the various types of families, is abstracted.		Child recognizes the essential components of both traditional and non-traditional families in terms of role relations and functions.

Portions of this table are based on Watson (1981). Studies testing portions of the table include Watson and Fischer (1977, 1980), Watson and Amgott-Kwan (in press), and Westerman (1979).

[a] Ages vary widely across tasks and conditions and are therefore given only for general developmental levels. These ages indicate when the skills at each level first appear in middle-class children.

[b] For the respective domains, examples are given only for steps actually assessed in the studies.

Agency. Before children can understand that people behave in terms of social roles, they need to understand that people act on their own as independent agents. The first step in the developmental sequence involves what seems to be the earliest form of this ability, the understanding that the self can be a cause of action. This understanding is evidenced by the 1-year-old's pretending to do something—to drink, to eat, to wash, to sleep (Bretherton & Bates, 1979; Harter, 1983; Rubin et al., 1983; Watson & Fischer, 1977).

Gradually, during the second year, children move from self to other, so that at approximately 2 years they can represent other people as active agents (Step 4). They can make a doll walk across the table as if it were walking on its own (Dasen, Inhelder, Lavalee, & Retschitzki, 1978; Watson & Fischer, 1977), and they can understand that an adult experimenter can carry out hidden actions that cannot be seen (Bertenthal & Fischer, 1983; Fischer & Jennings, 1981).

Behavioral Roles. By the age of 2, children understand both themselves and other people as independent actors, but they still cannot coordinate people's actions into social categories. The first understanding of such categories appears at approximately 3 years, when the child combines several related actions of an independent agent to form a behavioral category. For social roles, this category is called a "behavioral role" (Step 6), or a collection of behaviors and characteristics related to a specific social role but missing the complementary role. For example, a 3-year-old makes a doctor-doll wear a white coat and use a thermometer, a syringe, or an otolaryngoscope, but the doctor does not interact with the patient. The patient does not do anything at all, but is at best something to stick a thermometer and a syringe into. Most 3-year-olds understand a host of behavioral roles, including not only doctor, but also mother, father, child, baby, babysitter, and so forth. They seem to be able to understand any common role that is defined by concrete behaviors or characteristics.

Many of the roles most common in daily life relate to gender, and a number of studies indicate that 3-year-olds do understand behavioral categories for the sexes (Kuhn, Nash, & Brucken, 1978; Van Parys, 1981; Watson & Amgott-Kwan, 1983). The predominant gender categories seem to be boy, girl, man, and woman (Edwards, in press). Like gender, age defines a number of prominent social categories in all human societies, and children seem to understand many of the corresponding behavioral roles by the age of 3, at least in middle-class families in Western countries (Edwards, in press; Van Parys, 1981). Besides the gender-related age roles of boy, girl, man, and woman, 3-year-olds also understand categories such as baby, child, and adult.

Although these categories combine age and gender in real life, 3-year-olds do not seem to actually coordinate age and gender in their understandings (Edwards, in press; Van Parys, 1981). Instead, they treat the categories more simplistically, as if each one involved merely an independent type of person and not related dimensions of a person. In general, 3-year-olds seem unable to deal with more than one category at a time (Fischer, 1980; Fischer & Watson, 1981).

Another common dimension of social categorization across cultures is race, although the experience of racial differences is not universal. Those children who do have experience with race seem to develop categories for it by about 3 years of age (e.g., Clark & Clark, 1947; Katz, 1982; Van Parys, 1981). These categories enable 3-year-old American blacks, for example, to discriminate blacks from whites and to place values on each race that reflect the differential evaluation made in their society. We can predict that children of this age also form behavioral roles based on race, but to our knowledge there have been no direct tests for such skills.

Gender, age, and race define behavioral roles *per se*, and there are many other instances of behavioral roles that preschool children routinely learn, such as the complementary roles of student and teacher (Lee & Voivodas, 1977). In addition, preschoolers learn many kinds of behavioral categories that are not themselves roles, although they are relevant to roles. The categories of work and play, for example, are closely related to many roles, including those of adult and child. By 3 years of age, most children can understand such behavioral categories, although they cannot yet relate them to roles. Play is a set of behaviors such as throwing a ball, blowing a whistle, and digging in a sandbox. Work is an independent set of behaviors, such as cooking dinner, planting flowers, and sitting at a desk (Tucker, 1979).

The understanding of behavioral categories constitutes a major advance over the earlier understanding of agency alone, because it allows children to group behaviors together in socially appropriate clusters. The behavior of a 2-year-old boy illustrates what is missing when a child does not understand behavioral categories. The boy turned over his tricycle and pretended that it was a washing machine in which he was washing clothes, as his mother did in a real washing machine. When one of the authors asked him if he was pretending to be a mother, he acted confused and said that he was not a mother. Apparently, this 2-year-old was only carrying out a particular action, not acting out the behavioral role of mother. By the age of 3, most children can immediately understand such a question and elaborate other actions or characteristics that mothers do.

Social Roles.   The first social role (Step 8) appears about a year later, at age 4, when the child coordinates two behavioral roles into a social relationship, an integration of a role with its complement. In role theory, every social role is defined in terms of its relation to at least one other category, called a "complementary role." For example, doctor is defined in relation to patient, and mother in relation to child (Sarbin & Allen, 1968). A person in the role of medical doctor behaves according to a set of norms that require, among other things, that he or she display certain medical skills with a patient and try to help that patient overcome illness or stay healthy. Similarly, the person in the role of patient is expected to cooperate with the doctor in examination and treatment. Doctor and patient form a complementary role relation—a social role.

In pretend play, a child who understands the social role of doctor can make a doctor-doll examine a patient-doll, with the two interacting appropriately. This new capacity has important implications for children's social competence, because it allows them to understand much more about conventional relationships among people. For instance, two brothers, one 3 and one 4 1/2 years of age, repeatedly played storekeeper. The younger boy had a storekeeper-doll stock the shelves and work in the store, thus showing a behavioral role, but he did not have the storekeeper interact with other dolls. The older boy made the game much more sophisticated for both children, supplying what was missing in the younger boy's play. He had the storekeeper interact with customers, asking them what items they wanted to buy, accepting pay, and pretending to order and stock what the customers needed. Thus, he added the complementary role interactions that are typical of social, as opposed to behavioral, roles.

The ability to define social roles has significance for many aspects of children's behavior besides pretending. Children, of course, define themselves partially in terms of social categories (Harter, 1983; Kohlberg, 1966), and the development of social roles therefore affects their concepts of self. With this new ability, children can see the categories boy and girl as being specifically related: Lisa does not merely belong to the category of girl; she is a girl *as opposed to* a boy. Girl and woman are seen as specifically related in a different way: A girl is not merely a category of child, but she is a child who *will become* a woman. The ability to comprehend such relations for gender and age, and probably for race and social class, seems to first emerge at approximately 4 years of age (Connell, 1978; Edwards, in press; Katz, 1973, 1982; Ruble, Balaban, & Cooper, 1981; Van Parys, 1981; Watson & Amgott-Kwan, 1983; Westerman, 1980). Indeed, concepts that are defined in terms of such relations probably cannot be understood before this period. The concept of social class, for instance, involves the relation of at least two classes, such as poor and rich (Naimark, 1981).

The change in role understanding seems to affect social relationships as well. Indeed, at the age of 4, children seem to begin to focus on social relationships *per se*. Evidence suggests, for example, that children's friendships first become true relationships at this age, with each friend fulfilling an expected role, instead of being merely an enjoyable companion (Furman, 1982; Hartup, 1983).

Besides social roles themselves, a number of other skills based on the capacity to relate social categories seem to develop at this age (Fischer, 1980; Fischer & Watson, 1981; Hand, 1981a). Children begin to define many social categories in relational terms. The behavioral categories of work and play, for instance, are redefined in relation to adult and child: Adults work; children play (Tucker, 1979). The relations of adults to work and of children to play are clearly not social roles by the conventional definition, but they do involve the coordination of one social category with another.

Role Intersections. At 6 to 7 years, children move beyond the simple social role to an understanding of "role intersection" (Step 12), in which they coordinate two social roles for one agent with two social roles for a second agent to form a system of social roles. For example, one doll can act as both doctor and father to a second doll, who is both his patient and his daughter.

Older preschoolers struggling with the facts of role intersection often exhibit a concern about conflicting role expectations. For example, when one of the authors was a graduate student, his son asked if he would still be the boy's father when he became a psychologist. After the father explained that a person can be both a psychologist and a father, the boy then asked, "Yes, but are you a teacher or a student? You teach school, and you go to classes." He then asked how his father could be a teacher, a student, and a psychologist and still live at home. Clearly, the boy was struggling with role intersections. His concerns seemed to stem from his ability to understand social roles and the norms that accompany them, without being able to intersect multiple roles. Perhaps the genuine concerns of children in such situations provide the impetus for their development to higher steps of role understanding.

The capacity to understand role intersections allows children to eliminate many confusions that plagued them in earlier years. Not only can their "Daddy" be a teacher to his students, for example, but at the same time he can be their father and a husband to their mother, who is his wife. Starting at about 6 years, children can thus coordinate the roles of parent and spouse, because they can understand how both of their parents can fill two roles at once (Fischer & Watson, 1981; Watson & Amgott-Kwan, 1983).

Likewise, children can eliminate earlier confusions they may have had about work and play. It is not true that work is always done by adults and play by children; both adults and children can play or work. With this new understanding, the child may conceive of play as something that is fun and easy, while work is something that is not so much fun and hard (Tucker, 1979).

Major advances also occur in the understanding of roles and relations involving gender, age, race, and social class (Katz & Zalk, 1978; Leahy, 1981; Maccoby & Jacklin, 1974; Williams, Bennett, & Best, 1975). Children devise, for instance, a general schema for social class—a scale of goodness, wealth, or well-being on which individual people can be placed (Connell,

1978; Naimark, 1981). The ways in which this schema are understood still remain concrete, of course, involving clothes, cleanliness, type of speech, and the like. But the schema can be sophisticated enough to include even the conception of a middle class between lower and upper classes.

It is at 6 to 7 years, then, that children begin to sort out the complexities of role intersections and combinations and thus to move rapidly closer to adults' understandings of roles. This development apparently explains why so much previous research has seemed to find that children do not understand social roles until the elementary school years (Watson, 1981). Tasks that are designed to assess conceptions similar to those of adults are likely to underestimate preschoolers' social-cognitive abilities. Only when tasks are explicitly designed to test a specific level of skill can researchers be confident that they are correctly assessing what children can do (Bertenthal, 1981; Roberts, 1981).

Throughout the elementary school years, children build more and more complex and sophisticated forms of concrete role intersections. Then, beginning as early as 10 or 11 years of age, they can move beyond these concrete social categories and enter the next developmental cycle—the understanding of social systems and networks. The last steps in Table 1 (Steps 15 to 18) sketch part of this next cycle.

Other Research.   The series of studies that we conducted strongly supported the predicted developmental sequence for both the role of medical doctor with its complements and for the roles within the nuclear family. In addition, a number of studies from other laboratories support these findings. Generally, children's understandings of social categories have been found to progress from nonrelational categories based on salient behaviors to categories based on social relations to categories that involve role intersections. The studies cited in the preceding discussion constitute only a small portion of relevant investigations.

In general, studies in other laboratories have used less structured methods and more complex or unfamiliar tasks, and they have not assessed each developmental step independently. Consequently, these investigations have come to more pessimistic conclusions about the abilities of preschoolers (Anderson, 1977; Chambers & Tavuchis, 1976; Emmerich, 1959, 1961; Greenfield & Childs, 1977; Jordan, 1980). In most cases, the ages for a particular developmental step were 2 to 3 years later than in our studies. This lag is not surprising, since our methods were specifically designed to detect the first blossoming of preschool children's understandings of social roles.

Development of Concepts of Social Interaction: Mean and Nice

Social roles constitute only one of a number of types of important social categories. People also establish categories that specify, for example, scripts for how to behave in specific situations, as in restaurants or theaters (Schank & Abelson, 1977), and categories that reflect how they are perceived by others (Harter, 1982; Livesley & Bromley, 1973; Rosenberg, 1979). One of the most significant types of social category for the preschool child involves modes of social interaction—how people interact with each other and what kinds of rules they follow in those interactions.

Among categories for social interactions, there is one related pair that seems to be especially salient to preschool children—mean and nice. At an early age, children learn to discriminate between the types of concrete behaviors that are laudable and those that are deplorable in the eyes of others. In addition to simply labeling the categories, children also need to understand the relations between behaviors—how one person's nice behavior derives from another person's nice behavior, or how one person's mean behavior derives from another person's mean behavior.

Assimilating society's system for classifying different types of behaviors and comprehending the subtleties of social causality are not easy tasks for the child. Deep appreciation of the fine points of social interaction seems to require years of develpment and appears not to be completed until early adulthood or even later (Broughton, 1978; Fischer, Hand & Russell, 1983). Still, the development of this appreciation starts at a young age and occurs in a gradual step-by-step fashion throughout childhood. At each point in development, children have some way of classifying and accounting for social interaction.

Hand (1981a) studied the development of children's capacity to differentiate and explain opposite types of social interaction throughout early and middle childhood. The sequence that she studied, outlined in Table 2, is similar to the sequence of social role development, although some of the particular steps tested were different. To trace development in a detailed but comprehensive manner, she used a variety of experimental tasks. First, the imitative pretending technique from the social role research was used to detect children's early understandings of social interaction: Children acted out stories about people their own age being either nice or mean. Second, other more open-ended measures were included to assess the children's understanding in less structured settings: Children made up stories of their own instead of imitating the experimenter's, and they answered a series of interview questions about the social catergories of nice and mean, good and bad, and smart and dumb. Subjects were 72 middle-class boys and girls ranging in age from 3 to 12 years. In a strong-scalogram analysis, 70 of the 72 subjects fit the predicted sequence perfectly. The results for the more open-ended conditions, as well as supportive research from other laboratories, will be described later.

Behavioral Categories.   As with social roles, the development of social-interaction concepts seems to begin with the idea that people can act

TABLE 2 A Developmental Sequence for Understanding Nice and Mean Social Interactions

Level	Approximate Age of Emergence [a]	Step	Skill	Examples
I: Single Social Categories	2–3 years	1	*Active other agent:* A person performs at least one behavior not necessarily fitting a social-interaction category.	Child pretends that one doll picks up a ball or suggests playing with another doll.
		2	*Behavioral category:* A person performs at least two behaviors fitting an interaction category, such as "nice" or "mean."	Child has one doll act nice to another doll, giving it candy and saying, "I like you." The second doll can be passive.
		3	*Shifting behavioral categories:* One person performs at least two behaviors fitting the category "nice," as in Step 2, and then a second person performs at least two behaviors fitting the category "mean."	Child has one doll act nice to a second doll, giving it candy and saying, "Let's play." A third doll enters and acts mean to the second one, hitting it and saying, "Give me your ball!" in both cases, the second doll can be passive.
II: Relations between Social Categories	4–5 years	4a [b]	*Combination of opposite categories in a single person:* One person performs behaviors fitting two opposing categories, such as "nice" and "mean."	Child has one doll act nice to a second doll, saying, "Let's be friends" and giving the doll candy. The first doll then hits the second, saying "Since we're friends you should give me your ball!" The second doll can be passive throughout.
		4b [b]	*One-dimensional social influence:* The behaviors of one person fitting an interaction category such as "mean" produce reciprocal behaviors fitting that category in a second person.	Child has one doll say mean things and hit another doll, who responds by hitting and expressing dislike for the first one. The second one's behavior is clearly produced by the first one's behavior.

continued

TABLE 2 (cont.)

Level	Approximate Age of Emergence [a]	Step	Skill	Examples
		5	*One-dimensional social influence with three characters behaving in similar ways:* Same as Step 4b, but with three people interacting reciprocally according to a social category.	With three dolls, child has one tease the others, while a second one hits the others. The third doll rejects both of the first two because they are mean.
		6 [c]	*One-dimensional social influence with three characters behaving in opposite ways:* The behaviors of one person fitting a category such as "nice" and those of a second person fitting an opposite category such as "mean" produce reciprocal behaviors in the third person fitting the corresponding categories.	With three dolls, child has one share with the others, while a second one hits the others. The third doll responds nicely to the first doll and meanly to the second.
III: Systems of Social Categories	6–9 years	7	*Two-dimensional social influence:* Two people interact in ways fitting opposite categories, such that the first one acts, for example, both nice and mean, and the second one responds with reciprocal behaviors in the same categories.	Child has one doll initiate friendship with a second doll but in a mean way. The second one, confused about the discrepancy, declines the friendship because of the meanness. The first then apologizes and makes another friendly gesture, which the second one responds to accordingly.

continued

TABLE 2 (cont.)

Level	Approximate Age of Emergence [a]	Step	Skill	Examples
		8	*Two-dimensional social influence with three characters*: Same as Step 7 but with three people interacting reciprocally according to opposite categories.	With three dolls, child has one doll act friendly to a second one, while a third one initiates play in a mean way. The second doll acts friendly to the first one and rejects the third, pointing out the latter's meanness. The third then apologizes for being mean, while the first one does something new that is mean. The second doll accepts the third one's apology and rejects the first one, pointing out the change in his or her behavior.
IV: Abstractions	10 years and older	9	*Integration of opposite behaviors in terms of a single abstraction*: Two instances of interactions like that in Step 7 take place, and the relations between the two interactions are explained in terms of some general abstraction, such as that intentions matter more than actions.	With three dolls, child has one act friendly to a second, while a third initiates play in a mean way. The second doll responds to each accordingly, but then learns that the nice one had mean intentions while the mean one had nice intentions. The second doll then changes his or her behavior to each to match their intentions and explains that he or she cares more about people's intentions than their actions.

(continued)

TABLE 2   (cont.)

Level	Approximate Age of Emergence [a]	Step	Skill	Examples
		10	*Relation of two abstractions concerning opposite behaviors:* In interactions where people act in opposite ways to each other, as in Step 9, consideration of one abstraction about the inter-actions, such as that some people have greater needs than others, is used to modify consideration of a second abstraction, such as that intentions matter more than actions.	Child has two dolls act nice to a third doll to trick him or her into doing their homework for them. The third one recognizes the trick and rejects both dolls for having a mean intention behind their nice actions. But upon learning the needs that motivated the others, the third one is nice to the one that had special needs for help with homework, while rejecting the one who was simply lazy. He or she explains that his or her evaluation of their intention to trick was modified by their needs.

[a] Ages vary widely across tasks and conditions. Therefore, ages are listed only for general developmental levels, and they indicate when skills at that level first develop for middle-class children.

[b] Steps 4a and 4b develop at approximately the same time.

[c] Step 6 is transitional between Levels II and III. Apparently it can be mastered at Level II, but it is much easier to master at Level III.

Note: Portions of this table are based on Hand (1981a).

on their own as independent agents (Step 1). By the age of 3 years, most children can go beyond simple agency to use simple, concrete behavioral categories (Step 2), such as organizing two or more actions under the label "nice" (*e.g.*, giving someone candy and saying, "I like you"). Of course, the particular categories children use depend on the kinds of interactions to which they are exposed.

Most 3-year-olds have such good control of the categories "nice" and "mean" that they can easily shift back and forth between them, making one doll act nice and then making another doll act mean, or vice versa (Step 3). They are unable, however, to understand that the same person can act both ways in a short period of time. For example, Livesley and Bromley (1973) reported that preschoolers, who observed a person acting in opposite ways, tended to think they had seen two different people. 3-year-olds are also unable to understand reciprocal relations between social categories—how the nice or mean behavior of one person may cause the nice or mean behavior of another person. Thus, they cannot yet comprehend social causality or influence involving such categories.

Relating Categories of Interaction. By the age of 4 to 4 1/2 years, children have grown significantly in their ability to conceptualize social interaction. At this point, they begin to go beyond the separate behavioral categories of the 3-year-old and to integrate two or three categories of behavior into a relation. This ability is similar to the relating of two behavioral roles into a social role such as doctor with patient. They can understand, for example, the combination of opposite behaviors in a single person, as when the same person is nice at one moment and mean a short time later (Step 4a). And they can understand social influence, in which one person acts mean to another person because that other person acted mean to the first person (Step 4b).

The ability to relate two behavioral categories enables the child to participate in the social milieu in a more independent and self-directed way than ever before. The capacity to adopt both perspectives in an interaction increases children's knowledge of each perspective (Flavell, 1977; Lawler, 1981; Selman, 1980). The child who can consider both his or her own behavior and that of another person simultaneously can use his or her own actions more effectively to influence the other's behavior in the interaction (Westerman & Fischman-Havstad, 1982).

However, there remain important limits to the 4 1/2-year-old's thinking. Children this age cannot understand social influence as it relates to the combination of nice and mean. In other words, they cannot integrate their understanding that one person's behavior is caused by another person's behavior with their understanding that people can behave in both nice and mean ways. Consequently, they cannot comprehend how a set of social influences produces both positive and negative behaviors.

In addition, the 4 1/2-year-old's abilities to understand social influence by itself or the combination of nice and mean by itself are severely limited by context. In contexts that do not provide explicit support for relating social categories, such as unfamiliar situations and verbal interviews, children of this age tend to fall back on more primitive behaviors, such as treating nice and mean as separate categories (Hand, 1981b; Harter, 1982, 1983).

Integrating Multiple Characteristics of Interaction. Most 6- or 7-year-olds can integrate social influence with the combination of nice and mean to form a system for understanding social influence involving opposite behaviors. They can show how someone can act nice to one person and mean to a second person at the same time, because the first person acted nice and the other one acted mean (Step 6). Many children can also show an even more complex integration, in which one person acts both nice and mean to another person because that other person demonstrated both nice and mean behaviors (Step 7).

As with 4- and 5-year-olds, the social-interaction skills of elementary school children depend greatly on the amount of support provided by the situation. Without the help of a structured task, children typically show much less advanced behaviors (Hand, 1981b). The ability to understand social influence involving opposite behaviors seems to come and go depending upon the degree to which the situation helps children to structure their behavior appropriately (Hand, 1981a).

During the elementary school years, these skills are extended and consolidated so that they become less dependent on environmental support. Children gain the ability to understand social influence involving opposite behaviors even in more open-ended tasks. At the same time, they expand the range of categories in which they possess this understanding, applying it to situations involving more than two people and to pairs of social categories that are less concrete than nice and mean, such as smart and dumb or proud and sad (Hand, 1981a; Harter, 1977, 1982). In addition, children at this age can use an increasingly diverse range of antecedents to account for people's actions.

The new ability to integrate multiple characteristics of social interaction has major ramifications for the child—at least as far-reaching as those arising at about age 4 from the ability to relate interaction categories. The 6- or 7-year-old can begin to simultaneously take into account two aspects of each of two actors' behaviors in an interaction. For instance, she can not only consider both another person and herself, but she can also appreciate that both people have the capacity to act in positive and negative ways (Hand, 1981a; Harter, 1982). This capacity enables the child to coordinate her behavior with another person's in a much more effective and finely-tuned manner. Being able to think about her own positive and negative behaviors in relation to someone else's positive and negative behaviors means that the child can tailor her behavior closely to another person's. In this way, she becomes able to increase her social effectiveness, improving her chances of accomplishing what she wants while satisfying the needs of the other person.

These new abilities have significant limits, however. They are very much tied to concrete observable behaviors and situations, like the specific acts and events that cause the child's friends to act nice or mean. At this point, the child is still unable to go beyond these concrete generalizations to a more powerful, abstract conceptualization of social interaction (Biggs & Collis, 1982; Hand, 1981a; Harter, 1983; Rosenberg, 1979).

A broader, more abstract conception of human behavior awaits the onset of abstract thinking in early adolescence—occurring at about age 12 in Hand's (1981a) study of nice and mean behaviors. The advent of abstract thinking enables the person to move beyond explaining behavior via specific observable or easily inferable facts to begin positing durable traits, values, or social influences to explain human interactions and social systems. Some of the early developments in this new phase are outlined in Steps 9 and 10 of Table 2. It takes years of development, of course, for the school-age child, who can influence specific interactions, to change into the adult, who can operate in social systems and networks and influence society more broadly.

THE CONTRIBUTION OF CONTEXT TO DEVELOPMENT

Psychologists and educators sometimes describe skills as if they were unitary abilities, competencies that a child has in complete form. The child can read, the child understands conservation, the child comprehends social roles or social influence. Such statements imply that skills have a life of their own, separate from the contexts in which they are demonstrated. The evidence does not support such a view (Biggs & Collis, 1982; Feldman, 1980; Fischer, 1980; Flavell, 1971; Fleishman, 1982). The child who has mastered many basic reading skills is not able to read all material presented to him in school. The child who shows conservation of number commonly fails to show conservation of length. The child who can demonstrate an understanding of social categories in an imitative pretending task frequently cannot do so in an interview assessment (Hand, 1981a).

This absence of unitary cross-situational abilities follows logically from the fact that both the child and the environment contribute to performance. There could be unitary abilities only if environmental variations had minimal effects on behaviors. When describing children's skills, then, scientists and educators need to attend to the context in which each skill is manifested. All sorts of contextual variations typically produce significant differences in children's demonstrated level of ability. Factors that have been shown to affect developmental level include practice, familiarity, the presence of other people, the setting, and the form of the task (Cole & Riel, 1983; Jackson, Campos, & Fischer, 1978; Nicolich, 1978).

The Relation Between Competence and Spontaneous Performance

It would be unfortunate if all that could be said was that developmental level varies across contexts. Surely there must be order in the variations. Some recent findings suggest a type of order that would seem to have major implications for analyses of learning and development.

One of the most important dimensions along which contexts can vary seems to be the amount of structure or contextual support for children's behavior. Changes in the amount of support typically produce profound differences in the developmental level of behavior (Hand, 1981b; Vygotsky, 1978). In general, greater contextual support increases the probability that children will demonstrate their highest capabilities. With less contextual support, a wider variety of behaviors are observed, and hence a wider range of behavioral differences occur both among and within individuals.

In our various studies of the development of social roles and inter-actions, however, a systematic developmental change was found in this relation. At different points in social-cognitive development, the relation between children's behavior in structured settings and that in less structured, more open-ended settings shifted dramatically.

Early in the preschool years, between approximately 1 and 4 years of age, children tend spontaneously to demonstrate their most advanced competence not only in structured settings but also in more open-ended ones. Later in the preschool years, starting at about 4 years, the pattern changes abruptly. Older children seldom show their most advanced competence spontaneously, but seem to require a structured setting to consistently demonstrate the best they can do. The shift from the first pattern to the second occurs precisely at the point where children begin to integrate social categories into social roles, social influence, and the like (Hand, 1981b). According to skill theory, this point marks the shift to a new developmental level, beginning at about 4 years of age, at which children can relate categories or other kinds of representations within a single skill.

The research on social roles (Watson & Fischer, 1977, 1980) and on social interaction (Hand, 1981a) has shown this same pattern. In both sets of studies, children's competence was measured by a structured assessment and in two spontaneous conditions. The experimenter administered the structured assessment (employing the imitative pretending technique) and then left the room, asking the child to play with the experimental toys and make up stories of her own. After returning, the experimenter asked the child to tell the best story she could. The "best story" and the stories from the play period constituted the two spontaneous conditions, both of which were scored according to the same developmental sequence used in the structured assessment (shown in Tables 1 and 2, respectively, for the two sets of studies). Children's highest performances in the two spontaneous conditions were virtually identical.

The question asked was, "Did children show the same highest developmental step in the structured assessment and the two spontaneous assessments?" In the social role studies, the shift from the first pattern to the second occurred at the step where children's competence (their highest step in the structured assessment) was social roles or beyond (Steps 8 and higher in Table 1). That is, children whose competence was no higher than Step 7 typically demonstrated their competence in both spontaneous conditions, but children who were capable of combining two or more roles in a relation were unlikely to show their competence in the spontaneous conditions, as illustrated in Figure 1 (Watson & Fischer, 1977, 1980; see also Largo & Howard, 1979).

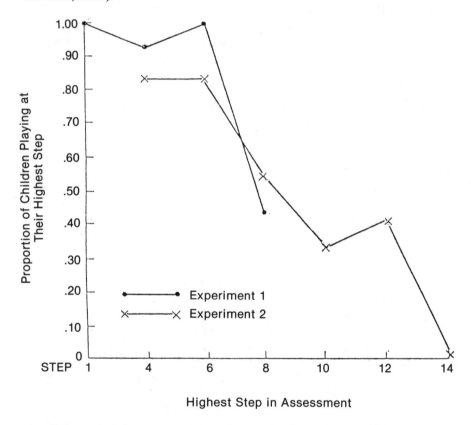

Figure 1:   Relation between Competence and Spontaneous Behavior in the Social Role Studies.*

*Adapted with permission from Watson and Fischer (1980).

Results from Hand's (1981b) study of social-interaction concepts showed a similar shift at the first step where children had to relate two inter-action categories (Step 4 in Table 2). Virtually all the children at this step demonstrated their most advanced level of competence in the spontaneous conditions, but virtually none of the children who were capable of relating two or more social categories exhibited this competence in the spontaneous conditions.

Thus, the evidence suggests that before children begin to relate social categories, they tend to perform spontaneously at their most advanced level of competence. Once they have begun to relate categories, however, more support from the environment seems to be required for them to demon-strate their competence involving relations of categories. Interestingly, the French psychologist Wallon (1970) described something similar to this phe-nomenon. Before the age of 4, he said, children tend to be driven to master whatever they encounter. Starting at 4, on the other hand, they come to assert their own goals and are no longer so driven by the demands of the im-mediate environment. However, Wallon's description seems to have been based primarily on informal observations of children, and he reported no research testing this hypothesis.

Surely more research is needed to determine the extent of this phe-nomenon. Does it occur in most domains of cognitive development, or only in a few? It could be, for example, that with tasks that are very important emotionally, children will be more likely to spontaneously show their most advanced competence. Our hypothesis, however, is that the phenomenon is highly general (Fischer, Hand, & Russell, 1983; Hand, 1981a). If this hy-pothesis proves to be accurate, then it would seem to require a recasting of what scientists mean by 'competence' (Rubin et al., 1983).

Implications for Education and Other Forms of Socialization

According to these findings, children of early preschool age seem to require little special environmental support to perform at their most advanced de-velopmental level. They seem naturally to engage with people and tasks in such a way that they directly practice and consolidate their newest skills. Thus, an educational program that maximizes opportunities to experiment with different materials and activities can be effective at this age. Likewise, in any socialization context, children of this age may tend naturally to func-tion at their most advanced competence, so long as the environment does not interfere.

At approximately age 4, however, when the child has developed the capacity to integrate categories in a relation, the situation seems to shift. More specific environmental support appears to become necessary to encour-age children to develop and use their skills at their most advanced level. This is not to say that a curriculum for the child at this age should be highly regimented and directive, although some structure and specific encouragement will be helpful to the child's development. Such structure and encouragement will probably be most effective when children are naturally motivated to pursue a particular activity. A sensitive teacher or parent who can follow a child's interests and intervene at propitious moments to suggest new or more effective ways of pursuing an activity is likely to facilitate the child's development across a wide range of domains.

THE INTERACTION BETWEEN COMPETENCE AND USE
OF SOCIAL CATEGORIES

Based on the research with structured assessments, the development of the understanding of social categories seems to be relatively straightforward, proceeding through three basic developmental levels in the preschool years. Infants cannot represent social categories, but at about 2 years of age, toddlers begin to understand agency—the ways that people can act on their own, independently of the child. By 2 1/2 to 3 years, children show the first level of true social categories. They can put together some of these independent actions to form their first *single social categories*— collections of behaviors and characteristics that form a class of social attributes. The second level, *simple relations of social categories,* first develops at approximately 4 years of age, when children can integrate two or more social categories into a skill for a social role, a type of social influence, or some other social relation. The third level, involving understandings of *complex systems of social categories,* first emerges at age 6 or 7 in forms such as social role intersections, social influence involving opposite behaviors, and multiple emotions in social interactions.

The portrait of social-category development clearly is not that simple, however, as demonstrated by the research on spontaneous performance. Structured assessments provide a good estimate of the child's best social abilities—his or her competence—but on the other hand, they also tend to constrain the child's behavior. As a result, much of the natural variability in behavior goes undetected in structured assessments. The best solution seems to be to use both structured assessments and measures of behavior in less structured contexts (Hand, 1981b).

Behavior in less structured contexts is particularly significant in the process of socialization. The way children contribute to their own socialization may be especially notable in situations where their behavior is not severely constrained. Children strive to understand their society's categories and rules and to behave in accordance with them, but when the context allows a range of behaviors, the relation between understanding and behavior may be complex and interesting.

Understanding a social category is not the same as using it. Understanding seems to be a prerequisite for effective use, but there is probably not a one-to-one relation between understanding and use. When investigators have tested for a relatively simple relation—for example, that greater understanding of sex roles will lead to closer adherence to those roles—they have found nothing so simple (Marcus & Overton, 1978).

The use of social categories is naturally affected not only by level of understanding but also by a host of other factors— the child's own goals, the affective valence of a category, the society's emphasis on the category, the exact nature of the connections among related categories, the demands of the immediate context. In addition, as we described above, the fact that a child has the competence to understand a category, as measured in a structured assessment, does not guarantee that he or she will demonstrate that competence in a different setting, particularly a less structured one. Thus, greater competence with a social category does not automatically lead to more use of that category or to more desirable behavior with respect to that category.

Unfortunately, there has been little research directly testing the relation between competence measured in a structured assessment and use in a less structured context. The paucity of research precludes any definitive conclusions, but the few existing studies do suggest systematic developmental changes in the relation. Each of the three major developmental levels of social categories seems to be characterized by certain kinds of distortions and biases in spontaneous use, which affect how children at each level comprehend and react to socialization pressures.

Middle Preschool: "Globbing" in Behavioral Categories

At the first developmental level, 3-year-olds build single behavioral categories. In spontaneous behavior, older children also use these categories in a manner that seems to be characteristic: they mix together components that in fact are separate, a process that we have called "globbing" (Fischer, Hand, & Russell, 1983). Because children do not relate categories, they cannot compare and differentiate them (Fischer, 1980; Werner, 1957). As a result, they have difficulty separating related social categories, which become mixed together in a "glob." Elements of one social category are combined with elements of a second one to create an original, but often unrealistic, globbed category.

Although our informal observations suggest that globbing of social categories is commonplace in 3- and 4-year-olds, research conducted on children of this age is scant, and we know of only two empirically documented examples of globbing—one involving age and one involving race. Edwards (in press) studied preschoolers' ability to discriminate photographs of people by age. Most 3- to 4-year-olds (mean age 3.9) could easily separate children into "little ones and big ones," but when asked to indicate which group they themselves belonged to, they made a systematic error. Most of the boys placed themselves with the big children, even though they in fact belonged with the little ones, while most of the girls placed themselves with the little children. By the age of 4 to 5 years (mean age 4.7), the effect had disappeared with children of both sexes placing themselves in the big category half of the time and in the little category half of the time. This distribution of responses was appropriate, since 4- and 5-year-olds were close to the age border between the small and large groups.

Edwards interpreted the younger children's systematic errors as reflecting a mixing together, or globbing, of size with gender. Since boys are males and men tend to be bigger than women, then boys must be big. Similarly, since girls are females and women tend to be smaller than men, then girls must be little. While this confusion of size with gender seems to disappear by 4 to 5 years of age, at least in simple tasks, a tendency to confuse size with another dimension, age, continues until 7 or 8, apparently because these two characteristics are in fact so closely related (Kratochwill & Goldman, 1973).

Van Parys (1981) uncovered a second instance of globbing in the use of the category of race by 3-year-old black children. Middle-class black and white children 3, 4, and 5 years of age sorted drawings of people into categories based on sex, age, and/or race. A number of black children, especially 3-year-old boys, systematically classified themselves incorrectly by race. When asked to place themselves in a black or white category, they placed themselves with the whites. Independently, these same children demonstrated both the competence to discriminate race accurately and the tendency to use race spontaneously: They showed good skill in classifying drawings of other people as black or white, and they tended to focus on other people's race in tasks where they could have focused on sex or age instead. By 5 years of age, the misclassification of self had disappeared. Similar confusions about race have been documented in several classic studies: young black children tend to classify themselves as white and to prefer white dolls and white playmates (Clark & Clark, 1947; Goodman, 1964; Porter, 1971), although there is some variation in these results across studies (Katz, 1982) and tasks (Van Parys, 1981).

In this instance of globbing, 3-year-olds seem to mix together goodness with white and badness with black, more often assigning negative characteristics to dark-skinned people than to light-skinned ones (Clark, Hocevar, & Dembo, 1980). According to this interpretation, they know that they themselves are good, and they think that it is better to be white than black. Consequently, they put themselves in the globbed category of "good" white, although they are in fact black.

Despite the paucity of research on early social categories, the child-psychoanalytic literature suggests that these instances may reflect a fundamental characteristic of the way young preschool children think (A. Freud, 1966; Mahler, Pine, & Bergman, 1975). Because of their primitive developmental level, young children consistently combine categories that do not belong together and thus construct categories that greatly distort social reality. This globbing process bears some similarity to what Sigmund Freud (1955) called condensation, a process in which two or more objects or people are combined in a single image or thought, as when a person in a dream seems to be the dreamer's spouse and parent at the same time. Contrary to Freud's interpretation, globbing does not need to be unconsciously motivated, since it seems to be a characteristic of certain levels of thinking (Feffer, 1982; Fischer & Pipp, in press–a).

Late Preschool: Oversimplified Relations Between Social Categories

By 4 to 4 1/2 years, most children can begin to relate two social categories and so move beyond gross distortions of behavioral categories. This new capacity leads to a major increase in sophistication, as shown in the research involving social roles and social interactions. Children can start to understand how doctors relate to patients, mothers to fathers, and so on—as well as how one person's actions towards another affect that second person's responses to the first.

In real-life situations, however, relations of social categories are usually complex. Each person occupies multiple social categories, often simultaneously, and the distinctions between categories are often subtle. Faced with these complexities, 4- to 6-year-olds tend to oversimplify the relations between categories. The oversimplifications seem to take at least two forms. First, children treat related categories as sharply distinct and miss the subtle differences—in effect, stereotyping social categories. Second, when relations in fact overlap, children mix them up, showing a form of globbing that is more sophisticated than that occurring at the previous level of understanding single categories.

Stereotyping. While there have been no definitive studies of the development of stereotyping in the preschool years, the emergence of the capacity to relate social categories often seems to lead to extreme stereotyping of salient social categories, including those involving gender, race, class, and age. Many children of this age show a remarkable surge of stereotyping, even in the face of blatantly contradictory evidence. Sex stereotyping seem to be especially common. One 4-year-old boy, for example, asserted that women wear dresses, even though his own mother almost always wore pants. A 4-year-old girl insisted on wearing pink dresses and party shoes, even on the playground.

Indeed, research on both sex-role and racial categories suggests that stereotyping may follow a standard developmental course. For sex roles, children show some evidence of stereotyping as early as 3 years of age, and sex stereotyping seems to be well established by 4 to 5 years (Kuhn et al., 1978; Williams, Bennett, & Best, 1975). The degree of stereotyping then appears to increase to a maximum at age 7 or 8 (Damon, 1977; Maccoby, 1980). During the elementary school years, the trend reverses, and stereotyping begins to slowly decrease, with children showing more flexibility about gender roles (Carter & Patterson, 1982).

For race categories, the first evidence for stereotyping of blacks and whites appears as early as 3 years of age. Then, there seems to be a surge in this stereotyping throughout the rest of the preschool years (Clark et al., 1980; Clark & Clark, 1947; Katz, 1982; Stevenson & Stewart, 1958). Stereotyping of black as negative and white as positive appears to peak in the late preschool and early elementary school years. After the age of 7 or 8, racial stereotyping appears to decrease systematically throughout the elementary school period (Clark et al., 1980; Katz, 1982; Katz & Zalk, 1978; Williams, Best, & Boswell, 1975). At the least, children in this period come to deal more accurately with the demands of the immediate situation, understanding, for example, that it is often undesirable to state a blatant stereotype.

A plausible interpretation of the data on racial stereotyping is that starting at 4 or 5 years, black children stop the extreme globbing of racial categories that is characteristic of the previous level. Now, instead of sometimes thinking of themselves as white, they gradually come to accept their race. In the late preschool years, however, children tend to stereotype black as negative; consequently, they may experience great difficulties with their racial self-image. Perhaps only in the elementary school years, when they can begin to deal with the complexities of racial categories, will these children be able to resolve the apparent conflict engendered by their earlier oversimplified understanding of race.

The developmental course for stereotyping suggested by these findings for gender and race can be divided into four main phases. (a) With the development of behavioral categories at approximately 3 years of age, children show evidence of some stereotyping. (b) At 4 to 5 years, there seems to be a surge in stereotyping, apparently arising from the fact that children gain the ability to understand role relations. For instance, they become capable of treating boys and girls as, in some senses, opposites. (c) Stereotyping seems to reach its peak or maximum between 6 and 8 years. By this age, children have had sufficient time to master the oversimplified role relations that they began to develop a few years earlier. In addition, children are moving into a new developmental level at this age, and one characteristic of the transition seems to be that skills from the previous level show a developmental spurt (see Fischer, Pipp, & Bullock, in press). Thus, children's oversimplifications may peak at this time. (d) After 7 or 8 years, stereotyping seems to decrease or become more qualified as children gain the ability to deal with complex relations among real-life social categories.

The development of other sorts of stereotyping may well follow this same model. Categories and attitudes toward social class or age, for example, may move through a similar progression (see Connell, 1978). Also, the distortion of role relations is not limited to emotionally loaded roles like those involving race and gender, but is also evident in less loaded social categories, such as work and play. Tucker (1979) found that many 4- and 5-year-olds believe work is what adults do, play is what children do. According to this stereotyped way of thinking, children cannot work and adults cannot play.

It is important to realize, however, that this developmental portrait of stereotyping will not hold for all definitions and measures of stereotyping. Only the simplest types of stereotyping will occur at these early ages. More complex types, such as those requiring conceptions of social institutions or networks, will of course not develop until later.

What seems to be characteristic of the late preschool years, is that for the first time children become competent enough to understand and use the concrete stereotypes that they encounter in their everyday social lives. Thus, stereotyping in this period arises naturally from the combination of the social reality they experience with the limitations of their ability to understand that reality.

Globbing. The oversimplified relations of categories in the late preschool years produce not only stereotyping but also a form of globbing. Of course, the globbing of relations of categories is not as primitive as the globbing of single categories at the previous level. Instead of mixing together individual categories, children seem to mix together category relations that overlap in real life.

The many overlapping social roles in the nuclear family appear to provide a particularly rich source for this type of globbing. A child's father is an adult, a male, a man, a husband, and a father, all at the same time. The man's daughter is a child, a female, a girl, a daughter, and often a sister. With so much overlapping, 4- to 6-year-olds cannot get all the relations straight. They can think about simple relations between categories, but they cannot form a broader framework to grasp the way each category relates to all the others. The several roles of parents seem to be especially likely to be globbed: husband/wife, father/mother, man/woman, and male/female are collapsed into a single role relation, usually referred to by the child with the labels "Mommy" and "Daddy." Children do not seem to be able to understand, for example, that their mother and father simultaneously fill both parent and spouse roles (Watson & Amgott-Kwan, 1983).

Globbing of the overlapping roles of parents seems to provide the basis for an emotional drama that is common in nuclear families—what Freud (1924/1961) called the Oedipus conflict. The essence of this conflict is that the child tries to take the place of the same-sex parent as the object of affection of the opposite-sex parent: the boy tries to replace his father, the girl her mother. The child can attempt such a simple substitution because he globs overlapping roles. In the collapsed role relation "Mommy"/"Daddy", the child focuses on the fact that "Mommy" and "Daddy" are a female and male who have a special relationship. Because other characteristics of "Mommy" and "Daddy" are overlooked, any male can substitute for "Daddy" or any female for "Mommy," and so a child can easily take the place of the same-sex parent (Fischer & Watson, 1981).

Presumably, many other examples of globbing of relations also occur in the late preschool years. Uncovering such distortions would seem to be particularly relevant to understanding emotional development during this age period. In the same way that globbing family relations seems to have emotional consequences in the family, globbing other types of relations would seem likely to have other important emotional consequences.

Effects of Social Evaluation.   Along with learning the most basic relations among social categories in their society, children 4 to 6 years of age also appear to learn society's evaluations of prominent social categories. Their new ability to understand relations enables them to compare social categories in order to evaluate them. Four- to 6-year-olds are thus able to determine the importance and value of categories such as male and female or black and white in their society.

Van Parys' (1981) study demonstrates how children learn and use such evaluations. She administered a number of choice tasks to seventy-two 3-, 4-, and 5-year-old black and white middle-class Denver children. Each child sorted drawings into categories that required him or her to choose among various combinations of gender, age, and race—putting together the ones that were similar to each other in some tasks and the ones that were like the self in other tasks. She thus obtained measures of the psychological salience or importance to the children of the three types of categories.

Three-year-olds did not show any consistent pattern of choice, except that many of them tended to ignore race. 4- and 5-year-olds, on the other hand, showed a pattern of choice that seemed to match the way middle-class adults use the categories. Gender was used most often, age next, and race least. This finding cannot be explained in terms of the physical salience of the categories in the drawings because the figures were drawn to minimize salience differences. In addition, if one category were physically most salient, it would have been age, since the children and adults in the drawings differed obviously in size. Also, research has shown that the age dimension is generally salient for both infants and toddlers (Brooks & Lewis, 1976; Edwards, in press).

Van Parys' results indicate that when gender, age, and race are in question, gender is the dimension that 4- and 5-year-olds attend to most, although they also attend frequently to age. In her sample, only a few children focused on race. However, different subgroups of children showed different rankings of categories as a function of their own gender and race. These differences seemed to reflect the statuses of the categories to which the children belonged. In white middle-class culture, males are generally valued more than females, and for tasks in which children were describing themselves, white boys and girls made choices that reflected this difference. Four- and 5-year-old white boys showed the general pattern, selecting on the basis of gender more than age, but white girls of the same ages de-emphasized gender and emphasized age, choosing on the basis of age more often than gender. Both groups used race the least often.

With black children the patterns of choice were different, apparently reflecting the more positive evaluation of females in black American culture (Weston & Mednick, 1970). Four- and 5-year-old black girls tended to follow the general pattern of selecting on the basis of gender more than age, but black boys of the same age de-emphasized gender and chose more often on the basis of age.

These complex effects of the children's own characteristics were further complicated by the effects of various tasks. Seemingly minor variations in the assessment tasks sometimes produced major changes in the patterns of choice. It is not known whether these task effects were the result of the young ages of the children participating in the study or whether they would also be characteristic of older children's and adults' choices. Studies that use only one task, it would seem, cannot make legitimate conclusions about the general patterns of choice in preschool children.

By 4 or 5 years of age, children seem to have learned the basic social categories that they encounter in their society and to have organized those categories into relations reflecting their society's reality and values. Because of the limits of their understanding, they tend to stereotype social relations, but their stereotypes are primarily exaggerations of the realities of their society. It might be said that 4- and 5-year-olds often understand the relations of social categories in their society all too well.

Elementary School: Realistic Systems of Social Categories

The social-cognitive advance that begins at 6 or 7 years has pervasive implications for children's social behavior. With the ability to integrate multiple social categories in complex relations such as role intersections, children can move past the distortions and confusions of earlier years and understand the social categories around them in concrete detail. Many societies acknowledge this ability to understand the complexities of social behavior by giving children new social responsibilities at this age (Rogoff, Sellers, Pirrotta, Fox, & White, 1975; Weisner & Gallimore, 1977). Starting at 6 or 7 years, children begin, for example, to take responsibility for care of younger siblings and for important chores, such as tending livestock and preparing food.

The advent of this new ability seems to explain why most previous research has found that social categories, especially social roles, are not understood until the elementary school years (*e.g.*, Bigner, 1974; Marcus & Overton, 1978; Piaget, 1924/1928). Although that conclusion was clearly overdrawn, it is true that preschool children cannot understand complex tasks dealing with social categories and that elementary school children can eliminate most of the distortions that are so common in preschoolers' use of categories.

Indeed, once children correct these distortions, they seem to reject them vehemently. Freud (1924/1961) reported, for example, that when elementary school children correct the Oedipal belief that they can substitute for their same-sex parent and marry their opposite-sex parent, they emotionally reject the idea of doing so, often finding the thought repulsive and denying that they ever entertained it. In a less emotional domain, Tucker (1979) discovered a similar phenomenon. After children correct their belief that work is what adults do and play is what children do, they have difficulty even pretending to have the belief. That is, in a game about work and play they often cannot make a doll act as if it believed that what adults do is work and what children do is play.

More generally, children's conceptions of social categories move toward an accurate reflection of the concrete realities of their society. The oversimplified stereotyping of the previous level gives way to a more moderate or qualified form that captures accurately the society's definitions of social relations. Even for difficult concrete concepts, reality seems to play a greater role at this age than earlier. For example, because they can begin to comprehend concepts like wealth, children come to understand social class better. Thus, although social class stereotyping may blossom, lower and upper classes are less likely to be confused with good and bad. Complex issues concerning occupation and status enter the child's interpretation of class (Connell, 1978; Leahy, 1981; Naimark, 1981).

The realistic systems of social categories at this age are not completely free of distortion, however. Their accuracy in mirroring concrete reality seems to produce a type of distortion—a literalness in the interpretation of social categories and relations. Because children of this age are not yet able to place social relations in the broader context of social systems, they show a rigid or literal adherence to many social rules, including those for gender (Kohlberg, 1966; Williams, Bennett, & Best, 1975) and for "proper" behavior (Adelson, 1975; Harter, 1983). One 8-year-old boy, for instance, was shopping with his mother and 1-year-old baby sister at the supermarket. At one point, his mother took a few steps away from the shopping cart in which the baby was sitting, and the 8-year-old self-righteously pointed to a sign on the cart and said, "Mother, it says right here, 'Do not leave baby unattended.'" A 7-year-old girl was upset when her father came to pick her up from school on Mothers' Visiting Day, because, she said, only mothers were allowed to be at school that day.

One of the best-documented facts of spontaneous social behavior in the elementary school years is that children separate into unisex groups (Maccoby & Jacklin, 1974). Girls play primarily with other girls, and boys primarily with other boys. Likewise, children of this age form close friendships almost exclusively with children of the same sex (Furman, 1982). These social patterns seem to be consistent with the children's concrete, stereotyped understandings of gender roles. Boys and girls are understood to be different in many specific ways and even considered to be opposites. Consequently, children associate with those who are like themselves—other children of the same sex.

Although we know of almost no research that has directly tested how children's understandings of social categories and rules mesh with their social behavior at this age, it would seem that many of the salient characteristics of elementary school behavior relate in a similar way to children's new understandings. For example, structured games become a major part of social interaction in the elementary school years. When children play cops and robbers, they need to keep track of role intersections, because each child fulfills both a pretend role (cop or robber) and a real role (Johnny the 9-year-old or Jason the 8-year-old). In games like hide-and-seek or dodge, they need to be able to keep track of rapidly changing roles: a minute ago Nicole was "It" and I had to avoid her, but now I am "It" and have to catch Nicole. In a similar vein, children at this age begin to strive to emulate attractive heroes or heroines in their lives. They are able to do so because they can consider the other's observable attributes in relation to their own, in order to modify their own behavior to become more like their idol's (Fischer & Watson, 1981; Kagan, 1958; Ruble, in press).

In general, children of elementary school age seem to have the capacity to understand the concrete realities of social life and thus to develop a new range of social skills, which allow them to act effectively in social relations.

CONCLUSIONS: INDIVIDUALS AND CULTURAL COMPLEXITY

Societies routinely teach children categories that define how everyone in the society is supposed to act. In scientists' analyses of this socialization process, the contribution of the developing child has typically been lost. Social categories are always realized in behavior through the child's understandings and motivations, and therefore a full analysis of socialization requires taking into account the child's understanding and use of social categories.

The portrait we have painted of the early development of social categories is straightforward. Children proceed from an awareness of single behavioral categories to simple relations of categories to complex systems of categories. For each of these developmental levels, children also seem to show characteristic modes of distortion when faced with situations that require more advanced skills than they can produce. With single behavioral categories, they demonstrate the process of globbing, in which several categories are mixed together. Simple relations of categories are characterized by stereotyping based on the evaluations of the categories by society; when faced with complex relations between categories, children also tend to mix up or glob relations that overlap in the real world. With respect to the third level, complex systems of categories, children construct realistic understandings of concrete social categories and the relations among them. The distortion that seems to be typical of this level is a rigid or literal adherence to the particulars of a social rule or category.

It is important, however, not to misinterpret this developmental sequence. An individual child is not at a single level in any simple sense. The levels are characteristic of specific combinations of child and environment, as noted earlier. Of the many explications of this proposition, three seem to be especially important.

First, children do not show the same developmental level in all situations. Instead, performance is uneven, with the same child showing large variations in developmental level in different contexts. The particular social categories that children understand at their highest level are those that are more generally emphasized or accentuated by the children's families and society. Different societies and different subcultures within a society will teach different social categories to their children (Edwards & Whiting, 1980; Weisner & Gallimore, 1977). In addition, children within one society or culture will also vary in their understanding and use of social categories.

Second, even for the same social categories measured in the same general situation, a child will often function at different developmental levels as a function of the degree of structure or support provided by the immediate context. The ages assigned to each step in the development of social categories reflect the period of the first appearance of the new capacity in middle-class children performing simple structured tasks specifically designed to elicit relevant behaviors. In most situations, most children will not show the respective skill at the designated earliest age.

Third, the degree of disparity between developmental level in structured and spontaneous contexts seems to increase in the late preschool years. Before approximately 4 years of age, children commonly appear to produce the highest developmental level of which they are capable, even when the situation does not demand it of them. After age 4, they become less likely to perform at their highest level unless the situation is structured to elicit such performance. Consequently, in spontaneous behavior 4- to 7-year-olds are unlikely to show evidence of high-level functioning. Even when capable of using systems of categories in structured tasks, children of this age will normally show one of the lower developmental levels in an unstructured task. When functioning at these lower levels, they will evidence distortions and confusions similar to those of younger children.

Although the development and use of social categories in the preschool years seems to be highly systematic, the systematicity cannot be understood by considering the child alone. Analysis of the collaboration between child and environment is required. Good teachers know how to take account of this fact in their everyday interactions with children, but researchers and theorists have only begun to deal with the processes by which child and environment collaborate to produce developing behavior.

REFERENCES

Adelson, J. The development of ideology in adolescence. In S. E. Dragastin & G. H. Elder, Jr. (Eds.), *Adolescence in the life cycle: Psychological change and social context.* New York: John Wiley & Sons, 1975.

Anderson, E. S. Young children's knowledge of role-related speech differences: A mommy is not a daddy is not a baby. *Papers and Reports in Child Language Development,* 1977, *13,* 83–90.

Bertenthal, B. I. The significance of developmental sequences for investigating the what and how of development. In K. W. Fischer (Ed.), *Cognitive development.* San Francisco: Jossey-Bass New Directions for Child Development (No. 12), 1981.

Bertenthal, B. I., & Fischer, K. W. The development of representation in search: A social-cognitive analysis. *Child Development,* 1983, *54,* 846–857.

Biggs, J., & Collis, K. *A system for evaluating learning outcomes: The SOLO taxonomy.* New York: Academic Press, 1982.

Bigner, J. Second borns' discrimination of sibling role concepts. *Developmental Psychology,* 1974, *10,* 564–573.

Bretherton, I., & Bates, E. The emergence of intentional communication. In I. C. Uzgiris (Ed.), *Social interaction and communication during infancy.* San Francisco: Jossey-Bass New Direction for Child Development (No. 4), 1979.

Brooks, J., & Lewis, M. Infants' responses to strangers: Midget, adult, and child. *Child Development,* 1976, *47,* 323–333.

Broughton, J. Development of concepts of self, mind, reality, and knowledge. In W. Damon (Ed.), *Social cognitiion.* San Francisco: Jossey-Bass New Directions for Child Development (No. 1), 1978.

Carter, D. B., & Patterson, C. J. Sex roles as social conventions: The development of children's conceptions of sex-role stereotypes. *Developmental Psychology,* 1982, *18,* 812–824.

Case, R., & Khanna, F. The missing links: Stages in children's progression from sensorimotor to logical thought. In K. W. Fischer (Ed.), *Cognitive development.* San Francisco: Jossey-Bass New Directions for Child Development (No. 12), 1981.

Chambers, J. C., & Tavuchis, N. Kids and kin: Children's understanding of American kin terms. *Journal of Child Language,* 1976, *3,* 63–80.

Clark, A., Hocevar, D., & Dembo, M. H. The role of cognitive development in children's explanations and preferences for skin color. *Developmental Psychology,* 1980, *16,* 332–339.

Clark, K. B., & Clark, M. P. Racial identification and preference in Negro children. In E. E. Maccoby, T. M. Newcomb, & E. L. Hartley (Eds.), *Readings in social psychology.* New York: Henry Holt & Company, 1947.

Cole, M., & Riel, M. Intelligence as cultural practice. In R. Sternberg (Ed.), *Handbook of human intelligence.* New York: Cambridge University Press, 1983.

Connell, R. W. Class consciousness in childhood. *Australian and New Zealand Journal of Sociology,* 1978, *6,* 87-99.

Corrigan, R. The development of representational skills. In K. W. Fischer (Ed.), *Levels in psychological development.* San Francisco: Jossey-Bass New Directions for Child Development (No. 21), 1983.

Damon, W. *The social world of the child.* San Francisco: Jossey-Bass, 1977.

Dasen, P., Inhelder, B., Lavalée, M., & Retschitzki, J. *Naissance de l'intelligence chez l'enfant baoulé de Côte d'Ivoire.* Berne, Switzerland: Hans Huber Medical Publisher, 1978.

Edwards, C. P. The age group labels and categories of preschool children. *Child Development,* in press.

Edwards, C. P., & Whiting, B. B. Differential socialization of girls and boys in the light of cross-cultural research. In C. M. Super & S. Harkness (Eds.), *Anthropological perspectives on child development.* San Francisco: Jossey-Bass New Directions for Child Development (No. 8), 1980.

Emmerich, W. Young children's discriminations of parent and child roles. *Child Development,* 1959, *30,* 403-419.

Emmerich, W. Family role concepts of children ages six to ten. *Child Development,* 1961, *32,* 609-624.

Feffer, M. H. *The structure of Freudian thought: The problem of immutability and discontinuity in developmental theory.* New York: International Universities Press, 1982.

Feldman, D. H. *Beyond universals in cognitive development.* Norwood, NJ: Ablex Publishing Corporation, 1980.

Fischer, K. W. A theory of cognitive development: The control and construction of hierarchies of skills. *Psychological Review,* 1980, *87,* 477-531.

Fischer, K. W, & Bullock, D. Patterns of data: Sequence, synchrony, and constraint in cognitive development. In K. W. Fischer (Ed.), *Cognitive development.* San Francisco: Jossey-Bass New Directions for Child Development (No. 12), 1981.

Fischer, K. W., & Corrigan, R. A skill approach to language development. In R. E. Stark (Ed.), *Language behavior in infancy and early childhood.* Amsterdam, Holland: Elsevier, The Netherlands, 1981.

Fischer, K. W., Hand, H. H., & Russell, S. The development of abstractions in adolescence and adulthood. In M. Commons, F. Richards, & C. Armon (Eds.), *Beyond formal operations.* New York: Praeger, 1983.

Fischer, K. W., & Jennings, S. The emergence of representation in search: Understanding the hider as an independent agent. *Developmental Review,* 1981, *1,* 18-30.

Fischer, K. W., & Pipp, S. L. Development of the structures of unconscious thought. In K. Bowers & D. Meichenbaum (Eds.), *The unconscious reconsidered.* New York: John Wiley & Sons, in press-a.

Fischer, K. W., & Pipp, S. L. Processes of cognitive development: Optimal level of skill acquisition. In R. L. Sternberg (Ed.), *Mechanisms of cognitive development.* San Francisco: W. H. Freeman & Co., in press-b.

Fischer, K. W., Pipp, S. L., & Bullock, D. Detecting discontinuities in development: Method and measurement. In R. N. Emde & R. Harmon (Eds.), *Continuities and discontinuities in development.* Norwood, NJ: Ablex Publishing Corporation, in press.

Fischer, K. W., & Watson, M. W. Explaining the Oedipus conflict. In K. W. Fischer (Ed.), *Cognitive development.* San Francisco: Jossey-Bass New Directions for Child Development (No. 12), 1981.

Flavell, J. H. Stage-related properties of cognitive development. *Cognitive Psychology,* 1971, *2,* 421–453.

Flavell, J. H. *Cognitive development.* Englewood Cliffs, NJ: Prentice-Hall, 1977.

Fleishman, E. A. Systems for describing human tasks. *American Psychologist,* 1982, *37,* 821–834.

Freud, A. *The ego and the mechanisms of defense* (C. Baines, trans.). New York: International Universities Press, 1966.

Freud, S. *The interpretation of dreams.* New York: Basic Books, 1955. (Originally published in 1900)

Freud, S. The dissolution of the Oedipus complex. In *The complete psychological works of Sigmund Freud* (Vol. 19) (J. Strachey, trans.). London: The Hogarth Press, 1961. (Originally published, 1924.)

Furman, W. Children's friendships. In T. Field, G. Finley, A. Huston, H. Quay, & L. Troll (Eds.), *Review of human development.* New York: John Wiley & Sons, 1982.

Gelman, R. Cognitive development. *Annual Review of Psychology,* 1978, *29,* 297–332.

Goodman, M. *Race awareness in young children.* New York: Crowell-Collier Press, 1964.

Greenfield, P. M., & Childs, C. P. Understanding sibling concepts: A developmental study of kin terms in Zinacantan. In P. Dasen (Ed.), *Cross-cultural Piagetian psychology.* New York: Gardner Press, 1977.

Guttman, L. A basis for scaling qualitative data. *American Sociological Review,* 1944, *9,* 139–150.

Hand, H. H. The development of concepts of social interaction: Children's understanding of nice and mean. (Unpublished doctoral dissertation, University of Denver, 1981.) *Dissertation Abstracts International,* in press. (1981a)

Hand, H. H. The relation between developmental level and spontaneous behavior: The importance of sampling contexts. In K. W. Fischer (Ed.), *Cognitive development.* San Francisco: Jossey-Bass New Directions for Child Development (No. 12), 1981b.

Harter, S. A cognitive-developmental approach to children's expression of conflicting feelings and a technique to facilitate such expression in play therapy. *Journal of Consulting and Clinical Psychology,* 1977, *45,* 417–432.

Harter, S. A cognitive-developmental approach to children's understanding of affect and trait labels. In F. C. Serafica (Ed.), *Social-cognitive development in context.* New York: The Guilford Press, 1982.

Harter, S. Developmental perspectives on the self system. In E. M. Hetherington (Ed.), *Socialization, personality, and social development*—Vol. 4 of P. H. Mussen (Ed.), *Carmichael's handbook of child psychology* (4th ed.). New York: John Wiley & Sons, 1983.

Hartup, W. W. Peer interaction and social organization. In P. H. Mussen (Ed.), *Carmichael's manual of child psychology* (3rd ed., Vol. 2). New York: John Wiley & Sons, 1970.

Hartup, W. W. Peer relations. In E. M. Hetherington (Ed.), *Socialization, personality, and social development*—Vol. 4 of P. H. Mussen (Ed.), *Carmichael's handbook of child psychology* (4th ed.). New York: John Wiley & Sons, 1983.

Jackson, E., Campos, J. J., & Fischer, K. W. The question of *decalage* between object permanence and person permanence. *Developmental Psychology*, 1978, *14,* 1–10.

Jordan, V. B. Conserving kinship concepts: A developmental study in social cognition. *Child Development,* 1980, *51,* 146–155.

Kagan, J. The concept of identification. *Psychological Review,* 1958, *65,* 296–305.

Katz, P. A. Perception of racial cues in preschool children. *Developmental Psychology,* 1973, *8,* 295–299.

*Katz, P. A. Development of children's racial awareness of intergroup attitudes. In L. G. Katz, C. H. Watkins, M. J. Spencer, & P. J. Wagemaker (Eds.), *Current topics in early childhood education* (Vol. 4). Norwood, NJ: Ablex Publishing Corporation, 1982. (ERIC Document Reproduction Service No. ED 207 675.)

Katz, P. A., & Zalk, S. R. Modification of children's racial attitudes. *Developmental Psychology,* 1978, *14,* 447–461.

Kaye, K. *The social and mental life of babies.* Chicago: University of Chicago Press, 1982.

Kitchener, K. S., & King, P. M. Reflective judgement: Concepts of justification and their relation to age and education. *Journal of Applied Developmental Psychology,* 1981, *2,* 89–116.

Kohlberg, L. A cognitive-developmental analysis of children's sex-role concepts and attitudes. In E. Maccoby (Ed.), *The development of sex differences.* Stanford, CA: Stanford University Press, 1966.

Kratochwill, T., & Goldman, J. A. Developmental changes in children's judgements of age. *Developmental Psychology,* 1973, *9,* 358–362.

Kuhn, D., Nash, S. C., & Brucken, L. Sex role concepts of two- and three-year-olds. *Child Development,* 1978, *49,* 445–451.

Largo, R. H., & Howard, J. A. Developmental progression in play behavior of children between nine and thirty months: I. Spontaneous Play and imitation. *Developmental Medicine and Child Neurology,* 1979, *21,* 299–310.

Lawler, R. W. *The articulation of complementary roles* (A. I. Memo 594). Cambridge, MA: Massachusetts Institute of Technology, Artificial Intelligence Laboratory, May 1981.

Leahy, R. L. The development of the conception of economic inequality: I. Descriptions and comparisons of rich and poor people. *Child Development,* 1981, *52,* 523–532.

Lee, P. C., & Voivodas, G. K. Sex role and pupil role in early childhood education. In L. G. Katz, M. Z. Glockner, S. T. Goodman, & M. J. Spencer (Eds.), *Current Topics in early childhood education* (Vol. 1). Norwood, NJ: Ablex Publishing Corporation, 1977.

Lerner, R. M., & Busch-Rossnagel, N. A. (Eds.), *Individuals as producers of their own development: A life-span perspective.* New York: Academic Press, 1981.

Linton, R. Age and sex categories. *American Sociological Review,* 1942, *7,* 589–603.

Livesley, W. J., & Bromley, D. B. *Person perception in childhood and adolescence.* New York: John Wiley & Sons, 1973.

Maccoby, E. E. *Social development: Psychological growth and the parent-child relationship.* New York: Harcourt Brace Jovanovich, 1980.

Maccoby, E. E., & Jacklin, C. N. *The psychology of sex differences.* Stanford, CA: Stanford University Press, 1974.

Mahler, M. S., Pine, F., & Bergman, A. *The psychological birth of the human infant: Symbiosis and individuation.* New York: Basic Books, 1975.

Marcus, D. E., & Overton, W. F. The development of cognitive gender constancy and sex role preferences. *Child Development,* 1978, *49,* 434–444.

Mead, G. H. *Mind, self, and society from the standpoint of a social behaviorist* (C. W. Morris, Ed.). Chicago: University of Chicago Press, 1934.

Naimark, H. *The development of the understanding of social class.* Unpublished doctoral dissertation, New York University, 1981.

Nicolich, L. M. *Symbolic play: Sequences of development and methods of assessment.* Paper presented at the Southeastern Regional Meeting of the Society for Research in Child Development, Atlanta, April 1978.

Piaget, J. *Judgement and reasoning in the child* (M. Warden, trans.). London: Routledge & Kegan Paul, 1928. (Originally published, 1924.)

Piaget, J. Le mécanisme du développement mental et les lois du groupement des opérations. *Archives de Psychologie, Genève,* 1941, *28,* 215–285.

Piaget, J. *Play, dreams, and imitation in childhood* (C. Gattegno & F. M. Hodgson, trans.). New York: W. W. Norton & Company, 1951. (Originally published, 1946.)

Piaget, J. *The origins of intelligence in children* (M. Cook, trans.). New York: W. W. Norton & Company, 1952. (Originally published, 1936.)

Porter, J. *Black child, white child: The development of racial attitudes.* Cambridge, MA: Harvard University Press, 1971.

Roberts, R. J. Errors and the assessment of cognitive development. In K. W. Fischer (Ed.), *Cognitive development*. San Francisco: Jossey-Bass New Directions for Child Development (No. 12), 1981.

Rogoff, B., Sellers, M. J., Pirrotta, S., Fox, N., & White, S. H. Age of assignment of roles and responsibilities to children. *Human Development, 1975, 18,* 353-369.

Rosenberg, M. *Conceiving the self.* New York: Basic Books, 1979.

Rubin, K. H., Fein, G. G., & Vandenberg, B. Play. In E. M. Hetherington (Ed.), *Socialization, personality, and social development*—Vol. 4 of P. H. Mussen (Ed.), *Carmichael's handbook of child psychology.* New York: John Wiley & Sons, 1983.

Ruble, D. N. The development of social comparison processes and their role in achievement-related self-socialization. In E. T. Higgins, D. N. Ruble, & W. W. Hartup (Eds.), *Social cognition and social development: A sociocultural perspective.* New York: Cambridge University Press, in press.

Ruble, D. N., Balaban, T., & Cooper, J. Gender constancy and the effects of sex-typed televised toy commercials. *Child Development, 1981, 52,* 667-673.

Sander, L. W. Infant and caretaking environment: Investigation and conceptualization of adaptive behavior in a system of increasing complexity. In E. J. Anthony (Ed.), *Explorations in child psychiatry.* New York: Plenum Press, 1975.

Sarbin, T. R., & Allen, V. L. Role theory. In G. Lindzey & E. Aronson (Eds.), *Handbook of social psychology* (Vol. 1). Reading, MA: Addison-Wesley Publishing Co, 1968.

Schank, R. C., & Abelson, R. *Scripts, plans, goals, and understanding.* Hillsdale, NJ: Lawrence Erlbaum Associates, 1977.

Selman, R. L. *The growth of interpersonal understanding: Developmental and clinical analyses.* New York: Academic Press, 1980.

Stevenson, H. W., & Stewart, E. C. A developmental study of race awareness in young children. *Child Development, 1958, 29,* 339-410.

Tronick, E. Z. (Ed.) *Social interchange in infancy: Affect, cognition, and communication.* Baltimore, MD: University Park Press, 1982.

Tucker, J. The concepts of and the attitudes toward work and play in children. (Unpublished doctoral dissertation, University of Denver, 1979.) *Dissertation Abstracts International, 1979, 40* (8B), 3987.

Van Parys, M. M. *Preschoolers in society: Use of the social roles of sex, age, and race for self and others by black and white children.* Paper presented at the sixth biennial meeting of the International Society for the Study of Behavioral Development, Toronto, Canada, August 1981.

Vygotsky, L. W. *Mind in society: The development of higher psychological processes* (M. Cole, V. John-Steiner, S. Scribner, & E. Souberman, Eds.). Cambridge, MA: Harvard University Press, 1978.

Wallon, H. *De l'acte a la pensée.* Paris, France: Flammarion et Cie, 1970.

Watson, M. W. The development of social roles: A sequence of social-cognitive development. In K. W. Fischer (Ed.), *Cognitive development*. San Francisco: Jossey-Bass New Directions for Child Development (No. 12), 1981.

Watson, M. W., & Amgott-Kwan, T. Transitions in children's understandings of parental roles. *Developmental Psychology, 1983, 19,* 659-666.

Watson, M. W., & Fischer, K. W. A developmental sequence of agent use in late infancy. *Child Development, 1977, 48,* 828-836.

Watson, M. W., & Fischer, K. W. Development of social roles in elicited and spontaneous behavior during the preschool years. *Developmental Psychology, 1980, 16,* 483-494.

Weisner, T. S., & Gallimore, R. My brother's keeper: Child and sibling caretaking. *Current Anthropology, 1977, 18,* 169-190.

Werner, H. The concept of development from a comparative and organismic point of view. In D. B. Harris (Ed.), *The concept of development*. Minneapolis: University of Minnesota Press, 1957.

Westerman, M. A. Differences in the organization of mother-child interaction in compliance problem and health dyads. (Unpublished doctoral dissertation, University of Southern California, 1979.) *Dissertation Abstracts International,* 1980, *40*(10B), 5031.

Westerman, M. A., & Fischman-Havstad, L. F. A pattern-oriented model of caretaker-child interaction, psychopathology, and control. In K. E. Nelson (Ed.), *Children's language* (Vol. 3). Hillsdale, NJ: Lawrence Erlbaum Associates, 1982.

Weston, P., & Mednick, M. T. Race, social class, and the motive to avoid success in women. *Journal of Cross-Cultural Psychology,* 1970, *1,* 284-291.

Williams, J. E., Bennett, S. M., & Best, D. L. Awareness and expression of sex stereotypes in young children. *Developmental Psychology,* 1975, *11,* 635-642.

Williams, J. E., Best, D. L., & Boswell, D. Children's racial attitudes in the early school years. *Child Development,* 1975, *46,* 494-500.

3

Children's Aesthetics

Ellis D. Evans

University of Washington

INTRODUCTION

A kindergarten teacher in Seattle, Washington regularly arranges for her class of 5-year-old children to visit an art gallery which showcases oil, acrylic, lithograph, and watercolor productions by regional artists. She also encourages her young students and their parents to attend light classical and "pops" concerts by the local symphony orchestra. Each year, this teacher schedules visits to her class by a puppeteer and members of a pantomime theater group to demonstrate their talents and converse with the children. As an active sculptress, she displays her own work in class as an impetus to children's clay modeling activities. Queried about these various experiences, this teacher maintains that she is stimulating children's aesthetic growth through exposure to the arts. Her sensitivity to the myriad opportunities for aesthetic experience seems exceeded only by her general enthusiasm for the arts in education.

But what, exactly, does it mean to speak of aesthetic growth and aesthetic education? What is the role of experience, such as exposure to the arts, in fostering aesthetic growth or development? By what mechanisms or processes do the young progress toward a mature aesthetic attitude?

These are but a few of the many questions about aesthetic development and education that challenge and perplex those scholars concerned with aesthetics. Scholars generally agree that aesthetic development is distinguished by the search for beauty, particularly within the context of art and artistic experience (Child, 1969; T. E. Curtis, 1981). Many also seem to agree that peak experiences of joy or wonderment inhere in this striving process, though undoubtedly occurring on different levels and in different forms across the lifespan. The experience of a jubilant preschooler at play with finger paints stands in marked contrast to an adult art critic who ponders the aesthetic qualities of a Van Gogh. Each in his or her own way may share some intrinsic sense of the sublime, but probably for entirely different reasons. Sublime experience, in turn, seems to underscore a quality of life that is uniquely human. Accordingly, any concept of education framed in relation to the "good life" will usually require some attention to aesthetics.

The issue of aesthetic education seems particularly timely in view of evidence from the continuing National Assessment of Educational Progress Study (NAEP, 1981). According to recent nationwide assessments, successive groups of children and adolescents are showing declines in their knowledge and appreciation of the arts, achievements that have not been particularly impressive in the past.

The very nature of aesthetic development, with its accompanying subjective experience, poses enormous problems for scholarly inquiry. Despite this, scholars press on toward solutions for these problems, hoping to achieve a fuller understanding of human aesthetic experience. Enlightenment about young children's aesthetic development and education is the major objective of this chapter. This begins with a clarification of some ideas about the nature and direction of aesthetic study. Subsequently, recent research on children's aesthetic development is reviewed with reflections on research issues and educational implications. Finally, the matter of formal attempts within the school to influence aesthetic development is addressed.

THE FORMAL STUDY OF AESTHETICS

Aesthetics as a field of formal inquiry bridges the disciplines of philosophy and psychology. As the senior discipline, philosophy has emphasized the analysis of beauty on rational, *a priori* grounds. Within psychology, an empirical research tradition known as experimental aesthetics has become a major force in the understanding of human aesthetic response (Hare, 1981). This tradition applies the methods of experimental science to questions of aesthetic sensitivity, preference, and judgement. A long-debated conceptual issue concerns whether aesthetic judgements are objective in the same sense that scientific judgements are, and, if so, what this commonality implies for any meaningful distinction between science and art (Winterbourne, 1981).

By what processes, in what sequences, and under what conditions humans develop and exercise an aesthetic attitude are basic psychological questions. Aesthetic attitude means an enduring predisposition to respond positively to beauty in all its forms, especially the arts.[1] The central cognitive component of aesthetic attitude is perception. Perception, in aesthetics, is said to be intrinsic (i.e., perception for perception's sake or, as Osborne (1979) puts it, "disinterested perception"). This means that a person attends to the qualities of a perceived object or event without accompanying utilitarian or ego concerns (e.g., concern for usefulness, economic value, moral considerations, or extraneous associations with past experiences).

Philosophers disagree about the role of pleasure or satisfaction in aesthetic perception. But the frequency with which scholars of various theoretical persuasions refer to aesthetic satisfaction or enjoyment suggests a legitimate place for pleasure in aesthetics study. The precise nature of pleasure remains at issue, but it is reasonable to suggest that aesthetic pleasure is immediately sensuous ("Isn't that marvelous!") and represents the affective dimension of a gradually more complex set of cognitive developments. These developments enable us to judge aesthetic properties and justify these judgements in a reflective manner (Beyer, 1974; Blanchee, 1974; Flannery, 1977; Kepperman, 1975). For artwork, it can be argued that goodness is proportionate to the satisfaction or interest it evokes or is capable of evoking in the perceiver. Satisfaction will be marked by an extension and clarification of consciousness, with emphases upon understanding, judgement, and decision making (Osborne, 1979).

A WORD ABOUT THEORY

Coherent theory may enable us to understand and account for individual differences in aesthetic growth. To date, however, a full theoretical picture has not been developed. The problem concerning emotion in art has been especially knotty. To some extent, the situation reflects a scholarly preoccupation with aesthetic *expression* (read: creative productivity). It seems that creative thinking and performance have been conveniently offered as the consummative index for aesthetic sensitivity when, in fact, one can appreciate without creating and create without showing aesthetic awareness. Readers haunted by the spectre of creativity and its attendant issues (e.g., nature and definitions, measurements, antecedents to, and education for) are referred elsewhere (Barron & Harrington, 1981; Stein, 1974). In the following paragraphs, theory is highlighted only as it relates to the psychological study of aesthetic response.

---

[1] Strictly speaking, aesthetics as a field of inquiry is neither synonymous with nor restricted to the arts. However, traditional sources of the aesthetic heritage—visual and theatre arts, spatial arts, music, dance, and literature—have provided the framework for most scholarly discourse.

In recent years, Gardner (1973b) has attempted to integrate developmental psychology with aesthetics in art. He holds that three psychological systems—perceiving, feeling, and making—become integrated to allow for the child's functional use of symbols. Symbolic activity is the fuel for a genuinely artistic process through which four streams of aesthetic experience gradually take shape, although these streams are not necessarily uniform in any one individual. Gardner argues that the essential raw material for three of these developmental streams—child as "maker," "audience member," and "performer"—is normally present by age 7 or 8. The fourth stream—child as "critic"—is thought to depend upon further qualitative change, notably the achievement of formal operational thought. More recently, Gardner has recognized special features of different symbol systems in a treatise on children's scribbling and drawing (Gardner, 1980a). He thus joins in a tradition built by earlier writers (see Selfe, 1980) concerned with the psychological significance of scribbling.

While Gardner explores nooks and crannies in the aesthetic labyrinth, psychobiology (Berlyne, 1971) provides insights about information processing and the pleasure derived from perceptual stimuli. These insights furnish a strong basis for recent experimental aesthetic studies. Other theoretical forces at work in the study of children's aesthetics are perhaps more familiar. Gestalt psychologists have persistently emphasized principles of perceptual development and learning in the grand manner of Kobler, Lewin, and Wertheimer (see Swenson, 1980). Contemporary cognitive psychologists prefer to view the arts as knowledge and ways of knowing. For children, knowledge is largely a function of their ability to sort, classify, and draw increasingly from concrete and symbolic characteristics that are found in artworks. Psychodynamic theories generally emphasize imaginative wish fulfillment and fantasy disposition in creative expression. Aesthetic emotion is secondary to more primary desires and conflicts of a personal, possibly unconscious nature; creativity is more often studied than aesthetic sensitivity per se. From humanistic psychology comes phenomenological nuances, giving particular attention to a perceiver's subjective experience with art. Aesthetic sensitivity is associated with the development of active, flexible, and open perceptual experience. Finally, and predictably, behavioral psychology (including social learning theory) focuses upon environmental variables that may exert control over aesthetic response. Behavioral analysis procedures are not widely visible in the aesthetic literature and seem generally incompatible with humanistic approaches on both philosophical and methodological grounds (Child, 1973).

STRATEGIES IN AESTHETICS RESEARCH

Sound data for an understanding of aesthetic sensitivity and judgement are dependent upon the validity and reliability of techniques used to gather them. We observe that measurement of aesthetic response is problematic for adults, to say nothing about young children. This section examines the three most common approaches to the problem: the general methodology for experimental aesthetics, aesthetics tests, and the structured interview procedure.[2]

Experimental Aesthetics

Controlled experimental aesthetics studies typically involve presenting individuals with one or two types of stimulus material and then monitoring some variety of consequent verbal or nonverbal response. The more conservative material consists of artificial stimuli such as nonsense shapes, geometric designs, or patterned line drawings. A more liberal approach involves acknowledged masterpieces of artistic creation or other genuine artworks generally defined by experts as being of lesser quality.

In either case, attempts are made to isolate or otherwise manipulate variables represented in the material that may influence aesthetic satisfaction, preference, or judgement. Several classes of independent variables are studied, including major groups of psychophysical or collative variables (Berlyne, 1971). Psychophysical variables concern some physical dimension of stimulus attributes, such as intensity, size, color, or auditory pitch. Collative variables encompass structural or formal aspects of stimulus patterns, including novelty, surprise, and complexity, with frequent attention to attributes such as proportion, symmetry, balance, rhythm, and consonance. Emphasis varies according to the precise nature of a stimulus pattern (visual, auditory, tactile, and so on).

For either class of independent variable, verbal judgements of preference, pleasure, interest, emotional meaning, or power of a stimulus to induce uncertainty or conflict normally serve as dependent variables for experimental study. A more recent technique includes the direct observation of exploratory behavior in the presence of aesthetic objects, duration of self-exposure to objects, direction of personal choice, and (occasionally) nonverbal expressions (e.g., posture, facial expression, smiling, or extent and volume of applause).

A basic assumption from such laboratory study is that verbal or nonverbal reactions approximate those that will occur in response to beauty (or ugliness) in nonexperimental settings. Thus, an experimental aesthetician will argue that data obtained under controlled conditions can assist us in explaining, predicting, and even controlling aesthetic behavior in the "natural" environment.

---

[2] Space limitations prevent the examination of a fourth strategy concerned with the analysis of children's artistic products. See Carothers and Gardner (1979) for an illustration of this methodology.

Testing for Aesthetic Sensitivity

With a notable exception, researchers in the field of experimental aesthetics have not studied extensively preschool and elementary school age children. Young children are more frequently represented in studies using tests of individual differences in aesthetic reaction. The most common standard for contemporary tests of aesthetic preference or judgment is the consensual evaluation of artworks by connoisseurs or experts. That is, the closer "naive" individuals agree with art judgments delivered by a group of recognized art or music authorities, the higher their aesthetic scores.

To illustrate, Child and Iwao (1973) constructed a series of six pairs of contrasting photographic prints to portray aesthetic qualities such as regularity and complexity. Upon exposure to these pairs, preschool and elementary school age children were asked to select their preferences. Picture preferences were neither strong nor reliable. Many children were attracted by the poorer artwork, although better work was chosen consistently by a small minority of children. This suggests an open road to the study of personal or background characteristics which differentiate children who prefer good or poor artwork.

A more recent and extensive measure is the *Visual Aesthetic Sensitivity Test* (Gotz, Borisy, Lynn, & Eysenck, 1979). This measure consists of 42 sets of two nonrepresentational pictures drawn by an artist of recognized competence, ordered in difficulty, with one picture in each set revealing certain intentional design faults. Theoretically, aesthetic choice should more frequently involve the unflawed picture. A consistent assumption is that the more "correct" choices one makes, the higher one's level of aesthetic development .

Still other tests of aesthetic sensitivity for use in research involve both art (Bell & Bell, 1979; Hill, 1972; Roosevelt, 1977; Salkind & Salkind, 1973) and music (L. Anderson, 1975; Bullock, 1973; Geringer, 1977; Shaw & Tomcala, 1976). As compared to other measurement strategies for aesthetics, such tests are more practical for field use. But their nemesis is technical adequacy (i.e., sufficient reliability and validity). As for most testing procedures, measurement reliability for aesthetic test increases with age of subjects. Since measurement validity cannot exceed reliability, the use of tests with younger children can be risky. And this says nothing about types of validity *per se*. Criterion-related validity is generally limited to the standard of expert adult judgement as indicated above. Further concurrent and predictive validity studies for aesthetic tests are sorely needed.

The Probing Interview Strategy

A popular alternative to testing for aesthetic reactions is the structured interview method. This less formal measurement signals the increasing presence of cognitive-developmental theory in aesthetic study. Piaget, for example, has influenced aesthetics research in two important ways: first, through researchers' use of the *methode clinique* to explore children's knowledge and conceptions of the arts (Gardner, Winner, & Kirscher, 1975) and second, as a source for the hypothesis that cognitive aspects of aesthetics-related behavior may develop in stage-sequential form parallel to, if not subsumed by, qualitative changes in logical thought structures. I hasten to add that Piagetian theory has little to say directly and specifically about aesthetic development. Rather, the theory guides aesthetics research by way of implication.

A typical interview study has children of different ages respond to open-ended questions about some work of art (a painting, a poem, or musical selection). Recorded protocols are then analyzed according to ideational content relevant to aesthetics (e.g., how art is produced, ways of describing art, and criteria for evaluating art). Categorizations of ideas are sought for comparative purposes across age groups. Any legitimate "stage grouping" of ideas is dependent upon the presence of reliable, age-related differences in aesthetics response which have a credible relationship to information processing and sequential change as represented by cognitive-developmental theory. A principal hazard to validity of results is excessive liberty in forcing gross verbal protocols of dubious reliability into conformity with a pre-existing theoretical framework.

Use of the structured interview method does not by itself betray a Piagetian bias; atheoretical studies have utilized the interview method. Moreover, some developmental studies are limited to descriptions of age-related art preferences with no probing of children about why they may like or dislike given artworks. Finally, this developmental approach to children's aesthetics is nearly exclusively cross-sectional in design methodology. The field lacks strong longitudinal research. For example, no studies based upon improved methods for lifespan developmental study (e.g., Baltes, Reese, & Lipsitt, 1980) have appeared to grace the journal literature.

MAINSTREAMS OF AESTHETIC RESEARCH

Having illustrated three major methods for children's aesthetics research, a sampling from the potpourri of related arts studies follows. These studies are organized into three clusters of research activity: developmental studies, with their emphasis upon age-related trends in aesthetic response; studies concerned primarily with sources of individual differences in aesthetic response (excepting age); and deliberate attempts to influence the course of aesthetic growth and development, including aesthetic education. At the onset it should be noted that, for reasons discussed elsewhere (Child, 1981), all three streams of research activity have been dominated by the visual arts.

Developmental studies have mostly involved experimental aesthetics meth-odology and the verbal probing strategy. Studies of individual differences usually are biased toward testing of one kind or another, as are intervention studies focused upon the impact of arranged aesthetic experience.

Developmental Studies

Preference for complexity.   Among the most frequently studied col-lative variables in children's aesthetic response is stimulus complexity. As Berlyne (1971) has observed, complexity in the arts varies by degree of orna-mentation or embellishment. Thus, elements are added to a basic pattern: lines, colors, scaled representations of objects, abstract symbols in paint-ings, and subsidiary notes in music. Or, deviations from a basic pattern are introduced, such as vibrato or rubato in music. The more independently selected elements in a given pattern, the greater the complexity or diversity. An important research question, then, concerns the effect of complexity or diversity on human aesthetic response and judgement.

Studies generally show that aesthetic preference across art forms changes with age in the direction of increased complexity (Chevrier & Delorme, 1980). This trend is presumably related to changes in perceptual ability, with preference based on some form of pleasure tied to perceptual functioning. Laboratory study of the phenomenon, however, is not always simply described. In part, the situation is affected by a researcher's choice of dependent measures: for example, voluntary looking time versus prefer-ence ratings. These measures do not have the same meaning for estimating an aesthetic reaction. In fact, these different measures underly an important distinction between "interestingness" and "pleasingness."

McWhinnie (1971), for example, emphasizes the *interest* value of in-creasing complexity in visual designs; finding such a design *pleasant* is a more characteristic response to simpler designs. Wohlwill (1975) also reports different results about the role of diversity in scenes of the physical environment and in constellations of postage stamps, depending upon which of the two criteria (looking time or preference) is used. For the envi-ronment scenes, diversity and looking time increased uniformly; for the postage stamp constellation, preference peaked at moderate or intermediate diversity. In neither case, however, were consistent age differences noted among children from grades one through eight. As Wohlwill observes, com-plexity alone may elicit both modes of response, but when meaningfulness is introduced (diversity in actual scenes versus random line drawings or non-sense shapes), the situation changes.

The difference in stimulus material has inspired a longstanding debate among suporters of the "old" and "new" experimental aesthetics. Purists fear contamination by anything but strictly objective stimulus material;

realists argue that the use of artificial stimuli begs the question about aesthetics in daily life. Thus, using real art (woodcuts) and photoreproductions of original art, a curvilinear relationship for complexity preference has been observed among children ages 6 to 10 (Farley & Weinstock, 1980). That is, for both stimulus modes and in contrast to adult preference for high complexity, the children were found to prefer moderate complexity to either high or low complexity. This relationship was particularly strong for the real art.

From these data, the authors suggest that real artworks of intermediate complexity are more likely to elicit aesthetic enjoyment for young school children. Such works could be used in classrooms to "capture or revive" children's interest in art. As for aesthetics research methodology, the message is more straightforward: The generalization power of visual art studies should increase when original artworks are used instead of reproductions. Quite inconsistent and unclear relationships between preference and complexity appear when artificial stimulus material (e.g., random polygons) is used, especially for preschool and primary grade children (Aitken & Hutt, 1974). In contrast, 4- to 6-year-old children (especially females) have presented a reliable age trend toward preference for complexity in book illustrations (Danset-Leger, 1975-76).

As for music, clear preferences for melodies with intermediate (versus low or high) complexity and low to moderate levels of melodic repetitiveness (redundancy) have been observed by grade four (McMullen, 1974). But later research is more equivocal. Eisenstein (1979) investigated the effect of complexity and redundancy conditions (as represented in musical form, dynamics, rhythm, and multiple combined elements) on the music selection and listening time behavior of musically naive primary and intermediate-level elementary school children. Patterns of music selection behavior were similar across grade levels, showing a predictable age trend in preference for increased complexity or less repetitive listening. Primary grade children, however, generally listened longer to a more varied range of music than did children at higher grade levels. The author courts tautology by concluding that music is more reinforcing for younger than for older children. Yet her data and those from related studies suggest an age-related convergence on preference for music of familiar styles, especially rock and easy-listening pop music, with spurious relationships to collative properties. Of course, nature and extent of musical training might make a difference in the power of collative properties to influence musical preference across styles. In fact, aural skills important for discriminating collative properties of music have been more strongly linked to number of years of piano study than to certain other experimental variables, such as extended instruction on single instruments and ensemble participation in either vocal or instrumental groups (May & Elliot, 1980).

To account for complexity preference and the impact of other collative variables, we can return to the hypothesis that human aesthetic reaction is based upon the positive hedonic value of (or pleasure derived from) a perceptual experience (Berlyne, 1971, 1974). Positive hedonic value is considered a function of arousal, the mechanisms for which are associated with reward and aversion systems in the brain. Accordingly, principles of neuropsychology have crept into the human aesthetics research camp. This research ultimately may be relevant to educators for understanding the arousal potential of stimulation as well as procedures for tension relief or de-arousal. That is, it is plausible to argue that aesthetic patterns can induce pleasure by first increasing then reducing arousal, as well as by encouraging an oscillation between the form and content of artistic works. Such pleasure could be a foundation for aesthetic appreciation. The anticipation of pleasure could therefore provide motivation for persons to seek out aesthetic experiences. This motivation can be described more simply as the "intrinsic appeal" of beauty in its various forms. The building of such motivation may constitute a long-term objective of aesthetic education. To reach this objective, however, we must learn what characteristics of aesthetic patterns can reliably incite inner activity in a positive sense. As a beginning, it seems clear that complexity is an important collative variable in aesthetic patterns. Hypotheses from rational aesthetics may also assist us toward better understanding (Beyer, 1974). Philosophers often stress some version of the principle *unity in variety* as central to genuine aesthetic experience. According to this interpretation, aesthetic delight derives from the active process of weaving contrasting parts of an artwork into a unified complex whole. Skilled perceptual weaving, then, may be taken as still another basic objective for aesthetic education.

Aesthetic discrimination and judgement.   Children's aesthetic discrimination and judgement have been assessed as they relate to four general categories within the arts: visual arts, music, literature, and related art forms (such as dance and theater arts).

Visual arts. Studies patterned on the *methode clinique* consistently reveal predictable age-related trends in children's thinking and judgements about visual art. Younger children's strong concern for subject matter and color gradually give way to increased interest in technical and thematic qualities: mood, theme, and surface features, such as configurations (Murphy, 1973; Rosensteil, Morison, Silverman, & Gardner, 1978). A shift from egocentricism to taking a greater perspective is also apparent in children's gradually increasing ability to separate subjective preference from a more objective analysis of art properties and to recognize attributes of a good artist and the feeling component of paintings (Clayton, 1975; Johnston, 1978; Parsons, Johnston, & Durham, 1978). Yet both primary- and intermediate-grade children often retain a preference for realistic paintings of familiar objects and brightly colored artworks (Rump, 1967, 1968). Thus, while criteria for sorting and analyzing artwork change with increasing age, concordant preferences may not.

More specifically, Burkett (1978) has documented a rough sequence in the development of children's classifications of objects as art or nonart. Within the age range of 5 to 8 years, children's concepts of art were focused upon manipulative activity (art as "making something"). The period from 9 to 12 years revealed greater intellectual analysis of art properties, with better understanding of imagination and creativity ("art as an idea"). This analytical approach continued among children past age 12 and included an increased attention to the expressive quality and cultural contents of art. Still more specifically, young children (ages 4 to 7) reportedly differ from older children in being more concrete, mechanistic, and legalistic in their response to probes about artwork (Gardner, Winner, & Kirscher, 1975). Younger children focused on the materials used to create artwork, the actions of production, and the rules or conventions about what is proper for making or changing artwork. Ideas about the origin of art were fuzzy, even if correct. Identities of works (as symbolic units) were not well understood, if even recognized. And the children's art evaluation, generally undifferentiated and egocentric ("It's good because I like it"), revealed little awareness of criteria apart from appeals to authority.

Murphy's (1973) study of children's affective reactions (e.g., "great," "terrible") to an oil painting by Chagall and a live opera performance sung in English corroborate the relatively primitive level of aesthetic development in young children. Eight criteria were used to analyze children's verbal professions: subject matter, sensory elements, formal properties, technical competence, expressive elements, general perceptual interest, extra aesthetic function (stimulus to further thought), and communication (symbolization or meaning). As predicted, younger children (ages 6 to 7 1/2) used fewer criteria—usually subject or sensory elements such as color and harmony. Occasionally, expressive elements (how a work affects feeling) were noted. Higher cognitive criteria were totally absent among the younger children; some were unable to find or use even one criterion. With advancing age, more criteria were referenced with greater age differences for painting than for opera, and impressive individual differences were evident within each age grouping from grades K to 12.

An instructive variation on the clinical method is the children's match-to-sample task. To illustrate, one recent study had children successively examine a series of pencil artworks matched according to the painting style of 10 different artists (DePorter & Kavanaugh, 1978). Each pair was accompanied by a choice array consisting of four additional reproductions. These 10 sets were divided equally into homogeneous (similar themes or subject matter for all paintings) and heterogeneous (varied subject matter) groups. For each trial, children were asked first to select a "match" for the paired paintings from the choice array, then to explain the reasons for their selections. Children's justifications were transcribed, then categorized and judged in three ways: subject matter or theme only, theme and general characteristics of a painting (e.g., clarity and color), and general characteristics of a painting, plus stylistic and technical details (e.g., brushwork, historical references). High scorers tended to be older (ages 12 and above) and were more apt to base judgements upon stylistic details than on subject matter.

This finding is compatible with earlier studies of sensitivity to style based upon similar match-to-sample procedures (Gardner, 1970; Gardner & Gardner, 1973). Altogether, these data dramatize the importance of basic conceptual development for style sensitivity, although cultural enrichment may enhance this ability to some degree. A broader conclusion is that both choice reliability and the use of aesthetic criteria for interpreting style are developments that occur relatively late in childhood or in early adolescence. Age-related changes in cognitive style (such as increased field independence and reflective, analytical information processing) surely are implicated. And this leads to an important implication for "training" children for aesthetic discrimination. Skill in discriminating style may require efforts to overcome children's natural tendency to center (sort and classify) artworks on a single criterion, such as subject matter or content. In Piagetian terms, preoperational children would seem to be poor candidates for such discrimination training, but transitional and early concrete operational children should be more easily trained. In any case, sound educational practice will have young children amply exposed to varied art forms before requiring systematic analysis or aesthetic criticism. This does not rule out strategic discrimination training, especially if artworks that are highly appealing to young children are used for this purpose.

To summarize thus far, related studies of children's response to visual arts yield evidence of age-related characteristics consistent with Piagetian stage-sequential development. But a claim that aesthetic growth is governed primarily by cognitive-developmental principles is risky before we know more about the affective components of human aesthetics (Paal, 1977) and the interplay of personality factors. Also puzzling is the educational meaning of young children's comparatively primitive state of aesthetic development. To the extent that aesthetic development may be constrained by maturational processes, attempts at early acceleration would seem ill-advised. Yet developmental studies nearly always involve children from the "natural environment" who have not benefited from specialized aesthetic experience. Thus, it remains for systematic intervention studies to determine how aesthetically capable young children actually can be. Meanwhile, there is scant but reliable evidence that by age 4 or 5, age-related increases occur in the ability to discriminate, describe, and group art styles, most clearly under conditions of direct tuition (Child, 1970, 1972).

Music. Explicit aesthetic qualities of young children's music experience have not been extensively researched. The attempt to integrate aesthetic experience into generic music education for children has a fairly short history as well (Gonzo, 1971). Apparently, technical performance has taken precedence over music appreciation in the past. Those studies from music appreciation most relevant to aesthetics concern music perception. For example, Child (1970, 1972) reports that by age 7 or 8 and thereafter, fairly reliable and knowing melodic perception can be observed; individual differences in pitch, harmony, and rhythm perception also appear as early as age 6, along with skills in rhythm reproduction, such as tapping.

More recently, normative sequences of the musical response among preschool-age children have been derived from direct observation, tests, and tape recordings of the singing of over 500 children (Moog, 1976). By age 3, for example, most children are capable of imitative singing. By age 6, the repetitive spontaneous motor movements to rhythmic music, characteristic of earlier age periods, have largely disappeared. Melody recognition (*sans* lyrics) is apparent by age 4, but by age 5 as many as one in four children still lack this ability. Awareness of harmony, or ability to analyze notes of different pitch when sounded simultaneously, is not reliably observed among normal preschool-age children.

Further normative study is addressed to advanced conceptual aspects of music. Research within a Piagetian framework has disclosed that children's ability to fully identify and understand meter in music is rare until around age 9 (Jones, 1976). Development up to that time is broadly consistent with Piaget's stage analysis of time concepts. In a more narrowly focused study of primary-grade children, Perney (1976) failed to confirm the Piagetian idea that conservation of metric time in music tasks develops in an invariant sequence.

These normative data are concerned largely with music perception and cannot tell a complete story about aesthetic growth. Schwadron (1975) offers evidence of heightened interest in music aesthetics and education research, arguing that the development of capacities for "sensitive-critical" music experience must be fused with growth in musical perception and response. This idea points to the basic issue of the precise qualities of an aesthetic response to music. Payne (1980) claims, with little empirical support, that a unique aesthetic emotion exists distinct from "ordinary" human moods that are influenced by music listening. If correct, Payne's work may fit well with broader psychobiology theory. Other factors in music appreciation concern *interest* more directly (Payne, 1980). These factors include the formal or textural structures of music, its historical significance, and instrumentation or orchestration, as well as (to a lesser degree) extra-musical implications (e.g., visual, dramatic, or philosophical). Taking musical interest as partly a function of understanding, musical training should exceed sheer familiarity with music in its power to enhance appreciation.

Working independently to define music aesthetics, Hargreaves and Colman (1981) offer five categories of aesthetic response to varied musical experiences: *categorical* (classifying music style or type as "classical," "traditional jazz," "folk"), *objective-analytic* (awareness of technical elements, such as tempo and instrumentation), *objective-global* (the intrinsic quality of music as a unified whole), *affective* (subjective emotional and evaluative responses, such as "sad," "awful," "strange"), and the *associative* (extramusical associations triggered by sounds, such as "birds in the jungle" or "wind and sea," although associations higher on the aesthetic scale, including relationships with other musical elements, belong here as well). The authors argue from data that the *affective* and *associative* elements are most apparent among children and naive adults. The *objective-analytic* response is more likely from trained musicians. At least, Hargreaves and Colman present a workable taxonomy for musical aesthetics. But the present data bank in music research is insufficient to portray clear sequences of developments across these categories.

A closely related area of study, however, involves the explanation and prediction of music preferences. LeBlanc (1980, 1981) proposes several major sources of variation in preference, which range from the stimulus properties of music, through social context factors, to the personal characteristics of the listener. LeBlanc has shown that fifth-grade children's musical preferences are strongly related to generic styles within the concert and popular music traditions, with tendencies to favor faster tempos and the instrumental (versus vocal) medium. LeBlanc suggests some sequences for introducing children to both jazz and art music, which provide a basis for further research. Elsewhere (Hargreaves, Messerschmidt, & Rubert, 1980) we learn that, as compared to naive peers, musically trained children give higher ratings of both quality and preference to unfamiliar music, although both groups respond more predictably to familiar music.

Perhaps closer to aesthetic experience in music is the developmental study of musical style sensitivity. Gardner (1973a) studied five groups of ten male and ten female children, whose modal ages were 6, 8, 11, 14, and 18 to 19. Style sensitivity was defined as skill in detecting whether two musical excerpts were drawn from the same piece of tape-recorded music. Baroque, classical, romantic, and modern styles were represented. Detection errors decreased progressively as age increased, with females generally surpassing males in accuracy. Except for the college-age group, error scores did not change upon subjects' hearing the same selection a second time. The important finding for early childhood educators is that bright primary-grade children reveal a dawning sensitivity to musical style for which select cue discrimination and decentering are requisite. Like most studies, Gardner's research is descriptive and provides no direct information about mechanisms or processes of style sensitivity. That some young children are alert to stylistic features in music, however, gives us sufficient reason for further investigation.

Finally, a series of studies by Zenatti (1976a, 1976b, 1976c) brings together concern for young children's musical preference and interest with background factors and individual differences. Marked preferences for consonance, tonality, and rhythmic patterns were noted by age 5, again with females excelling over males in measures of music appreciation. Clear signs of musical interest in harmony and melody were seen as early as age 4, with strong definition by age 7. Background factors most highly associated with musical interest, in order of importance, were paternal occupational status, emphasis upon music appreciation in the home, and beginning voice or instrument training. The apparent influence of musical acculturation on children's levels of aesthetic judgement was manifest as early as age 4 1/2 vis-a-vis children's sharp preferences for certain rhythmic patterns (especially pulsation) and on a perceptual level in terms of melodic versus nonmelodic versus nonmelodic contexts for rhythm.

Since Zenatti's studies involve French children, their findings cannot be generalized unequivocally for America. They do, however, support a growing belief that very young children are capable of more complete musical aesthetics than has formerly been thought (Schwadron, 1975). It seems reasonable to conclude that important foundation experiences for early aesthetic development are to be found in the home. Unfortunately, almost nothing is known about children's concepts of the "beautiful" in music, notwithstanding studies of musical taste. Neither has any semblance of understanding been reached about music improvisational behavior. Because music improvisation is characterized by a substantial affective display, usually spontaneous and impassioned, the origins and development of this form of musical expression seem ripe for aesthetics research.

Literature. Literature is usually presented to preschool and elementary schoolchildren as part of a "language arts" program, although children's literature is rarely treated as an art form (Greene, 1976). That it can and should be are increasingly popular notions among aesthetically minded educators. These intentions are praiseworthy, but psychological research about children's response to literature has yet to furnish a distinctly aesthetic flavor. One early toehold for understanding children's sensitivity to literary style comes from a study of children in grades one, three, six, and nine (Gardner & Gardner, 1971). Not surprisingly, older children showed greater ability to recognize and work with different storytelling styles. Though stylistic awareness was rather weak throughout the sample, a few individuals excelled at each grade level, again highlighting a wide range of individual differences.

Heeding the call for more definitive research, a second study involved oral presentations of prose and poetry to children at ages 7, 11, 14, and 19

(Gardner & Lohman, 1975). The task required matching and discriminating differences among various stylistic features of the literature (e.g., narrative, rhythm, word use, syntax, mood, and sentence types). Reasons given by the subjects were probed in the manner of the *methode clinique*. By this measure, explicit awareness of stylistic features was shown to be generally absent until early adolescence. A strong *figural* orientation was characteristic of younger children. That is, their attention was drawn more to specific elements (names, objects, plot details, and common objectives) than to matters of style. Yet, even the 14-year-olds seemed insecure in making judgements, and figural elements were still prominent in their interpretation. Oldest subjects gave clear indications of style sensitivity, but individual differences were remarkable even at this advanced level. All told, the authors infer that, as compared to art and music, literary style sensitivity proceeds somewhat slower, at least in the absence of specific training. Finally, the authors underscore the importance of cognitive development level for literary style and analysis. Such analysis often requires attention first to a work's semantic properties and second to the way in which prose or poetry is ordered to achieve given meanings. This secondary step probably depends upon formal operational thinking, a development not observed much before middle adolescence.

Closer to early childhood, Juscyk (1977) studied first- and third-grade children's appreciation of poetic devices, including rhyme, rhythm, and alliteration. Rhyme and rhythm attributes influenced children's preferences in positive fashion, with rhyme especially influential for the younger subjects. Alliteration had no apparent effect. First graders, in fact, had problems in attending to alliteration. An understanding of how poetic devices function was generally low throughout the entire sample. Similarly, preschools have expressed a greater liking for stories in verse than in prose (Hayes, Chemelsky, & Palmer, 1982), although story event retention was stronger for prose.

Both the Juscyk and Hayes et al. studies dramatize the importance of cognitive development for children's response to literature. Juscyk illustrates how limited young children can be in their understanding of form and content relationships in literary art. The Hayes et al. findings challenge a popular belief in early childhood education about the facilitative effect of rhyme on young children's story comprehension.

Concerning prose, Guthrie (1977) points to the value of structure for story comprehension and maintains that young listeners and readers quickly develop an expectation that stories are governed by select rules that pertain to setting, theme, plot, and resolution. But young children's awareness and appreciation of structural variations in stories has not been studied much. Applebee (1979) has taken promising steps to provide observational and anecdotal data about how children as young as age 2 1/2 begin to distinguish storytelling from other language functions. It is tempting to argue that aesthetic satisfaction may result as children search for meaning in stories and master the rules for story structure.

Beyond these few studies, most research about chidren's response to literature involves secondary-school age subjects and is lean in specifics about any aesthetic experience. Linguistic experience, however, may provide a breakthrough in adjoining aesthetics across diverse art forms, most particularly through children's metaphoric understanding. Possible relationships between verbal and visual metaphor and the role of metaphoric thinking in aesthetics constitute exciting topics for developmental study (see, for example, Gardner, 1980b; Greenberg, 1979; Kogan, Conner, Gross, & Fava, 1980; and Winner, Rosensteil, & Gardner, 1976).

Related art forms. Related art forms, such as dance and theater arts, have received little attention from research aestheticians. At a theoretical level, issues such as expressive versus cognitive theories for the analysis of dance aesthetics are noteworthy (Snoeyenbos & Knapp, 1979). Best (1974) discusses problems in studying dance aesthetics, and McColl (1979) extrapolates from aesthetics theory to explain how the dance can serve as a medium for dance education. A model for studying (and teaching) creative movement, based upon Guilford's (1967) factor analytic work about creative production (fluency, flexibility, originality, and elaboration), has also been proposed, but has apparently remained untested (Dodds, 1978). Some authorities might place the study of children's dance within the broader movement education literature (S. Curtis, 1982; Gilliom, 1970). But writers ordinarily distinguish the content of children's dance from movement education by emphasizing expressivity or improvisation and aesthetic elements that appear to some extent in all art forms (e.g., mood or theme, form, rhythm and balance, contrast, symmetry/asymmetry, and accent). Theoretically inclined readers should see Sandle (1972) for a basic statement about aesthetics and qualitative movement. For the empirically minded, Parsons and Lindauer (1980) provide one of the few psychological studies about dance experience and aesthetic characteristics of dance participants, albeit based upon adult subjects. On balance, the dance and theater arts represent uncharted territory for early childhood aesthetics research. This, despite a long-standing tradition of research on children's play which, of course, often takes form in creative movement and dramatics.

Aside from the dance, aesthetics research of likely interest to students of early childhood include areas in which only beginning steps have been taken: the aesthetics of visual literacy in relation to television and the cinema (Feldman, 1976; Kelly & Gardner, 1981; Sudano, 1978), consumer aesthetics (Holbrook & Huber, 1979), the aesthetic in sport (Best, 1974), and the aesthetics of environmental planning and design (Basch, 1972; Honig, 1978). Concerns for the latter topic illustrate the wide range of aesthetics theory and research. A provocative twist on aesthetics consistent with Berlyne's (1971) theory is that the stimulus characteristics of objects or events that elicit aesthetic pleasure in general (such as complexity, novelty, unexpectedness) may also apply to the enjoyment that individuals reportedly experience from performing destructive acts such as vandalism or property damage. Support for this idea comes from a unique experiment with college students about glass breakage. Greenberger and Allen (1980) found that a person's destructive behavior is strongly influenced by anticipation of exertion effort and complexity effects consequent to demolition. In general, the more effort believed necessary to destroy and the more complex or sensational the expected effects of demolition, the more satisfying the destructive act. It is not unreasonable to suggest that young children may behave similarly under such conditions. One needs to look no further than the toy-room for anecdotal evidence.

Individual and Group Differences

The study of psychology requires the study of individual differences, and aesthetics tests have been widely used for this purpose. One important step in the direction is cross-cultural comparative research to determine any degree of transcultural similarity in aesthetic response (Child, 1981). Thus, the visual aesthetic reactions of culturally different male and female children ages 7 and over have been assessed by the Visual Aesthetic Sensitivity Test (Chan, Eysenck, & Gotz, 1980). Considerable similarity among these children was observed, especially for females. As a group, children from Hong Kong scored somewhat lower and German children substantially higher than did their Japanese and English counterparts. Within-culture factors cannot be overlooked because the findings ran parallel to the comparatively lower and higher socioeconomic status of the samples from Hong Kong and Germany, respectively. Socioeconomic background has also surfaced in related studies, including preferences for sensory attributes as a basis for sorting objects. Seaman (1974), for example, found that 5-year-old middle- and lower-class children consistently used form and color, respectively, for this type of task. Much remains to be known about the reliability of and reasons for any socioeconomic status differences in aesthetic development. (Our current aesthetics data base has been established to an overwhelming extent using middle-class subjects.)

Further study of cultural variables has yielded puzzling results. For example, one large-scale comparative study of aesthetic sensitivity involved American and Japanese children, of both sexes, in grades one, four, seven, and ten (Harris, DeLissovoy, & Enami, 1975). Children's art appreciation scores were determined by extent of conformity to experts' judgements of 60 pairs of art reproductions presented in the form of slide photographs. First graders' preferences showed highest agreement with the experts, a result unaccounted for by degree of picture brightness, realism, or familiarity. Agreement with experts declined to grade seven with a "rebound" occuring at grade ten, except for the Japanese males, who continued their wayward response. The exclusive use of Western art in this study is suspect. Even so, Japanese children as a whole showed higher absolute appreciation scores that did their American peers. This suggests a possible cultural influence and may include a difference in educational experience. Results from other cross-cultural studies tease us about the role of biological, hereditary, and maturational factors for a general aesthetic dimension of human development (Brody, 1972; Burt, 1960; Farley & Ahn, 1973). Yet a striking impression from such studies is that American children and youth infrequently appear as top scorers on tests of aesthetic reaction.

Within United States culture, the application of similar measurement methods has more consistently illuminated relationships between aesthetic reaction and personality. Among the more reliable personality correlates of aesthetic sensitivity in older subjects are cognitive openness and flexibility, field independence, autonomy of judgement, tolerance of ambiguity, and empathy (Child, 1972; Machotka, 1970; McWhinnie, 1971). Since these correlates have developmental histories, there is reason to believe that their relationship to aesthetic sensitivity could also be documented at younger age levels. Measurement problems complicate this search. Discerning readers will note that a similar cluster of personality characteristics is often associated with high creativity ratings (Wallach, 1970). Yet creativity—especially as assessed narrowly by measures of divergent thinking— is not uniformly correlated with aesthetic sensitivity among older subjects (F. E. Anderson, 1971). Unfortunately, with so little data available, one cannot say much about the reliability of such relationships.

Because many of the personality correlates of aesthetic sensitivity resemble dimensions of perceptual development (including fine perceptual discrimination) it is tempting to argue for a strong cognitive-skills analysis of the aesthetic response. Indeed, Bilotta and Lindauer (1980) conclude that selected cognitive skills may be more important than conventional artistic training insofar as our capacity to respond to the arts is concerned. Along these lines, preference for either linear or "painterly" art styles has been associated with cognitive styles among college-age youth (Savarese & Miller, 1979). But the critical questions for early childhood educators call for data about the origins of perceptual style differences, how affective development may be interwined with them, and what early learning experiences may influence the quality of perceptual development vis-a-vis aesthetics.

Very little direct information is available to help us with these questions. Both parental attitudes and early home stimulation may figure prominently as sources of developmental influence on aesthetic perception (Freeman, 1976), and these sources may be linked to socioeconomic status, as mentioned earlier. Gardner's (1976) intensive longitudinal study of five first-born children from infancy onward suggests that individual differences in styles of inquiry or exploration are apparent as early as age 2. Possibly these stylistic differences are linked to parental teaching style. Though difficult to extrapolate, infant perception research may eventually be instructive to aestheticians. For example, preference for vertical symmetry (versus horizontal symmetry and asymmetry) can occur as early as age 1 (Bornstein, Ferdinandsen, & Gross, 1981). Developmental study indicates that, by age 9, children's perceptions of symmetry are similar to those of adults. Common maturational processes are surely at work here (Brody, 1970). Provocative hypotheses about aesthetics and neuropsychology, including the matter of hemispheric dominance, may result in fruitful research (see Ellis & Miller, 1981; Foster, 1977). Once again, a major limitation of most existing aesthetics research is its relative lack of participants below the kindergarten/ primary grade level.

Intervention Research

Common experience tells us that many, if not most, children gradually become aesthetically sensitive to some degree—at least on an intuitive basis. Aesthetically inclined educators, however, prefer not to leave this development to chance. Neither are they apt to be satisfied with an intuitive or otherwise unrefined state of aesthetic development. So education in some form is seen to enable some extent of control over children's aesthetic development. Thus, Broudy (1976) argues for the importance of aesthetic education because "imaginative perception and perceptive imagination need to be cultivated in everyone" (p. 29). Smith (1976) concurs by championing an educational policy for aesthetics that is capable of "inducting persons into the artworld" and sharpening "basic aesthetic skills...in the art of appreciation" (p. 7). Similarly, Eisner (1976) heralds the value of "educational connoisseurship," meaning appreciation in the sense of an awareness and understanding of all aesthetic experience. Appreciation is seen as the basis for advanced aesthetic judgement and criticism.

No one expects that young children necesarily could or even should become precocious connoisseurs of the arts. But important precursors of connoisseurship as may be subject to controlled experience and that reside in perceptual skill, attitude development, and knowledge about art are important issues for psychological or educational research. For convenience of discussion, the few existing intervention or manipulative studies about children's aesthetics are classified into two related groups. The first group concern specific attempts to "train" one or more aspects of aesthetic response under relatively well-controlled conditions. The second group involves broader scale, more general programmatic interventions.

Training studies. Aesthetic response training studies are largely characterized by specific attempts to modify specific aspects of aesthetic response. Thus, Gardner (1972) has shown that children as young as age 7 can be accurately instructed to sort paintings according to stylistic criteria. Children's skill in detecting recurrent *Gestalten* was not necessarily dependent upon a full capacity for concrete operational thought. Even children of kindergarten age have demonstrated the ability to form and generalize concepts from visually complex art under conditions of instruction (Clark, 1972). Kindergarten children have also responded well to systematic training for texture discrimination (rough/smooth), using appropriate accompanying vocabulary, by subsequently incorporating texture into their drawings and describing texture in the artistic works of others (Seefeldt, 1979).

Type and quality of training, together with extent of longer-term effects, are clearly at issue in this research. Considering young children's developmental levels, multisensory approaches would seem advantageous. Further, training may be more sensible in contexts explicitly conducive to aesthetic expression. Precedent comes from a study of 4-year-old children who experienced a "multisensory-cognitive curriculum" in a specially designed aesthetic environment (Taylor & Trujillo, 1973). These children revealed substantially greater aesthetic qualities in their own artworks, as compared to controls who enjoyed the same curriculum in a conventional environment. Critical judgement abilities were unaffected in both groups.

Similar findings about training selected components of aesthetic response appears in music research. The major assumption underlying much of this research is that finer early music discrimination skills will predispose qualitatively better aesthetic development. Thus, Jetter (1978) established a systematic aural/visual identification procedure for instructing young children in a heirarchy of music learning tasks: identification of instrument timbres, exact melodic repetition, and half-step intervals. Most 4-year-olds in urban day care and suburban preschools who received this instruction demonstrated mastery level achievement on these tasks, regardless of their musical aptitude differences. Hair (1973) also provides clear evidence that first-grade children can be efficiently trained to perform basic harmonic discriminations (i.e., to determine differences between chords and associate tones with chords, according to conventional tonal construction).

Convinced that primary grade children normally do not know how to listen to "high quality" music with understanding and enjoyment, Trammell (1978) established a brief, five-session listening program based upon repetition and guidance. This involved alerting children to technical aspects of music (mood, tone, color, melody, form, and rhythm). As compared to controls, guided children increased their self-reported enjoyment of music. Lack of follow-up or transfer of training assessment suggests that these results be interpreted with caution.

As in art skills training, contextual factors in music training studies cannot be overlooked. Both teacher and peer influences are noteworthy. One of the apparently few aesthetics studies based upon behavior analysis procedures involved a contingent teacher approval/disapproval feedback strategy tailored to individual elementary-school children (Dorow, 1977). Contingency management was associated with changes in frequency of music listening behavior and attentiveness during music concerts. It is not known how such behavior may have generalized beyond the school setting. A basic conceptual problem with contingent reinforcement, of course, is the possibly insidious conditioning of musical tastes according to teacher preference. Specificity of tastes, at best, is incidental to more basic tasks of perceptual development, aesthetic pleasure, and gradual understanding of criteria useful for aesthetic criticism.

Flohr and Brown (1979) report that both preschool and kindergarten children showed significantly more idiosyncratic expressive movement to music while blindfolded than when working in groups within sight of their peers. This strong imitative effect highlights a possible constraining or inhibiting force in aesthetic movement. Perhaps imitative tendencies could also be harnessed by a creative model (peer *or* teacher) to enhance the range of expressive movement among children. Either way, the study reminds us of the importance of social context in studying aesthetic behavior.

Hypothesized effects of planned intervention or incidental classroom learning are not always observed in aesthetics studies. Brown (1977), for example, reports no differences in musical preference behavior, cognitive music skills, or attitudes about school music between controls and children, ranging from 3 1/2 to 5 1/2 years of age, provided with aural discrimination training for either instrumental or vocal music. In short, knowing does not necessarily result in valuing. Depending upon the type and extent of training, certain variables (e.g., age, sensory modality, preference, and musical aptitude) may interact with treatment. Many puzzles remain to be solved along these lines, especially for music aptitude (Schleuter & Deyarman, 1977). To date, aptitude- or trait-treatment interaction methodology for aesthetics study is not much in evidence.

To conclude, recent training for selected aspects of aesthetic response is more often efficacious than not, at least in the short run. More meaningful advances in aesthetic sensitivity require that a child come to understand how artworks can be grouped and analyzed in alternative ways. In visual art, this means utilizing criteria beyond single classifications, such as subject matter or color. Yet we know that young children's response to artwork is clearly dominated by subject matter. Awareness of formal properties is a relatively late development, at least in the absence of training. Even training, however, may be mediated by more basic cognitive or affective developments, especially multiple classification skills and openness to new experience. Such developments are probably relevant in music as well. Critical listening skills have a key role and, unfortunately, methodologies for promoting them are not commonly found in music materials for teachers of preschool- and primary-grade children (Hair, 1973). Some semblance of formal training can perhaps be justified on the grounds that it increases children's awareness of aesthetic properties, thus increasing their enjoyment of art in a more general sense.

It is somewhat paradoxical, however, that beyond simple queries about children's aesthetic preference, there is little research evidence concerning children's feelings about artwork. In any case, it seems reaonable to argue that training and tests for generalization should occur in a context of experience with real art. This will require careful teacher attention to the aesthetic qualities of the classroom or day care setting. Except for scattered pilot projects, there are few indications that teachers are trained in the art of designing an aesthetic learning environment for young children. And the problem of teacher training is embedded within the broader issue of comprehensive aesthetic education programs in the schools.

Broader programmatic interventions.   Provision for organized aesthetic education in school settings requires attention to major issues common to all kinds of educational programming (Smith, 1976). These issues include program rationale, goals, and objectives; curriculum content and sequencing; instructional methods; staff preparation; and evaluation procedures. An assumption implicit in the literature is that aesthetics research and theory can provide a basis for resolving these issues. Even if true, slow progress toward this end has been exceeded by bold, often intuitive or largely philosophical structures for curriculum development. That is, the relationship between aesthetics research and aesthetic education programming is obscure. The rationale for aesthetic education is especially controversial. Purists argue for aesthetic education on intrinsic grounds; pragmatists more often view the arts as instrumental—as a means to foster comprehensive cognitive/ intellectual development. The balance of professional opinion seems in favor of a unified or integrated arts approach to aesthetic education, with rationales and goals varying from one context to another. This stands in contrast to more traditional and recurrent practices whereby the arts are segmented from the general curriculum or, at best, are supplementary to mainstream education. In this latter case, any systematic aesthetic education depends mostly upon the qualities of individual teachers— arts specialists, in particular. In true form, however, aesthetic education is not discipline bound. Rather, it concerns sensory utilization, cognition, and affect in the process of art appreciation. Additionally, the values of creative performance and aesthetic criticism will be embedded in a total school ecology that can be experienced and analyzed in aesthetic terms (T. E. Curtis, 1981).

As with most human endeavor, large discrepancies can be observed between the real and ideal for aesthetic education. Though numerous aesthetic education projects can be culled from the literature, many seem to have passed by the educational establishment like proverbial ships in the night. Or else their influence has been confined to narrow boundaries, if implementation has occurred at all (see, for example, Colwell, 1970). Programs of general interest to early childhood education include Project AIM (Arts in Motion) (Ramsey, 1980), Project Impact (see Plummer, 1977), Project KAP (Kindergarten Art Program) (Castrup, Ain, & Scott, 1972), and The Bee Hive (Richard & Medeja, 1974). The Bee Hive, for example, is a kindergarten program inspired in part by the British Infant School Model. The arts and play serve as a medium to personalize learning experiences in relation to skill development for sensorimotor language activity and creative expression. Special emphasis is placed upon design of the physical environment and a humanistic climate for learning. Original field implementation involved 2 years of operation with successive groups of 25 and 19 children. Evaluation data, at least in the original report, are neither extensive nor based upon rigorous measurement. Thus, potential consumers must be content with testimonials about program impact which, incidentally, are guardedly optimistic.

Several less comprehensive educational programs germane to young children's aesthetic growth have appeared. None, however, concern preschool settings. Piper and Shoemaker (1973) describe a prescriptive teaching approach to promote achievement of musical concepts (rhythm, melody, harmony, form, timbre, and dynamics). This program takes form in a series of lessons, complete with behavioral objectives, for weekly integration into regular kindergarten programs. Evaluation data suggest respectable internal validity for this approach to music education. In this same genre, Bradley (1974) evaluated a year-long comparative study of a "traditional and experimental" music education program stressing active listening, cooperative learning, and performance skills. Experimental children showed superior aural acuity and visual-perceptual skills at year's end. No follow-up data are reported, but the immediate results attest to a more dynamic and integrated approach to music than is customarily found in elementary classrooms.

Apparently the most visible, highly developed, and widely implemented single program of comprehensive aesthetics education comes from Central Midwestern Regional Educational Laboratory (CEMREL) (Madeja, 1976, 1977). A project of interdisciplinary planning, this kindergarten to grade six multimedia program is intended to enhance aesthetic perception and provide arts instruction to complement existing art programs. The curriculum takes the form of integrated arts for general education. Daily arts study at each grade level is advised. Visual arts, music, dance, theatre, literature, and films provide core content for implementation by the generalist classroom teacher. Curriculum units are available for the following topics: aesthetics and the physical world, arts elements, the artist, the creative process, the culture, and the environment.

Formative evaluation procedures for the CEMREL program, based primarily on qualitative methods, have shaped the development of various units for use at kindergarten and first grade levels (Hall, 1982). At the time of this writing, summative evaluation data are not available, if they exist. The trend for evaluation of aesthetic education at CEMREL apparently is an ethnographic approach to idiosyncratic programming by teachers who sample from the CEMREL aesthetics smorgasbord.

A FINAL WORD

Generally speaking, evaluation research on aesthetic education has been weak and sporadic (Wilson, 1974). Longitudinal investigations are in short supply, with little known about long-term gains and transfer beyond the school situation. The state of measurement practice is a particularly sore point. Process evaluation to attest to adequacy of program implementation is conspicuous by its absence from most aesthetic education studies. Stake (1976) is among the few authorities on evaluation to have addressed these problems. He favors extensive use of observation and interview methods in a framework of responsive evaluation. Applications of Stake's methodology are not widely reported. One attempt (Stake & Hoke, 1976) fell short of providing convincing evidence about either program success or failure. It can be argued, of course, that the inquiry process itself can help educators toward a fuller understanding of their programs.

A key figure in this process is the teacher who, unfortunately, is rarely trained to think like an evaluator. Even barring this role, the issue of teacher training for effective aesthetic education is a serious one. Inspection of normative teacher education curricula reveals comparatively little emphasis upon the arts. Practicing teachers commonly express insecurity and low confidence about bringing effective multi-arts experience to their young charges. It is encouraging that some precedent for improving upon this state of affairs can be found in the Child Development Associate Training Program (Research for Better Schools, 1976) and scattered training projects for aspiring teachers (Kaufman, 1975).

In addition to nurturing enthusiasm for the arts and coordinating participatory arts experiences, the classroom teacher has a key role in guiding the development of children's aesthetic judgment (Feldman, 1973, 1976). For this task, a teacher's level of technical skill is probably less important than a rich background of cultural experience. This may be one factor that distinguishes aesthetic value for children in British Infant Schools from their counterparts in the typical American early school setting. At least, generic American teacher education programs could provide fuller and more focused experiences in aesthetic criticism for their recipients.

Clearly, much work remains to be done to successfully realize our collective human potential for aesthetic growth. We must begin by seeking universal support for stronger arts acculturation in preservice and inservice teacher education, including the formal study of aesthetics and human development. Simultaneously, a skeptical public must be persuaded that aesthetic education is a critical attribute for any concept of basic education. All of this is based, of course, on the assumption that some form of organized aesthetics education can make a positive difference in young children's aesthetic perceptions. Training studies give us reason to be encouraged. Teachers skilled in designing an aesthetic learning environment, using real artworks for children's sensory discrimination ability training, coordinating home and school aesthetic experiences, and encouraging children's aesthetic expressiveness are the basic ingredient for any degree of success in aesthetic education. It would appear, however, that a thoroughgoing, comprehensive experiment with aesthetic education, complete with longitudinal evaluation procedures, has yet to be attempted in early childhood education.

REFERENCES

Aitken, P. P., & Hutt, C. Do children find complex patterns interesting or pleasing? *Child Development,* 1974, *45*(2), 425–431.

Anderson, F. E. Aesthetic sensitivity, dogmatism, and the Eisner Art Inventory. *Studies in Art Education,* 1971, *12,* 49–55.

Anderson, L. The effects of music literature in developing aesthetic sensitivity to music. *Journal of Research in Music Education,* 1975, *23*(1), 78–84.

Applebee, A. N. Children and stories: Learning the rules of the game. *Language Arts,* 1979, *56,* 641–646.

Baltes, P. B., Reese, H. W., & Lipsitt, L. P. Life span developmental psychology. *Annual Review of Psychology,* 1980, *31,* 65–110.

Barron, F., & Harrington, D. M. Creativity, intelligence, and personality. *Annual Review of Psychology,* 1981, *32,* 439–476.

Basch, D. The uses of aesthetics in planning: A critical review. *Journal of Aesthetic Education,* 1972, *6*(3), 39–56.

Bell, R., & Bell, G. Individual differences in children's preferences among recent paintings. *British Journal of Educational Psychology,* 1979, *49*(2), 182–187.

Berlyne, D. E. *Aesthetics and psychobiology.* New York: Appleton-Century-Crofts, 1971.

Berlyne, D. E. *Studies in the new experimental aesthetics: Steps toward an objective psychology of aesthetic appreciation.* Washington, D.C.: Hemisphere Publishing, 1974.

Best, D. N. The aesthetic in sport. *British Journal of Aesthetics,* 1974, *14*(3), 197–213.

Best, D. N. Some problems in the aesthetics of dance. *Journal of Aesthetic Education,* 1975, *9*(3), 105–112.

Beyer, L. E. Objectivity, autonomy, and aesthetic evaluation. *Journal of Aesthetic Education,* 1974, *8*(3), 107–116.

Bilotta, J., & Lindauer, M. S. Artistic and nonartistic backgrounds as determinants of the cognitive response to the arts. *Bulletin of the Psychonomic Society,* 1980, *15*(5), 354–356.

Blanchee, R. On the subjectivity of aesthetic judgment. *Journal de Psychologie Normale et Pathologique,* 1974, *71*(2), 181–201.

Bornstein, M. H., Ferdinandsen, K., & Gross, C. G. Perception of symmetry in infancy. *Developmental Psychology,* 1981, *17,* 82–86.

Bradley, I. L. Development and aural and visual perception through creative processes. *Journal of Research in Music Education,* 1974, *22*(3), 234–240.

Brody, G. F. The development of visual aesthetic preferences in young children. *Sciences de l'Art,* 1970, *7*(1-2), 27–31.

Brody, G. F. The development of aesthetic preferences: A comparison of American and Jamaican children. *Proceedings of the Annual Convention of the American Psychological Association,* 1972, *7,* 307–308.

Broudy, H. S. Some reactions to a concept of aesthetic education. *Journal of Aesthetic Education,* 1976, *10*(3-4), 29–37.

Brown, A. L. The effect of televised cognitive skills instruction in local instrumental music on student music selection, music skills, and attitudes. *Dissertation Abstracts International,* 1977, *37*(9-A), 5670.

Bullock, W. J. A review of measures of musico-aesthetic attitude. *Journal of Research in Music Education,* 1973, *21*(4), 331–344.

Burkett, M. F. Concepts of art as verbally expressed by children aged 5 through 15 years. *Dissertation Abstracts International,* 1978, *38*(12-A), 7084.

Burt, C. The general aesthetic factor, III. *British Journal of Psychology, Statistical Section,* 1960, *13,* 90–92.

Carothers, T., & Gardner, H. When children's drawings become art: The emergence of aesthetic production and perception. *Development Psychology,* 1979, *15,* 570–580.

Castrup, J., Ain, E., & Scott, R. Art skills of preschool children. *Studies in Art Education,* 1972, *13*(3), 62–69.

Chan, J., Eysenck, H. J., & Gotz, K. O. A new visual aesthetic sensitivity test: III. Cross-cultural comparison between Hong Kong children and adults, and English and Japanese samples. *Perceptual and Motor Skills,* 1980, *50*(3, pt. 2), 1325–1326.

Chevrier, J., & Delorme, A. Aesthetic preferences: Influence of perceptual ability, age, and complexity of stimulus. *Perceptual and Motor Skills,* 1980, *50,* 839–849.

Child, I. L. Esthetics. In G. Lindzey & E. Aronson (Eds.), *The handbook of social psychology* (Vol. 1, 2nd ed.). Reading, MA: Addison-Wesley Publishing Co., 1969.

Child, I. L. Aesthetic judgment in children. *Transaction,* 1970, *7,* 45–51.

Child, I. L. Esthetics. *Annual Review of Psychology,* 1972,*23,* 669–694.

Child, I. L. *Humanistic psychology and the research tradition: Their several virtues.* New York: John Wiley & Sons, 1973.

Child, I. L. Bases of transcultural agreement in response to art. In H. I. Day (Ed.), *Advances in intrinsic motivation and esthetics.* New York: Plenum Press, 1981.

Child, I. L., & Iwao, S. Personality and esthetic sensitivity. *Journal of Personality and Social Psychology,* 1968, *8,* 308–312.

*Child, I. L., and Iwao, S. *Responses of children to art: Final report.* Washington, D.C.: Office of Education (DHEW), Bureau of Research, 1973. (ERIC Document Reproduction Service No. ED 083 089)

Clark, G. A. Children's abilities to form and generalize visual concepts from visually complex art. *Dissertation Abstracts International,* 1972, *32*(12-A, 6848.

Clayton, J. R. An investigation into the possibility of developmental trends in aesthetics. *Dissertation Abstracts International,* 1975, *35*(11-A), 7149–7150.

*Colwell, R. *An approach to aesthetic education: Final report.* Washington, D.C.: Office of Education (DHEW), Bureau of Research, 1970. (ERIC Document Nos. ED 048 315 & ED 048 316)

Curtis, S. *The joy of movement in early childhood.* New York: Teachers College Press, Columbia University, 1982.

Curtis, T. E. *Aesthetic education and the quality of life.* Bloomington, IN: Phi Delta Kappa Educational Foundation, 1981.

Danset-Leger, J. Reaction of children to complexity in illustrations from children's books. *Bulletin de Psychologie,* 1975-76, *29*(4-7), 319–336.

DePorter, D. A., & Kavanaugh, R. D. Parameters of children's sensitivity to painting styles. *Studies in Art Education,* 1978, *20*(1), 43–48.

Dodds, P. Creativity in movement: Models for analysis. *Journal of Creative Behavior,* 1978, *12*(4).

Dorow, L. E. The effect of teacher approval/disapproval ratios on student music selection behavior and concert attentiveness. *Journal of Research in Music Education,* 1977, *25,* 32–40.

Eisenstein, S. R. Grade/age levels and the reinforcement value of the collative properties of music. *Journal of Research in Music Education,* 1979, *27*(2), 76–85.

Eisner, E. W. Educational connoisseurship and criticism: The form and function in educational evaluation. *Journal of Aesthetic Education,* 1976, *10*(3–4), 135–150.

Ellis, A. W., & Miller, D. Left and wrong in adverts: Neuropsychological correlates of aesthetic preference. *British Journal of Psychology,* 1981, *72,* 225–229.

Farley, F. H., & Ahn, S. H. Experimental aesthetics: Visual aesthetic preference in five cultures. *Studies in Art Education,* 1973, *15,* 44–48.

Farley, F. H., & Weinstock, C. A. Experimental aesthetics: Children's complexity preference in original art and photoreproductions. *Bulletin of the Psychometric Society,* 1980, *15,* 194–196.

Feldman, E. B. The teacher as model critic. *Journal of Aesthetic Education,* 1973, *7*(1), 50–57.

Feldman, E. B. Visual literacy. *Journal of Aesthetic Education,* 1976, *10*(3–4), 195–200.

Flannery, M. The aesthetic behavior of children. *Art Education,* 1977, *30*(1), 18–23.

Flohr, J. W., & Brown, J. The influence of peer imitation on expressive movement to music. *Journal of Research in Music Education,* 1979, *27*(3), 143–148.

Foster, S. Hemispheric dominance and the art process. *Art Education,* 1977, *30*(2), 28–29.

Freeman, J. Developmental influences on children's perception. *Educational Research,* 1976, *19*(1), 69–75.

Gardner, H. Children's sensitivity to painting styles. *Child Development,* 1970, *41,* 813–821.

Gardner, H. The development of sensitivity to figural and stylistic aspects of paintings. *British Journal of Psychology,* 1972, 63, 605–615.

Gardner, H. Children's sensitivity to musical styles. *Merrill-Palmer Quarterly,* 1973, *19*(1), 67–77. (1973a)

Gardner, H. *The arts and human development: A psychological study of the artistic process.* New York: Wiley-Interscience, 1973b.

Gardner, H. Promising paths toward artistic knowledge: A report from Harvard Project Zero. *Journal of Aesthetic Education,* 1976, *10*(3 & 4), 201–207.

Gardner, H. *Artful scribbles: The significance of children's drawings.* New York: Basic Books, 1980a.

Gardner, H. Children's literary development: The realms of metaphors and stories. In P. McGee & A. Chapman (Eds.), *Children's humor.* New York: John Wiley & Sons, 1980b.

Gardner, H., & Gardner, J. Children's literary skills. *Journal of Experimental Education,* 1971, *39*(4), 42–46.

Gardner, H. & Gardner, J. Developmental trends in sensitivity to form and subject matter in paintings. *Studies in Art Education,* 1973, *14*(2), 52–56.

Gardner, H., and Lohman, W. Children's sensitivity to literary styles. *Merrill-Palmer Quarterly,* 1975, *21*(2), 113–126.

Gardner, H., Winner, E., & Kirscher, M. Children's conception of the arts. *Journal of Aesthetic Education,* 1975, *9*(3), 60–77.

Geringer, J. M. An assessment of children's musical instrument preferences. *Journal of Music Therapy,* 1977, *14,* 172–179.

Gilliom B. *Basic movement education: Rationale and teaching units.* Reading, MA: Addison-Wesley Publishing Co., 1970.

Gonzo, C. Aesthetic experience: A coming of age in music education. *Music Educators' Journal,* 1971, *58,* 4–10.

Gotz, K. L., Borisy, A. R., Lynn, R., & Eysenck, H. J. A new visual aesthetic sensitivity test: I. Construction and psychometric properties. *Perceptual and Motor Skills,* 1979, *49,* 795–802.

Greenberg, J. The child's capacity to perceive metaphors in art objects. A paradigmatic case of aesthetic development. *Journal of Creative Behavior,* 1979, *13*(4), 232–246.

Greenberger, D. B., & Allen, V. L. Instruction and complexity: An application of aesthetic theory. *Personality and Social Psychology Bulletin,* 1980, *6*(3), 479–483.

Greene, M. Literature in aesthetic education. *Journal of Aesthetic Education,* 1976, *10*(3 & 4), 61–76.

Guilford, J. P. *The nature of human intelligence.* New York: McGraw-Hill Book Company, 1967.

Guthrie, J. T. Research views: Story comprehension. *Reading Teacher,* 1977, *30*(5), 574–577.

Hair, H. I. The effect of training on the harmonic discrimination of first grade children. *Journal of Research in Music Education,* 1973, *21*(1), 85–90.

Hall, B. W. Personal correspondence from CEMREL, April 12, 1982.

Hare, F. C. Recent developments in experimental aesthetics. In H. I. Day (Ed.), *Advances in intrinsic instruction and aesthetics.* New York: Plenum Press, 1981.

Hargreaves, D. J., & Colman, A. M. The dimensions of aesthetic reactions to music. *Psychology of Music,* 1981, *9*(1), 15–20.

Hargreaves, D. J., Messerschmidt, P., & Rubert, C. Musical preference and evaluation. *Psychology of Music,* 1980, *8*(1), 13–18.

Harris, D. B., DeLissovoy, V., & Enami, J. The aesthetic sensitivity of Japanese and American children. *Journal of Aesthetic Education,* 1975, *9*(4), 81–95.

Hayes, D. S., Chemelsky, B. E., & Palmer, M. Nursery rhymes and prose passages: Preschooler's liking and short-term retention of story events. *Developmental Psychology,* 1982, *18*(1), 49–56.

Hill, W. B. A technique for assessing aesthetic predispositions: Mosaic Construction Test. *Journal of Creative Behavior,* 1972, *6*(40), 225–235.

Holbrook, M. B., & Huber, J. Separating perceptual dimensions from affective overtones: An application to consumer aesthetics. *Journal of Consumer Research,* 1979, *5,* 272–283.

Honig, A. S. Aesthetics in Asian child care settings. *Child Education,* 1978, *54,* 251–255.

Jetter, J. T. An instructional model for teaching identification and naming of music phenomena to preschool children. *Journal of Research in Music Education,* 1978, *26*(20), 97–110.

Johnston, M. A. An investigation into the possibility of cognitive-developmental stages of the aesthetic experience of children. *Dissertation Abstracts International,* 1978, *38*(11-A), 6435.

Jones, R. L. The development of the child's conception of meter in music. *Journal of Research in Music Education,* 1976, *24*(3), 142–154.

Juscyk, P. W. Rhymes and reasons: Some aspects of the child's appreciation of poetic form. *Developmental Psychology,* 1977, *13*(6), 599–607.

Kaufman, M. Teaching with artists. *Elementary School Journal,* 1975, *75*(6), 350–356.

Kelly, H., & Gardner, H. *Viewing children through television.* San Francisco: Jossey-Bass, 1981.

Kepperman, J. Art and aesthetic experience. *British Journal of Aesthetics,* 1975, *15*(1), 29–39.

Kogan, N., Conner, K., Gross, A., & Fava, D. Understanding visual metaphor: Developmental and individual differences. *Monographs of the Society for Research in Child Development,* 1980, *45,* 1–85.

LeBlanc, A. Outline of a proposed model of sources of imitation in musical taste. *Bulletin of the Council for Research in Music Education,* 1980, *61,* 29–34.

LeBlanc, A. Effects of style, tempo, and performing medium on children's music preference. *Journal of Research in Music Education,* 1981, *29*(2), 143–156.

Machotka, P. Visual aesthetics and learning. *Journal of Aesthetic Education,* 1970, *4,* 117–130.

Madeja, S. S. The CEMREL Aesthetic Education Program: A report. *Journal of Research in Music Education,* 1976, *10*(3-4), 209–216.

Madeja, S. S. *Through the arts to the aesthetic: The CEMREL aesthetic education curriculum.* St. Louis, Mo.: Central Midwestern Regional Educational Laboratory, 1977.

May, W. V., & Elliot, C. A. Relationship among ensemble participation, private instruction, and skill development. *Journal of Research in Music Education,* 1980, *28*(3), 155–161.

McColl, S. L. Dance as aesthetic education. *Journal of Physical Education and Recreation,* 1979, *50*(7), 44–46.

McMullen, P. T. Influence of number of different pitches and melodic redundancy on preference responses. *Journal of Research in Music Education,* 1974, *22*(3), 198–204.

McWhinnie, H. J. A review of selected aspects of empirical aesthetics: III. *Journal of Aesthetic Education,* 1971, *5*(4), 115–126.

Moog, H. The development of musical experience in children of preschool age. *Psychology of Music,* 1976, *4*(2), 38–45.

*Murphy, D. T. A developmental study of the criteria used by children to justify their affective response to art experiences. Paper presented at Annual Meeting of the American Educational Research Association, New Orleans, Louisiana, February 28, 1973. (ERIC Document Reproduction Service No. ED 079 182).

NAEP Music 1971–1979. *Results from the second national music assessment (No. 10-MU-01) and Art 1974–1979: Results from the second national art assessment (No. 10-A-01).* Denver: National Assessment Distribution Center, 1981.

Osborne, H. Some theories of aesthetic judgment. *Journal of Aesthetics and Art Criticism,* 1979, *38*(2), 135–144.

Paal, Akos. Aesthetic qualities of children's drawings at the age of six to twelve years. *Magyar Pszichologiai Szemle,* 1977, *34,* 492–504.

Parsons, C., & Lindauer, M. S. Dance and theater: Their psychological importance and the aesthetic characteristics of their participants. *Catalog of Selected Documents in Psychology,* 1980, *10,* 88. Ms. 2143, 25 pp.

Parsons, M., Johnston, M., & Durham, R. Developmental stages in children's aesthetic responses. *Journal of Aesthetic Education,* 1978, *12*(1), 83–104.

Payne, R. Towards an understanding of music appreciation. *Psychology of Music,* 1980, *8*(2), 31–41.

Perney, J. Musical tasks related to the development of the conservation of metric time. *Journal of Research in Music Education,* 1976, *24*(4), 159–169.

Piper, R. M., & Shoemaker, D. M. Formative evaluation of kindergarten music program based on behavioral objectives. *Journal of Research in Music Education,* 1973, *21*(3), 145–152.

Plummer, G. S. Children's art judgment. *Journal of Creative Behavior,* 1977, *11*(3), 176–181.

Ramsey, M. Learning through the arts. *Today's Education,* 1980, *69*(4), 66–68.

Research for Better Schools. *Child development associate training program.* Unit V: *Expressive experiences for young chidren.* Module 1: *Exposing, appreciating, and communicating through expressive experiences for young children.* Philadelphia: Philadelphia School District, Research for Better Schools, 1976.

Richard, N., & Madeja, S. S. *The Bee Hive: The arts in early education.* St. Louis, Mo.: Central Midwestern Regional Educational Laboratory, 1974.

Roosevelt, R. K. Development of an instrument to measure qualitative discrimination based on visual perception responses to art. *Dissertation Abstracts International,* 1977, *38*(4-A), 1827–1828.

Rosenstiel, A. K., Morison, P., Silverman, J., & Gardner, H. Critical judgment: A developmental study. *Journal of Aesthetic Education,* 1978, *12*(4), 95–107.

Rump, E. E. Variables affecting appreciation in relation to age. *British Journal of Educational Psychology,* 1967, *37,* 58–70.

Rump, E. E. Relative preference as a function of number of elements in an abstract design. *Australian Journal of Psychology,* 1968, *20*(1), 39–48.

Salkind, L., & Salkind, N. A measure of aesthetic preference. *Studies in Art Education,* 1973, *15,* 21–27.

Sandle, D. Aesthetics and the psychology of qualitative movement. In J. E. Kane (Ed.), *Psychological aspects of physical education and sport.* London: Routledge & Kegan Paul, 1972.

Saverese, J. M., & Miller, R. J. Artistic preferences and cognitive-perceptual style. *Studies in Art Education,* 1979, *20*(2), 45–51.

Schleuter, S. L., & Deyarman, R. Musical aptitude stability among primary school children. *Bulletin of the Council for Research in Music Education,* 1977, *51,* 14–22.

Schwadron, A. A. Research directions in comparative music aesthetics and music education. *Journal of Aesthetic Education,* 1975, *9*(1), 99–109.

Seaman, A. C. Responses of lower- and middle-class 5-year-old children to achromatic and chromatic color and form stimuli. *Perceptual and Motor Skills,* 1974, *38*(3, pt. 2), 1257–1258.

Seefeldt, C. The effects of a program designed to increase young children's perception of texture. *Studies in Art Education,* 1979, *20*(2), 40–44.

Selfe, L. A review of current theories in psychology of children's drawings. British Journal of Aesthetics, 1980, 20(2), 160–164.

Shaw, C. N., & Tomcala, M. A music attitude scale for use with upper elementary school children. *Journal of Research in Music Education,* 1976, *24*(2), 73–80.

Smith, R. A. On the third domain: The aesthetic intent and public policy. *Journal of Aesthetic Education,* 1976, *10,* 5–9.

Snoeyenbos, M. H., & Knapp, C. A. Dance theory and dance education. *Journal of Aesthetic Education,* 1979, *13*(3), 17–30.

Stake, R. E. To evaluate an art program. *Journal of Aesthetic Education,* 1976, *10*(3 & 4), 115–133.

Stake, R. E., & Hoke, G. A. Evaluating an arts program: Movement and dance in a downstate district. *National Elementary Principal,* 1976, *55*(3), 52–59.

Stein, M. I. *Stimulating creativity.* New York: Academic Press, 1974.

Swenson, L. C. *Theories of learning.* Belmont, CA: Wadsworth, 1980.

Sudano, G. R. Television and the development of aesthetic literacy in children. *Contemporary Education,* 1978, *49,* 223–227.

Taylor, A. P., & Trujillo, J. L. The effects of selected stimuli on the art products, concept promotion, and aesthetic judgmental decisions of 4-year-old children. *Studies in Art Education,* 1973, *14*(2), 57–66.

Trammell, P. T. An investigation of the effectiveness of repetition and guided listening in developing enjoyable music listening experiences for second grade students. *Dissertation Abstracts International,* 1978, *38*(9-A), 5323–5324.

Wallach, M. A. Creativity. In P. H. Mussen (Ed.), *Carmichael's manual of child psychology.* New York: John Wiley & Sons, 1970.

Wilson, B. One view of the past and future of research in aesthetic education. *Journal of Aesthetic Education,* 1974, *8*(3), 59–67.

Winner, E., Rosenstiel, A., & Gardner, H. The development of metaphoric understanding. Developmental Psychology, 1976, *12,* 289–297.

Winterbourne, A. T. Objectivity in science and aesthetics. *British Journal of Aesthetics,* 1981, *21,* 253–260.

Wohlwill, J. F. Children's responses to meaningful pictures varying in diversity: Exploration time vs. preference. *Journal of Experimental Child Psychology,* 1975, *20,* 341–351.

Zenatti, A. Children's aesthetic judgment about musical consonance, tonality, and isochromism of the rhythmic beat. *Psychologie Francais,* 1976a *21,* 175–184.

Zenatti, A. Influence of some sociocultural variables on musical development in children. *Psychologie Francais,* 1976b, *21,* 185–190.

Zenatti, A. Esthetic judgment and perception in rhythm tests in children between 4 and 10 years old. *Anne Psychologique,* 1976c, *76,* 93–115.

4

Microcomputers in Early Childhood Education

Mima Spencer and Linda Baskin

*ERIC Clearinghouse on Elementary and
Early Childhood Education*

Not too long ago, an "apple" was a fruit, a "pet" was a cat or dog, and computers were strictly for adults. Today in some classrooms, a preschooler may be able to learn to discriminate between "above" and "below" on an Apple microcomputer, a first grader might practice arithmetic problems on her classroom TRS-80, and a second grader might check his spelling on a Commodore PET. No longer the exclusive property of highly specialized computer scientists, computers today are used in an increasing number of offices, schools, and homes. Preschools and day care centers are also starting to use microcomputers to teach and entertain children and to keep business records.

As computers become easier to use and more widely available, children will begin to take them for granted, just as many of today's adults learned to take television for granted when they were children. The development of software (the instructions for the computer or the computer program) suitable for children is likely to accelerate this process. Many major publishers now have electronic publishing divisions and are either commissioning or producing software for school and home computers.

Manufacturing efforts to produce better hardware and software have coincided with schools' attempts to provide greater accessibility to computers for children. According to a report by the National Center for Educational Statistics, more than half of the schools in the nation had acquired at least one computer by 1981 (National Center for Educational Statistics, 1981). A later survey conducted by Market Data Retrieval of Westport, Connecticut, reported that the number of schools having a computer had increased by 60% in the last year (Minnesota Schools Winning the Microcomputer Race, 1982). Many of these computers were being used primarily for administrative, record keeping, and accounting purposes, but the use of computers for instructional purposes was also increasing as teachers became more aware of the microcomputer's capabilities and more knowledgeable about educational software.

The age at which children first encounter computers in school has been steadily decreasing. There are now a number of research reports on children as young as 3 and 4 using computers successfully. Piestrup (1981) found that children, even at this early age, can be taught to operate a computer to the point of inserting floppy disks into the machine. Preschool teacher Sally Larsen reports teaching almost three hundred 4- to 12-year-old children to write short programs in Basic (Campbell, 1982). Other instances of children's use of computers are discussed in a report from the Institute for Communication Research at Stanford University (Paisley & Chen,1982). Kindergarten programs on computer literacy are also becoming more common (Hungate, 1982; Rosen, 1982), and microcomputer learning activities are being introduced in many preschools and day care centers (Lewis, 1981; Swigger & Campbell, 1981).

Perhaps most surprising about the schools' rapid acquisition of microcomputers is the fact that even though microcomputers were not readily available in significant numbers until the late 1970s, the new technology earned an early and rapid acceptance in school settings. Even allowing for aggressive marketing techniques, microcomputers appeared to offer something intriguing to educators.

Quite apart from the obvious utility of learning to use computers in a society increasingly making use of high technology, microcomputers offered the potential to change the nature of education. Even though other technological developments, such as television, have been heralded as having the capability to change educational theory and practice, the interactive nature of computers makes them significantly different from former technologies.

New patterns of classroom teaching and learning are part of the changes anticipated by many administrators and teachers. Among the areas potentially affected are methods of presenting factual information, methods of testing children's achievement, the role of the teacher in instruction, and aspects of the relationship between home and school. In addition, teacher education, curriculum planning, and traditional concepts of grade levels and sequences of instruction may be changed. More important than any single effect, however, is the possibility that using microcomputers will affect the way children think and learn.

COMPUTER LITERACY

As computer use becomes more common in society, what kinds of computer-related skills or knowledge may be needed by children and adults? Presently, people are expected to be able to use the telephone system; operate simple machines such as television sets, stoves, or typewriters; and know the rudiments of using a checking account. Understanding how to do these things is considered a normal requirement for adult life. It appears that knowing about computers and how to use them is also becoming essential, and that teaching about computers will ultimately be the responsibility of the schools. The term "computer literacy" is often used to describe such computer-related skills and knowledge.

Despite wide use of the term, there is as yet no consensus as to what constitutes computer literacy. Computer literacy has variously been defined as learning about computers and what they can do, learning to program, or a combination of these activities. Some define computer literacy as the ability to read and write via computer—that is, to read and write computer programs. Computer literacy has also been defined as the ability to use computer programs, rather than to create them. Other definitions include the study of the history of computers, the way computers work, and the potential impact of computers on society. Projects are currently underway to explore the concept of computer literacy in schools (Hunter, 1980; Bitter, 1982). Despite a variety of opinions, whatever definition of computer literacy is accepted by educators will be reflected in the curriculum materials and activities used to teach children to be computer literate.

Some people suggest that the rush to teach computer literacy is premature. They believe that instead of having to teach the technical terms and skills necessary to use computers today, future computers should be designed so that people can use them easily without special training. This point of view may prove to be increasingly sensible as more "user friendly" software is developed and marketed. Though much of the user friendly software is still disappointingly difficult to use, the urgent need for such software is being articulated by most software users, and producers are beginning to respond.

If most computer software becomes user friendly and if computers become widely available, much of what is now considered essential knowledge about computers will no longer be necessary, and the concept of computer literacy may become as outmoded as the concept of "telephone literacy." Just as children now learn to use telephones by watching their parents at home, playing with toy telephones, and later using the real phone, so computers will become a commonplace part of children's daily lives.

Given today's interest in children's learning to use computers, it seems likely that efforts will be made to include computers in most early childhood curricula. Early childhood educators are already beginning to explore the question of what young children can and should learn about computers and what they should learn first. For example, should a child first learn about the parts of a computer and how they are used? Or would using computers in an exploratory way to find out what happens when keys are pressed or a program is run be a better first exposure? What concepts are most relevant for young children? Does it make sense to explain a memory chip to a 3-year-old or teach a 5-year-old to program?

While no firm answers to these questions exist, appropriate approaches and content may depend on a child's age and developmental level. When more research evidence on children's use of computers has been collected and teachers have had more experience in working with children and computers, more reliable information should be available for making decisions on how best to introduce computers. Some educators question the value of having young children learn about computers and are asking for more evidence as to the potential positive and negative effects before proceeding to use them. Despite their concerns, it seems unlikely that the move towards computer use in early childhood education will be reversed. What may be more important is that thoughtful educators and parents continue to become knowledgeable about computers and to influence the way computers are used with children.

MICROCOMPUTER EXPERIENCES FOR YOUNG CHILDREN

According to most reports, parents and teachers are very positive about children's experiences with microcomputers. The children themselves are both enthusiastic and less inhibited than adults in learning how to use microcomputers. But teachers and parents also ask about the effects of computer use on children and wonder whether such activities as playing games or learning numbers on the computer will be helpful to children's development. Specifically, some questions asked are, "Will computerized lessons help children learn to read more easily than standardized or conventional methods?"; "Can children learn to solve problems more quickly when challenged by an interactive computer program that provides feedback about answers?"; and, "Will use of the computer isolate children from one another?"

Effects of Microcomputers on Children

Even though extensive research on microcomputer use with children is still to come, reports on the effects of using large mainframe computer systems developed in the 1960s and 1970s, such as the PLATO or TICCIT systems, are available. Hallworth and Brebner (1980) reviewed studies of computer assisted instruction (CAI) intended for age groups ranging from kindergarten through college. Two results were consistent across studies: (a) individuals were able to learn as well using computers as they did using more conventional materials and methods, and (b) they enjoyed learning in this manner.

The report also indicates that certain children, especially those who learn slowly or need to repeat lessons, appear to learn more readily when they can proceed at their own pace through the computerized lessons and can repeat each lesson as often as they choose. Similarly, exceptionally capable children, who are often bored or restless during periods of repetitive teaching or times when they must wait for others to learn, adapt readily to CAI. When able to proceed through lessons as rapidly as they choose, children progress more quickly through materials and appear to enjoy controlling the pace of their work.

Computer feedback to children on how they are doing during lessons also appears to motivate them, reduces the time needed to do each task and improves attitudes towards learning. In programs that automatically move the learner to a higher level of difficulty when the previous level has been mastered, children were able to cover more material then they might otherwise have done in the same period of time (Hallworth & Brebner, 1980).

The research on use of large computer systems is consistent with early results on microcomputer use. Although often describing studies of short duration or research conducted with small samples, preliminary reports on microcomputer use—as well as reports by teachers already working with children and microcomputers—also indicate improved learning and enthusiasm in children. For example, at the 1982 meeting of the Association for Educational Data Systems in Orlando, Florida, teachers who had brought children from their classes to demonstrate the use of microcomputers stated that the children's learning improved and that their enthusiasm for working with computers, plus computer feedback, provided learning motivation. At the Bing Nursery School on the Stanford University campus, Piestrup (1981) worked with fifty-five 3- and 4-year-old children, helping them learn reading readiness concepts such as "above," "below," "left," and "right" on an Apple II microcomputer. She reports that both teachers and children were enthusiastic and that criterion tests on the four reading skill concepts showed that children improved after the 3-week period with the computer.

Economically disadvantaged kindergarten children at a San Francisco Bay Area school worked weekly with Commodore PET microcomputers from October 1980 to May 1981. Programs focused on basic mathematics, visual discrimination, and name and telephone number practice. Each of the 12 children involved had a computer to use and was allowed to explore the keyboard extensively and learn the connection between pressing a key and seeing something new appear on the screen. Gradually, the children learned to work the computer and go through the programs, increasing the amount of time they could work with the computer from 15 minutes to more than 35 minutes. In later tests of the children's ability to learn from the computerized instruction, four children performed better on certain math, counting, and telephone number tasks than six children who had not used the computer (Hungate, 1982).

Sheingold (1983) suggests that microcomputers might be used to help children get in touch with the symbolic aspects of what they already know or are learning about from other kinds of experiences. For example, by having real chick eggs incubating in a preschool classroom at the same time a computer simulation of the development of a chick inside an egg is available in class, children might be encouraged to make connections between the real world and the image on the computer.

Although the reports of improved learning and children's eagerness to spend time with microcomputers are positive, teachers and parents have posed additional questions. Two of the most common of these are, "How much time on the microcomputer is the right amount for a young child?"; and, "Will children's social development be negatively affected by early exposure to computers?" A fairly obvious answer to these questions seems to be that there is probably no such thing as a "right" amount of time on the computer. Children need to engage in a variety of activities: play with their friends, spend time outdoors, and interact with computers as one of the many experiences they will have. Sheingold (1983) suggests that early childhood educators learn to think of the microcomputer as one of many learning tools that children might use, rather than as a replacement for other activities.

Contrary to earlier fears that using a computer might prove to be an isolating experience, mutual consulting, cooperation, and collaboration among children has been reported often by teachers and by children themselves. It may be that the computer contributes to sociability. Another social effect of using computers appears to be that a child's self-esteem is fostered by the confidence and satisfaction generated by having control of the computer, making choices during a program, learning to program, and so on. Self-concept development has been noted by several teachers working with young children. At one preschool, a shy child gained the respect of class members and improved his social skills as a result of his "expertise" on the computer.

Teachers report that children often gain a sense of power by using computers (Damarin, 1982; Paisley & Chen, 1982). For instance, the child who is working alone at the computer is independent of adults or other children. His or her own actions determine whether the computer will work or the program will run, providing a sense of control. Failure to do well the first time is not humiliating; the child can return to the beginning and try again. The computer is patient, if somewhat rigid in its requirements for responses. The interaction between child and computer is self-reinforcing, and artificial kinds of reinforcement (a smiling face or musical salute produced by the computer) may become unnecessary. Motivation is strong to try another letter, redo a sum, or press a different key so that the child can continue. According to some reports, children enjoy the privacy of working alone at a computer. The freedom to make mistakes and correct errors without other children or the teacher noticing or commenting on them appears to be a plus. Also, when a child working at the computer wants to save something discovered or created, it can easily be done.

These reports, which reflect educators' experiences in working with children and computers, indicate that computers can provide exciting and instructive experiences, perhaps in ways not yet conceived of by educators. Although none of these effects occurs all of the time or applies to every child or situation, the initial results of using computers in elementary and early childhood education settings are encouraging.

Computer Applications for Young Children

Before teachers and administrators can begin to plan for computer applications in early childhood education, it is important for them to become aware of the various ways in which computers can be used with young children. The following categories are neither exhaustive nor mutually exclusive but suggest some of the more important ways computers might be used with this age group.

Computer literacy. As has already been suggested, the primary goal of any use of computers with young children might be considered computer literacy (i.e., teaching children what computers can do and how to use them). Computer literacy can include teaching children how to use the computer as a tool (a medium with which to calculate, draw, or write), as a tutor (to provide instruction), as a tutee (to be programmed), or as a combination of these three (Taylor, 1980).

Computer Assisted Instruction (CAI). When the computer is used as a tutor, concepts, information, or skills normally presented through conventional teaching methods are taught by computer. For example, 4- or 5-year-old children can learn the alphabet, counting, or how to discriminate between similar and different objects by interacting with a computer programed to present information, receive responses, and offer new information based on the children's responses.

Computer programming. One of the reasons given for teaching young children to program (in other words, to learn to use a computer language to give the computer instructions) is to promote computer literacy and to prepare children for a computer-oriented future. Another reason for teaching children to program is related to cognitive development. Specifically, programming requires the child who works with the computer to do certain things: to appreciate the fact that there may be many ways to solve a problem, analyze a task, pose alternative solutions to problems, understand how to sequence instructions, and use logic. These kinds of skills are viewed as valuable in themselves and may be generalized to situations and learning experiences other than those involving computers.

Computer art.   A teacher working with young children may introduce computers to them by illustrating how the computer can be used to draw pictures or designs. Children (like many adults) appear to be fascinated by computer graphics and quickly learn the instructions or activities necessary to create their own designs and pictures. In a way, the computer used in this manner functions as a very powerful tool or medium for expression. As children become more skilled, they are able to produce valuable and interesting art based on increasingly complex programs. Through using computer graphics, children gain personal satisfaction as well as an increased understanding of design, composition, and use of color (Piestrup, 1982).

Word processing.   Primary school children can use computers as tools to create their own text and practice writing and reading. Word processing programs can encourage young children to experiment with language as well as to record their own writing (Classroom Computer News Forum, 1983).

Administrative uses.   Although not part of children's direct involvement with computers, administrative uses of computers may free educators from routine record keeping to spend more time in instructional activities and at the same time help them to develop computer literacy. Computers in offices are frequently used for accounting, reports, word processing, attendance, personnel records, and budget preparation or management. (A computer purchase can often be justified for administrative purposes and the computer later used for instructional purposes as well.)

The diversity of computer applications suggests that learning how to incorporate a computer in early childhood education is a matter of deciding from among many possible uses. The trend of the late 1970s and early 1980s seems to be for educators to select one or two applications at first, probably on the basis of primary need and funds or equipment available. Until further research is available, educators may have to continue to choose appropriate computer applications according to perceived needs, reports from other educators, and budget considerations. Of particular interest to those involved with young children may be three of the six applications already mentioned: CAI, computer programming, and word processing.

COMPUTER ASSISTED INSTRUCTION

One way to use computers in education is to transfer to the computer a part of the job of teaching children. Although computers do not have a regular classroom teacher's flexibility and comprehensive view of each child's needs, they are powerful, patient machines that can be programmed for many instructional activities.

For example, a computer system can present new material or concepts to children, ask questions, and record responses. Or a child may practice arithmetic problems presented by a computer and receive feedback on his or her answers. These kinds of uses are referred to as computer assisted instruction (CAI). CAI is not new, but a variety of CAI software for microcomputers has recently become available. CAI can be used to teach almost any subject and, as in most teaching, content can be presented in a variety of ways. Since the 1960s, when CAI began, several formats, based in part on traditional educational methods, have evolved. These formats, now conventions for presenting CAI, include drill and practice, educational games, simulations, and tutorials.

Drill and practice refers to programs which allow students to review and practice basic concepts and skills. For example, a computer can present arithmetic problems appropriate for each child's stage of development, give feedback, provide supplementary information, or present easier or more difficult problems based on the student's responses (Suppes, 1980).

In early childhood education, programs asking the child to match letters or numbers to specific keys on the keyboard, discriminate between "same" and "different," or supply the next number in a series are all examples of drill and practice. Some drill and practice programs can also provide teachers with a report on each child's progress or responses. Such programs can be used to provide practice of lessons introduced earlier by the teacher or as a separate activity.

Educational games on the computer are designed to help the child learn almost as a by-product of playing the game. A child's enjoyment of the game appears to provide motivation to spend more time than might be spent if the game material were presented in another format (Malone, 1980). An example of an educational game for young children might be one that asked the children to practice the directions left and right by finding their way through a maze displayed on the computer screen. Another game might invite children to guess the name of an animal stored in the computer memory based on computer responses to the children's listing of animal attributes (fur, hooves, etc.).

Simulations are programs in which a child takes a role in a model situation set up by the computer. The situation can be either realistic or fantastic. For example, a realistic simulation might involve the child in buying the family groceries and deciding what to choose from the different food groups displayed on the screen. An older child might be asked to spend only a certain amount to acquire the necessary groceries. A more fanciful simulation might portray an ocean bottom and ask the child to make choices, such as what a fish should do when a shark appears or a hook comes down into the water. While it is important to remember that a simulation only deals with a small part of a situation, it is expected that children experiencing simulations will acquire concepts that would be more difficult (or less fun) to acquire in other ways.

Tutorials are programs in which the computer, as the teacher, presents information to the child and asks the child to respond. Questions may be asked and the child may choose between different alternatives; the computer then provides feedback based on the responses. For example, in an early reading program, children might be shown a story and then asked to identify actors or actions from the story. One of the limitations of a tutorial program is that all students' responses must be anticipated and built into the program. Therefore, there is no room for the spontaneity or major strategy changes that a classroom teacher might introduce. Another limitation for early childhood uses are the reading skills required by most tutorials available today. Nonetheless, tutorial programs can be helpful in presenting new material or reinforcing concepts.

Despite the general need for the child to possess reading skills, computer assisted lessons have been developed for children as young as 3 and 4 years of age. When children are too young to read, graphics or an audiotape can be used to present information or instructions. At this time, only a limited number of software programs use graphics and audiotapes for younger children, but the number is expected to increase in the near future as more microcomputers are purchased for homes and early childhood centers.

COMPUTER PROGRAMMING

The computer may have a greater impact on education by introducing new concepts about teaching and new ideas about learning than by automating teaching practices and providing learning experiences that have been available for decades. Learning to program at an early age, particularly using computer languages developed especially for children, may affect the way children approach problems or think about their environment. Although children are being taught to program in several languages (for example, Basic and Pilot) the Logo language is of particular interest to early childhood educators. In his book *Mindstorms*, Seymour Papert (1980) describes Logo as based on a Piagetian model in which children are builders of their own intellectual structures and learn through programming the importance of exploration and discovery. Although Papert does not always agree with Piaget on the ages at which children can profit from different learning experiences, the ideas underlying the Logo language substantially draw from Piaget's developmental theories.

A language that allows even young children to create their own programs for the computer, Logo was developed under Papert's direction at the Massachusetts Institute of Technology (M.I.T.) in the 1960s. As part of the early testing of Logo with young children, a mechanical toy—a turtle that could be controlled by the computer—was developed. Children as young as 4 were able to use Logo to instruct the turtle to draw shapes on paper taped to the floor. In later versions of Logo, the turtle became a triangular shape on the computer screen; programming this turtle resulted in pictures on the computer screen (Lough, 1983).

The Logo commands that control the turtle are simple ones. For example, if a child enters the command "Forward 100," the turtle on the screen will draw a line 100 turtle steps long (about 3 inches) in the direction it was facing. The command "Right 90" tells the turtle to turn 90 degrees to the right. Repeating this sequence of commands three more times would therefore result in a square. The child might store this group of commands under the name "Square." From then on, the simple command "Do Square" would invoke the longer list of commands to create the picture of a square on the screen. According to Papert, it is not necessary to teach children that a square is an enclosed figure with four equal sides and right angles because Logo, a tool which "speaks math", gives them access to and personal knowledge of mathematical concepts. Using Logo additionally teaches about problem solving, analyzing a task, sequencing, and refining multiple strategies or approaches.

Papert also describes Logo as an "object to think with." He believes children can learn to communicate with computers as naturally as they learn to communicate with other people and that this communication can change the way children learn about other things. In other words, the experiences a child has with the computer can create models, strategies, or skills related to learning that can transfer to other areas of activity.

Preschool, elementary, and secondary school-age children have been exposed to Logo in research and educational settings. The Lamplighter School, a private school in Dallas, Texas, was the site of a 4-year project using Logo with children 3 to 9 years old. The project was a collaboration between the M.I.T. Logo group, Texas Instruments, and the school. In most instances, children demonstrated increased understanding of the concepts of mathematics and enjoyment of things mathematical, although they did not necessarily improve their performance on standardized tests (Watt, 1982).

The nature of the learning experience provided by use of a language such as Logo is different from that resulting from computer assisted instruction (CAI). In CAI, the learner is basically a responder who is to progress through computerized lessons preselected by educators. In a sense, the content is fixed: an answer on a drill and practice problem in math is either right or wrong. In contrast, Logo is a more expressive tool, one that permits the child to learn about mathematics and other concepts through experimentation and discovery. Logo is also nonjudgmental in that there are no right or wrong answers in designing a program. One of the reasons for educators' interest in Logo is this open-ended quality.

WORD PROCESSING

Computer word processing programs, which allow children to write and modify their own work, may have the same impact on children's learning language arts as Logo appears to have had on mathematics learning. The use of a word processing program, which lets children easily insert or delete text, may encourage them to write more freely and fully than they would have without the help of such a program. Another benefit is that a word processor with a printer produces more attractive, "grown-up looking" text than children's handwritten copy. Older children can edit their own work, easily move chunks of text around, and otherwise revise work without having to recopy. Teachers report that this freedom encourages children to write more and that the quality of writing is improved (Classroom Computer News Forum, 1982; Levin & Kareev, 1980). As children are introduced to keyboards at earlier and earlier ages, typing (even one letter at a time) also becomes a more natural part of the writing process. According to "Classroom Computer News Forum" (1982), word processing programs are being developed especially for use by children.

When is a child old enough to effectively use a word processing program to type letters of the alphabet, numbers, and other symbols? At what point can a word processor aid a child in beginning to write simple sentences, paragraphs, stories, or poems? There are no easy answers to these questions: A child's maturity, capability to identify keys, and the availability of adult assistance in teaching use of the program are all factors in determining when word processing can be successfully introduced.

As soon as a child has command of sufficient vocabulary and syntax to begin expressing thoughts in writing—perhaps in the primary grades—a word processor can be a useful tool. Even though the child may only be able to write simple sentences, such as "The boy runs" or "The dog eats," the word processor permits changing the noun or verb in either sentence to create two new sentences without losing the originals. The teacher can correct errors, leaving the sentence in its original form for the child to see the difference. As the child learns new words or expands ideas, they can be added to the original work that has been stored, in several versions if necessary, until he or she is satisfied with the creation. In one sense, using a word processor documents the child's progress both to the child and to the teacher. A printout for parents can also be made for reporting purposes.

Improved reading comprehension is another potential benefit of using word processing programs to assist language development. Children highly motivated to interact with the computer learn quickly that reading is an essential step to getting the computer to respond as they want. Reading to understand directions or to determine which answer is needed by the computer for the program to progress gives children a reason for developing proficiency, immediate reinforcement when they do become proficient, and the ability to move to more complex programs requiring more sophisticated reading skills.

TRAINING FOR EDUCATORS

Training in the use of computers is cited repeatedly as a major need for educators at all levels (Clements, 1983; Oliver, 1983; Sheingold, 1981). In addition to learning how to use a computer, teachers and administrators need information and experience before they can evaluate and choose from among the increasing number of computer applications. For example, a teacher who learns Basic programming as part of a computer literacy course in college may be less interested in using computer assisted instruction (CAI) or Logo than in using the computer to teach children programming.

Lack of sufficient training can be costly. Too often a school system spends a great deal of money to purchase hardware and software but spends very little on teaching the teachers and administrators to integrate computer use into their regular activities. As a result, the computers are seldom used or are stored until someone learns more about them. Educators are often expected to spend their own time acquiring the necessary information to use the equipment. In this situation, one teacher may eventually learn about the computer and teach others—or may be the only one to use the computer. In the latter case, others may find it too difficult to gain access to the computer or may decide the computer is too complicated to master. An enthusiastic teacher or principal can help other staff members learn about the computer, but inservice sessions are needed and should be considered an integral part of the school's plan to bring computers into the classroom.

The ideal training situation is one which is relatively labor-intensive. It takes many hours of an instructor's time to acquaint teachers with the full range of a computer's potential. Particularly important is hands-on experience, which gives teachers an opportunity to become familiar with the computer by actually using it. Hands-on practice necessitates access to a number of computers and a variety of software, as well as good teaching skills on the part of the trainer. Different learning styles and possible feelings of anxiety or reluctance to learn about computers on the part of teachers should also be considered in planning training sessions.

Training is also occurring outside of work settings. Many university colleges of education are now responding to demands for information with preservice and inservice courses on computer literacy, CAI, and programming. Most colleges that have started such programs, particularly for practicing teachers, have been overwhelmed with the number of students who sign up to take classes. Often a relatively general course, such as introductory programming or an overview of computer applications, is offered to try to meet the needs of most students. An increase in short courses, weekend and evening classes, and workshops is still needed in most communities.

Early childhood educators should be concerned that the training offered to future and practicing teachers be relevant to the needs of younger children. How many colleges presently offer coursework in Logo for young children, provide information on input devices for nontypists, or teach about voice output for nonreaders? At the graduate level, seminars, independent study, or special-problems courses might focus on ways in which interaction with computers can address the special needs of children (Clements, 1983).

INVOLVEMENT OF EARLY CHILDHOOD EDUCATORS

Important issues related to young children and computers have yet to be fully addressed by specialists in early childhood education. These issues range from such basic considerations as how computer use affects children and how computers should be used in classrooms to policy and curriculum issues about what should be taught, when, and how. Investigators have already begun to collect data on some of these subjects, but more time is needed before answers are forthcoming.

Another factor related to the successful use of computers in teaching young children may be the degree to which educators choose to become actively involved in developing plans for integrating computer use into existing curricula. Teachers' input is also needed in the development and critical review of early childhood education software if computer-related activities are to be all that they could be.

Two possiblities exist with regard to development of software. Early childhood education software may become primarily a computerized version of traditional materials, incorporating traditional methods, or it may be designed to take advantage of computer power to introduce new and different learning experiences. Teachers' involvement, especially at this early stage of software development, can make a difference. The alternative to involvement may be to have to accept by default the products of this new technology.

REFERENCES

Bitter, G. G. The road to computer literacy: A scope and sequence model. *Electronic Learning,* September, 1982, 60–63.

Campbell, L. Computers: Relevant issues for Montessorians. *American Montessori Society Magazine,* 1982, *9*(4), 4–8.

Classroom Computer News Forum—Word processing: How will it shape the student as writer? *Classroom Computer News,* 1982, *3*(2), 24–27; 74–76.

*Clements, D. H. *Microcomputers in early education: Rationale and outline for teacher training.* Kent, OH: Kent State University, 1983. (ERIC Document Reproduction Service No. ED 223 328)

*Damarin, S. K. *The impact of computer technology on children.* Symposium presented at the American Society for Information Science Conference on the Impact of Computer Technology on Children, Columbus, Ohio, 1982. Unpublished manuscript.

*Hallworth, H. J., & Brebner, A. *Computer assisted instruction in schools: Achievements, present developments, and projections for the future.* Calgary, Canada: Calgary University, 1980. (ERIC Document Reproduction Service No. ED 200 187)

Hungate, H. Computers in the kindergarten. *The Computing Teacher,* January, 1982, 15–18.

*Hunter, B. *An approach to integrating computer literacy into the K-8 curriculum,* 1980. (ERIC Document Reproduction Service No. ED 195 247)

Levin, J. A., & Kareev, Y. *Personal computers and education: The challenge to schools.* San Diego, CA: University of California Center for Human Information Processing (Report No. 98), 1980.

*Lewis, C. L. A study of preschool children's use of computer programs. In D. Harris & L. Nelson-Heern, *Proceedings of the Third National Educational Computing Conference,* Denton, Texas: North Texas State University, June 1981. (ERIC Document Reproduction Service No. ED 207 526)

Lough, T. Logo. *Electronic Learning,* March, 1983, 49–53.

Malone, T. W. *What makes things fun to learn? A study of intrinsically motivating computer games.* Palo Alto, CA: Xerox Research Center, 1980.

"Minnesota Schools Winning the Microcomputer Race." *Education Daily, 15*(231), December 3, 1982, 1.

National Center for Educational Statistics (United States Department of Education). *Student use of computers in the schools* (Fast Response Survey System Early Release). March 20, 1981, pp. 1.

Oliver, P. An administrator's round-table: Technology and education—Issues and answers. *Electronic Learning,* February 1983, 63–66.

*Paisley, W., & Chen, M. *Children and electronic text: Challenge and opportunities of the "New Literacy."* Stanford, CA: Stanford University Institute for Communication Research, 1982. (ERIC Document Reproduction Service No. ED 225 530)

Papert, S. *Mindstorms: Children, computers, and powerful ideas.* New York: Basic Books, 1980.

*Piestrup, A. M. Preschool children use Apple II to test reading skills programs. 1981. (ERIC Document Reproduction Service No. ED 202 476)

*Piestrup, A. M. Young children use computer graphics. *Harvard Computer Graphics Week,* Harvard University Graduate School of Design, 1982. (ERIC Document Reproduction Service No. ED 224 564)

Rosen, S. Texas lighting the way via video. *Learning*, October 1982, 34–36.

*Sheingold, K. Issues related to the implementation of computer technology in schools: A cross-sectional study. *Children's Electronic Laboratory,* Memo No. 1, 1981. (ERIC Document Reproduction Service No. ED 205 165)

Sheingold, K. Young children in our technological society: The impact of microcomputers. Paper presented at the University of Maryland Conference on Young Children in Our Technological Environment, March 1983.

Suppes, P. Computer-based mathematics instruction. In R. P. Taylor (Ed.), *The computer in the school: Tutor, tool, tutee.* New York: Teachers College Press, Columbia University, 1980.

*Swigger, K. M., & Cambell, J. Computers and the nursery school. In D. Harris & L. Nelson-Heern, *Proceedings of the Third Annual National Educational Computing Conference,* Denton, Texas: North Texas State University, June 1981. (ERIC Document Reproduction Service No. ED 207 526)

Taylor, R. P. (Ed.). *The computer in the school: Tutor, tool, tutee.* New York: Teachers College Press, Columbia University, 1980.

Watt, D. Logo in the schools. *Byte*, August, 1982, 116–134.

5

Enhancing the Effectiveness of Parent Education: An Analysis of Program Assumptions

Douglas R. Powell

Purdue University

The field of parent education is flourishing. The number of programs for parents is growing rapidly as professionals and policymakers give increased attention to the influence of families on early childhood development, and to the stresses of parenthood. The diverse array of programs now in existence has caused the parent education field to take on a fragmented and diffuse character, with parent programs varying considerably in terms of aims, methods, and theoretical orientations to child development. In spite of the long history of parent education, never before have there been so many program models and tested ways to work with parents of young children.

Questions which surface frequently in discussions of parent education pertain to effective ways to provide programs for parents: "What is the most successful approach?"; and "What really works?" These and similar questions gain importance as interest in parent education increases, the diversity of program approaches expands, and resources for program support become scarce. The answers are not as readily available as the questions, of course. This is partially due to a limited empirical data base. Also, the variety of programs makes it difficult to generalize findings from one program to other programs or settings. More importantly, though, the lack of thorough answers to questions relating to program effectiveness reflects a narrowly defined view of the issues which must be confronted when carrying out an effective parent education program.

This chapter addresses questions of program effectiveness by analyzing selected assumptions about the ways in which programs attempt to influence parents. An important step toward the improvement of program effectiveness is the identification and clarification of assumptions which prompt and sustain specific program structures and operations. These assumptions often are implicit or unacknowledged in the design and delivery of programs, but they play a central role in providing a framework for program efforts to change parents' childrearing beliefs, knowledge, and skills. A careful investigation of the underlying suppositions or theoretical origins of specific program operations—at a general level as well as within individual programs—may establish a firm foundation for considering strategies to enhance program effectiveness.

The following dimensions of parent programs are examined: (a) the expertise and role of the professional in working with parents, (b) the development of program standards of "good parenting," and (c) conceptions of how parents change. The intent is to explore each of these areas in terms of the relationship between prevailing assumptions and program practices. As a preface to analysis of these areas, current trends and developments in the parent education field are considered.

THE GREENING OF PARENT EDUCATION

In recent years, the parent education label has come to represent many different types of programs. The term is no longer limited to conventional didactic instruction in child development. The field now encompasses such varied efforts as home-based parent training, small clusters of parents who functions as self-help groups, short-term lecture/discussion courses on family relations conducted in work settings, and educational experiences which seek to strengthen parents' use of community institutions. There is great variation among programs in terms of frequency and duration of contact with parents, structure, personnel, curriculum content, and inclusion or exclusion of the child.

The broadening of the parent education field is exemplified in the changes which have taken place in programmatic approaches to early childhood intervention in the past decade. The focus of many intervention programs has expanded recently to include the family as well as the preschool child (see Zigler & Berman, 1983). This shift is partly in response to the growing body of research data which suggest that the benefits of early education may be maximized if there is a significant level of parent involvement (Bronfenbrenner, 1974). This reorientation also is based on the argument that a focus on parents is more cost-effective than a child-only focus, because the parent program ultimately may affect siblings other than the target child, the benefits may be sustained by the parent after the program ends, and there may be an unintended by-product of self-growth in the parent, such as job training (Powell, 1982a).

The ways in which early intervention programs work with parents vary considerably. The experience of Head Start provides a case in point. Although parent involvement has been an important part of Head Start since its beginning, recent developments have moved many Head Start programs toward a family focus. Three program models within Head Start give particular emphasis to parents and the entire family: Home Start, the Parent Child Centers, and the Child and Family Resource Program. The latter program, launched in 11 locations throughout the United States in 1973, is the most family-focused demonstration program ever undertaken within Head Start. The unit of enrollment is the family rather than the child. A key element of the program is an assessment which examines needs, strengths, and goals of the family. This leads to a Family Action Plan which addresses an array of family needs (i.e., health, social services, education, child care) and includes specific steps toward realization of a family's goals (O'Keefe, 1979). A recent review of Head Start by a distinguished group of scholars and national leaders recommended that components of the Child and Family Resource Program be incorporated into existing Head Start programs (United States Department of Health and Human Services, 1980).

Perhaps the "newest kids on the block" in the parent education field are members of the growing group of parent or family support programs. These programs may be distinguished from traditional parent education programs in their lack of a predetermined curriculum or imposed content, and in their emphasis on individual or family functioning. Instead of (or in addition to) focusing on the parent's direct contribution to the child's cognitive development, support programs tend to deal with the parent's experiences in the parental role and in managing the affairs of everyday life. In some programs, for instance, there is no established curriculum of lessons on child development; rather, the content of parent group discussions is determined largely by parents' interests (Powell, in press; Wandersman, Wandersman, & Kahn, 1980). Parent or family support programs usually capitalize on the value of meaningful interpersonal ties with peers in adjusting to the demands of childrearing and typically do not place staff in a dominant role in "teaching" parents. As will be discussed later, support programs represent a markedly different orientation to working with parents in terms of assumptions about parents' needs, interests, and processes of change.

A recent major trend in the parent education field is the increased attention to the social contexts in which parents function. A conclusion of Bronfenbrenner's (1974) analysis of the effectiveness of early intervention programs was that ecological intervention in the form of family support systems would be an effective way to enhance the development of children. The goals and activities of a growing number of programs are consistent with this notion of intervention. The focus is on a parent's or family's relationship with its immediate environment. For instance, a major goal of the Child and Family Resource Program within Head Start is to link families to community resources (O'Keefe, 1979). Environmental forces, such as neighborhoods and local human services, have an important influence on the quality of childrearing, and thus are appropriate targets of intervention (Powell, 1979). This approach contrasts markedly with parent education programs which view the quality of childrearing to be largely a function of a parent's child development knowledge.

It is debatable whether programs which emphasize support and/or have concern for a family's relations with its community fall within the parent education field. White (1977) has noted the distinction between parent education and "family welfare" programs, arguing that professional educators are qualified to deal with educational issues and not with such matters as poor jobs and inadequate housing. No doubt this question creates one of the most disturbing tensions in the field today. What are the boundaries of the parent education field? The issue is difficult to resolve partly because it is not clear when a program activity is "noneducational." Is helping a parent learn skills to make effective use of a local resource, such as a medical clinic, an educational or a welfare matter? The issue also is problematic in that traditional parent education as well as family-oriented and parent support programs generally have the same ultimate goal—the improvement of child development. In addition, the labels assigned to programs may be superficial, if not misleading, representations of the actual programs. Indeed, this writer has observed a number of family and parent "support" programs where it appeared that the concept of support actually was a new euphemism for subtle but intentional professional directives on how to educate a preschool child.

The parent education field, then, is maturing. It is experiencing substantive expansion and differentiation. The field has transcended the traditional education of parents about child development to include a focus on the entire family and to embrace an interest in a parent's or a family's relations with the environment. Programs differ in terms of their emphasis on child development, parent development, and family development. Questions about the field's identity—what parent education is and is not—emerge as new ways are developed to help parents become better parents. Conflicts arise as experts debate the merits of, for example, teaching a parent a cognitive stimulation technique versus helping a family function more effectively.

Another indication of the field's maturity is the increasing realization that parent education is not a panacea for society's ills. The current wave of interest in parent programs was ushered in with high expectations. Federal education officials argued that "every child has a right to a trained parent" (Bell, 1975), while researchers demonstrated the strong influence of parents on child growth and development (see Schaefer, 1972, for a review). For many, the key to a new, better society began with the education of parents. For example, Rheingold (1973) proposed a new profession (composed of "scientists of rearing") which would acquire and test knowledge on the rearing of children. To her, the need for these scientists was obvious:

> Parents-to-be must be certified as to their competence, and a practical examination is better than a paper one. We must take an examination to obtain a license to drive a car. The child deserves no less; the good of the country demands much more. (p. 45)

Unfortunately, Rheingold did not address seriously the problems of determining and measuring parental competence. A major issue in parent education surrounds the question of who is to determine what constitutes "good parenting." Rheingold also assumed that parental knowledge is the primary influence on parent behavior, thereby ignoring the potentially significant impact of socioecological forces (such as unemployment). Moreover, child development is influenced by more than parents.

Viewing parental influences in isolation from other forces in the child's life is as inadequate as viewing schools as totally responsible for a child's achievement (Schlossman, 1978). By examining carefully what Cremin (1978) calls the "configurations of education" (i.e., home, school, church) historically and for the present day, we begin to understand that many interconnected agencies are involved in a child's life. Whether more realistic expectations of the outcome of parent education will be sustained on a long-term basis remains to be seen. An examination of the history of parent education in the United States suggests that new waves of interest have been characterized by high hopes for an improved social order (Schlossman, 1976).

This brief review of current trends in the parent education field underscores the longstanding, dominant assumption in our culture that parents require training in the rearing of young children. Inherent in all theories of the child is the notion that lay people—especially parents—need expert advice in the care of children (Kessen, 1979).

Historically, a prevalent assumption has been that low-income parents are in particular need of training. For example, a major goal of the Parent Teacher Association (PTA) in the early 1900s (then known as the National Congress of Mothers) was to work with poor families. Mothers' clubs for women of limited financial resources were led by PTA members in an effort to disseminate current knowledge on child care and family life (Schlossman, 1976). In the 1960s and early 1970s, research on mother/child interaction was interpreted as suggesting that low-income home environments were "culturally disadvantaged" and that this deprivation was the cause of poor academic achievement among children from low-income families. The white middle-class bias in this deficit model orientation has been criticized heavily

(Lightfoot, 1978) and, more recently, there has been an emphasis on differences between children from varied social and racial backgrounds, rather than a focus on deficiencies. A recent study, for instance, suggests that differences between lower- and middle-class children may represent "stylistic patterns rather than capacity differences" (Yando, Seitz, & Zigler, 1979, p. 107).

The tendency to view low-income groups as in greater need of parent education than other groups points to a critical issue in the field today: Who needs parent education? Even with the deficit model discarded, persuasive arguments exist that low-income population groups need parent programs more than middle-class populations due to the stressful conditions of poverty. Bronfenbrenner (1978) has answered this question by proposing that the groups most in need of parent education are those who do not yet or never will have children. He suggests that the progressive fragmentation and isolation of the family in its childrearing role leads to the need to re-educate society's decision makers about the necessary and sufficient conditions for making human beings human. Bronfenbrenner has argued that parent education should focus on the conditions of parenthood—forces external to the family which impinge on childrearing—and that an effective way to improve the conditions of parenthood is to educate "workers, neighbors, friends... members of organizations, committees and boards" (p. 783) about the difficult circumstances which affect the capacity of the family to function.

It is impossible to decide who needs parent education without specifying the type of program potentially of greatest value. A more useful question, then, is, "Who needs what type of parent education?" This enables consideration of the *match* between specific population groups and the particular goals and methods of programs. An examination of the match between program and participant necessitates an analysis of assumptions behind the design and delivery of parent education programs.

PROFESSIONAL EXPERTISE AND ROLES

A core component of a parent education program is the interpersonal relationship between parents and program staff. Parent education, like all other education, is a "people-changing" enterprise; the aim of most programs is to enhance parent/child interaction by changing some aspect of parents' behavior, knowledge, or attitudes. It is through the management of a parent/ professional relationship that staff attempt to influence parents. Interactions with parents typically are concerned with change (e.g., introducing a concept or a skill) or with monitoring parents' behaviors (e.g., determining whether a knowledge or a skill level is acceptable). Program workers are not mere deliverers of a curriculum or treatment plan; indeed, program content is shaped significantly by the way in which it is handled by staff (e.g., one staff member may highlight a point that another staff member ignores, even though both were "trained" according to the same curriculum).

The parent education literature has given minimal attention to the role of staff in working with parents. It appears that interest in curriculum development has overshadowed concern for the way in which a curriculum is implemented. However, recent work raises questions about the importance of particular curriculum approaches in influencing parent and child outcomes in parent education programs. A study of the effects of three different curricula (language, cognitive, and social) in a home-based parent education program for mothers of toddlers found no differences in children's IQ test competence in relation to curriculum type (Kessen, Fein, Clarke-Stewart, & Starr, 1975). Similarly, in an analysis of the effects of 28 parent training programs, Goodson and Hess (1976) found no relationship between the content of the curriculum and the degree of program impact on children's cognitive skills. These findings are similar to the results of a curriculum comparison study in early childhood education by Weikart, Epstein, Schweinhart, and Bond (1978). The lack of difference in children's cognitive growth in relation to different curricula prompted the conclusion that the principal issue in early education is not which curriculum to use but how to manage any curriculum to achieve positive results.

Most parent education workers are keenly aware of the importance of their relations with parents. Staff members expend a good deal of energy in the development and maintenance of credibility and acceptance vis-a-vis parents. The "presentation of self" generally is not treated lightly; such details as dress, disclosure of personal and/or professional background, and style of engaging parents are crucial ingredients in exchanges with parents. As one parent program worker put it recently, "What parent would believe me if I weren't seen as knowledgeable and approachable?" There is an important assumption in this statement: A parent's perception of the professional as credible and warm is a prerequisite to the parent's acceptance and implementation of the program's messages. A more fundamental assumption of this staff member's statement, however, is that the professional has something to say which the parent should believe. This assumption appears to be dominant in the vast majority of parent education programs today. Professional roles and behaviors are based on a view of the professional as a *giver* and the parent as a *receiver* of expert knowledge. It is assumed that the professional knows something that the parent does not know and, moreover, that it is in the best interests of the parent to find out what the professional knows.

The professional-as-expert orientation increasingly is under attack in the parent education field as questions are raised about the value of professional involvement in such intimate family matters as childrearing (Lasch,

1977). Dokecki, Roberts, and Moroney (1979) have suggested that the view of professionals as knowledge-givers and parents as knowledge-receivers is an inappropriate conceptualization of parent education: "Parent educators typically assume that parents are less than competent adults, with limited experiential knowledge of children and little basic childrearing information" (p. 11). This approach, they argue, is the major problem with parent education today and accounts for the low levels of participation and relatively low effectiveness of many formal parent education programs.

To what extent is there an expert knowledge base that professionals can impart to parents and which parents would find to be useful? The traditional response is that a good deal of child development research and theory is relevant to parents and, if disseminated or "packaged" properly, parents would find it useful. This assumption supports the notion that the ideal parent has been trained and authorized by experts; there is a body of knowledge which must be mastered prior to the granting of "licensure" in parenting. At the other extreme is the idea that child development research data are too inconclusive, too contradictory, and too general to be taken as hard facts. This orientation was aired in a recent *New York Times* (1981) article ("The Childhood 'Industry': Conflicting Advice") in which statements such as the following were attributed to nationally renowned research psychologists: "Parents should trust no one . . . they should always be skeptical when the conclusion comes from the discoverers themselves"; and "Why do we need all this (expert childrearing) advice? Much of it is bubba psychology—from the Russian word for grandmother. What are these people selling that a grandmother couldn't tell you?"

There is a small but growing number of parent programs which seem to reflect this latter perspective. One example is a project initiated in Syracuse, New York, by Urie Bronfenbrenner and Moncrieff Cochran and their colleagues at Cornell University. A central belief of this program is that

> the most valid and useful knowledge about the rearing of children is lodged among the people—across generations, in the networks, in the historical folkways of ethnic and cultural traditions, rather than in the heads of college professors, trained professionals or the books written by the so-called experts. (Cochran & Woolever, 1983, pp. 228-229)

In this program, then, parents are viewed as the experts. The child development knowledge base is generated by parents, not professionals. Home visitors learn about the parent's view of the child and seek out examples of activities that are carried out successfully (in the parent's judgment) with the child. Descriptions of these parent/child activities (e.g., cooking, setting table for a meal) are prepared by the home visitor and then shared with other parents.

A middle position, perhaps, in the question of useful childrearing knowledge is that professional knowledge is different from the knowledge of parents; it is not superior, but complementary. Professionals possess information about children as a group and about children in particular situations (e.g., within a laboratory situation), while parents have much information about their child as an individual and about his or her behaviors in specific settings. Both knowledge bases, if creatively combined, may be useful in enhancing the development of children (Dokecki et al., 1979). Many child development experts are organizing the presentation of research literature in ways that permit a useful application of research knowledge to practical situations (see Zigler & Kagan, 1982).

The interest in a partnership or *collaborative* relationship between parents and professionals stems partly from dissatisfaction with the professional-as-expert paradigm (Kessen et al., 1975; Weikart et al., 1978). There appears to be a variety of ways in which this concept may be implemented. One variant of this arrangement is to combine the professional's *general* information about children and the parent's *particular* information about the child. For instance, a collaborative approach to the problem of how a parent might handle a child's separation anxiety may be realized through a pooling of the professional's knowledge of attachment behavior in general and a parent's information about a particular child's responses to separation from a parent. Presumably this approach requires a significant amount of mutual respect and basic understanding about how the partners are to determine what information is useful and legitimate. The parent-as-expert approach in the Cornell project also is suggestive of a collaborative relationship, although here the collaboration is not toward pooling separate sources of knowledge (the parent's and professional's) but toward the development of the parent-determined base of knowledge about childrearing—the professional collaborates with the parent as a facilitator. Interestingly, the program worker does not appear to lose expert status in this arrangement. The expertise is in facilitation, not child development, however. More attention will be given to the notion of collaboration in the next section of this chapter.

The question of whether professionals possess useful knowledge for working with parents is delicate because it tampers with the professional status of those who work with young children and parents. One of the attributes of a profession is to claim control of a body of knowledge that serves as the technology of the occupational group (Hughes, 1971). The more sophisticated and complex the knowledge base, the higher the professional status of the occupation. A fundamental problem of the child care field—and presumably parent education as well—is the perceived lack of a distinctive body of knowledge that provides a foundation for the field (Joffe, 1977; Powell, 1982b). To "take away" or diminish in some way the child development knowledge base of parent education, then, has implications for professional status as well as professional roles unless a new form of expertise (e.g., facilitating group discussion among parents) is substituted.

Without claim to some type of specialty, what distinguishes the program worker from the parent?

Clearly, parents differ significantly in what they find to be "useful" information from a parent education program. There are different needs for parent education; quite simply, some parents have an easier time with childrearing than others. Should not professional roles be determined partly by the type of assistance a parent seems to require? Dokecki et al. (1979) have conceptualized a continuum of parent education needs and corresponding professional responses. The continuum may be expressed in terms of four levels which are not static or mutually exclusive. Level 1 includes parents "who provide well for their children on a day-to-day basis and... [who] evidence no obvious parent education needs" (p. 16). The appropriate professional response is a "prospective mode" wherein the program worker "looks forward" to future developmental needs of the child and provides anticipatory guidance. This is the least intrusive professional role in the continuum of responses. Level II consists of parents who "manage well most of the time, but who are somewhat uneasy about specific childrearing skills" and who "unknowingly engage in certain childrearing practices that are likely to lead to difficulties in the future" (p. 16). It is suggested that the professional response be a "resource mode" wherein the professional is available to parents who inquire about specific childrearing matters.

Level III of the Dokecki et al. (1979) continuum includes those whose parent education needs are "obvious" because their children have difficulty in relating to others, including their parents. However, this group of parents may be "doing many things well" and is "a long way from abdicating the parent role" (p. 17). The professional response is a "collaborative mode"; the parent and professional work together to identify possible solutions to problems causing difficulty for the child. Level IV involves parents whose "social, emotional, and material resources are not sufficient to provide for the growth and developmental needs of their child" (p. 17). Here the professional may need to act in a "protective mode" to protect the child and/or parent.

This typology of parent needs and professional responses raises the question of who determines the parent's need level. Who decides, for instance, that a parent is relating to a child in ways which may lead to difficulties? The assessment of parent education needs is a sensitive matter which entails careful consideration of value differences in childrearing. It is to this issue that we now turn.

PROGRAM STANDARDS OF "GOOD PARENTING"

All well-functioning parent education programs include a general understanding or concept of what constitutes "good parenting." That is, there is at least a minimum level of agreement about appropriate and inappropriate parental goals, attitudes, and behaviors. It appears that in most cases this concept is of an implicit nature and that its development is influenced primarily by program staff. As Clarke-Stewart (1978) has noted, the assumption of most programs is "that the mother's goals for herself and her child are the same as the program designer's—or would be if the mother knew better" (p. 90). This assumption has been questioned vigorously, especially from the standpoint of professionals imposing their values on parents. There is debate as to whether value conflicts actually exist and, if so, what strategies might be effective in remedying the problem.

Concern about the extent to which parent education programs respect existing parental practices stems from the growing recognition and acceptance of cultural pluralism and sociocultural diversity in parents' behavior. Laosa (1983) has described the concern in this manner:

> To some, the current parent education movement seems yet another attempt to melt away sociocultural diversity by imposing one group's standard of parenting over others. The "melting pot" view of American society called for the amalgamation of all subcultures into a new and superior culture. It now seems clear that an amalgamation model, when directed by a dominant class, leads to the melting away of the other subcultures and to the preponderance of one group over the others (p. 337).

This issue may be particularly critical in programs where middle-class professionals deal with low-income parents. The matter of sex role socialization is an example of potential conflict. Middle-class professionals typically support parental behavior which reduces conventional sex role typing; it is appropriate, for example, for boys to play with dolls. Many working-class and low-income parents (especially fathers) do not object to conventional sex roles and probably would have a strong negative reaction to their young sons playing with dolls. Childrearing values, not scientific data, are in conflict (Powell, 1982a). Criticisms also have been made of the practice of having parents function as classroom aides to teachers, where the expectation is that parents will incorporate some or most of the curriculum into the home. The apparent assumption is that the teacher's behavior is superior to the parent's. But should the school culture dominate the home (see Powell, 1982a)? Will the status of the parent be diminished from the child's perspective if the parent functions in the shadow of the teacher's authority (see Fein, 1980)?

There are no systematic data with regard to the prevalence of value conflicts between parents and staff in parent education programs. In fact, several studies indicate that conflicts are minimal or nonexistent. Levenstein (1971) found that the low-income mothers in her home-based parent education program had aspirations for their children which paralleled those of middle-class mothers. Similarly, Elardo and Caldwell (1973) found that parents and teachers involved in an inner-city intervention program in Little Rock, Arkansas shared similar objectives and goals for children (e.g., to know concepts such as smooth, round, scratchy; to follow teachers' requests; to ask "Why" questions). While there were several areas of disagreement (e.g., exhibiting aggression in schools), the researchers concluded that far more consonance than dissonance exists in childrearing values among parents and teachers. Given the potential (if not the actual) problem of parent/staff value conflicts, an important question is how to establish standards of parental behavior in parent education programs. How might a concept of "good parenting" be established which represents the values of parents and staff?

The idea of a "shared partnership" or a collaborative relationship between parents and staff often is suggested as a method for dealing with real or potential value conflicts. This approach was discussed earlier in this chapter in terms of respecting and utilizing parents' information about their children. Collaboration is a promising concept which appears to be favored among a growing number of parent education programs. Unfortunately, little is known about the ways in which the idea is operationalized. Exactly how do parents and professionals identify and resolve differences of opinion? What types of negotiation processes occur? Is there in fact a genuine collaboration, or do some programs merely use the label because it is in vogue?

One way to structure parental input into the development of program activities and policies is to place parents in decision-making roles. In the early childhood field there have been attempts to guarantee respect for the rights of parents by giving power to parents for such matters as personnel selection (see Fein, 1980, for a critique). The original Head Start mandate, for example, called for the "maximum feasible participation" of parents (Valentine & Stark, 1979). It appears that this strategy has not been used extensively in parent education programs, probably because of the obvious threat to professional autonomy and the inherent conflict in having the recipient or client of a service (parents) also serve to make decisions about the scope, content, and delivery of the service.

Parent support programs offer an alternative way to deal with parent/staff value differences. The expectation here is that staff would help parents achieve goals which parents themselves would define. External values and assumptions would not be imposed on parents in the form of a preconceived intervention. More research is needed on the inner workings of such programs. It is questionable whether professionals can and should go about their work within a value-free (versus value-specific) framework. Is it possible or desirable for a program worker to support parental goals that conflict markedly with those of the worker?

Again we see a violation of traditional conceptions of professionalism in the roles of professionals in collaborative relationships with parents and in support programs. A characteristic of a well-established profession is that the professional, not the client, defines client needs and prescribes a remedy (Powell, 1982b). It is unusual for professionals to assume roles where the client has considerable influence on the formulation of needs and goals. This issue is heightened in the early childhood field because significant parental involvement may be viewed as a threat of lay control over an occupational group that has a fledgling professional identity (Joffe, 1977).

Another strategy to deal with the problem of conflicting values and goals in a parent education program is to admit only parents who are sympathetic to the program orientation. A self-selection process among parents might accomplish the same goal if program values are communicated clearly during the recruitment of participants. Presumably this is what happens with many parent discussion groups where there is a particular theoretical framework (e.g., commitment to behavioristic principles versus a psychoanalytic orientation). Self-selection serves to reduce struggles about appropriate approaches to childrearing and probably provides an important common bond or identity among participants. This strategy is unlikely to be effective, at least politically, for community-based programs which attempt to serve populations defined by geographic boundaries rather than by childrearing value orientations.

The use of community paraprofessionals sometimes is viewed as a way to make programs sensitive to the childrearing values of parents, especially where low-income populations are served. Many programs use paraprofessionals as primary staff persons (e.g., home visitors, discussion group leaders). Paraprofessionals are expected to bring unique skills, perspectives, and affiliations which strengthen a parent's relations with his or her community and program participants. A major problem with this strategy is to maintain the integrity of the paraprofessional role. There is a tendency among some professional staff to diminish the significance of this unique role (e.g., to disregard paraprofessionals' ideas for program content), thereby threatening paraprofessionals' liaison role with the community and program participants (Gottlieb, 1981). There is a significant role difference between a paraprofessional who functions as a catalyst for program responsiveness to parents and a paraprofessional who serves as a messenger in a one-way communication channel from professional to parent (Powell, in press).

While the focus of this section has been on parent/staff relationships in the development of program standards of appropriate parental behavior, it is important to comment briefly on the assumption underlying the content of increasing numbers of parent programs. The content in question pertains to the "parents-as-teachers" approach to parent education. Many programs today emphasize parents' contributions to a child's academic skills and engage parents in activities and roles which parallel the typical functions of a teacher. Clearly there is potential benefit in enhancing the teaching behaviors and orientations of parents. But traditional teaching behaviors differ qualitatively from parenting behaviors. Recent research indicates there are differences in the child care patterns of parents and preschool teachers (Hess, Price, Dickson, & Conroy, 1981), and Katz (1980) has set forth major theoretical distinctions between parenting and teaching in such areas as attachment level, intensity of affect, degree of spontaneity, and scope of responsibility. The question is whether distinctions between parenting and teaching are recognized in "parents-as-teachers" educational programs. Are behaviors and attitudes traditionally associated with parenting (e.g., unconditional love) supported alongside an emphasis on teaching behaviors, or is the main message that appropriate parental behaviors approximate those of a teacher? Katz cites the case of a mother whose participation in a teaching-oriented parent education program led to confusion about her role and to a deterioration of the mother/son relationship due to her anxiety in carrying out program expectations. The parent's tension was accompanied by the realization that "the boy had no mother" in terms of her usual soft, nondemanding approach. A difficult task for parent programs, then, is to introduce concepts and processes without undermining valuable, existing dimensions of the parent/child relationship.

CONCEPTIONS OF HOW PARENTS CHANGE

A critical and yet usually ignored attribute of parent programs in terms of overall effectiveness deals with conceptions of how parents change. What assumptions underlie particular program strategies regarding efforts to influence parents' behaviors and beliefs? What are the images of how parents respond to information, program activities, and experiences?

A dominant assumption in most parent education programs is that parents respond to expert opinion and information. It is assumed that parents will change in the intended direction upon receipt of information or advice from a program worker or fellow program participant. While this assumption seems quite plausible, there is not a convincing set of research data to support the idea. In a critical review of parent training programs, Clarke-Stewart (1978) concluded that parents' childrearing behaviors and attitudes are connected to sociocultural traditions and socioeconomic circumstances, and that there is no evidence that childrearing practices are determined by expert opinion or literature on child care and development. In view of the paucity of carefully designed studies on this topic, it seems premature to conclude that expert opinion cannot affect parental practices. Longitudinal research with different population groups is needed to determine the relative impact of different influences on parent's childrearing behaviors and knowledge. Especially needed is an understanding of the conditions under which parents carry out the suggestions of experts (e.g., when expert advice is consistent with existing ideas?).

Unfortunately, little is known about the ways in which parents respond to program information or experiences. It appears that the socioecological contexts in which parents function play an important role in mediating program influence. For instance, a parent's personal social network ties (relations with relatives, friends, neighbors) have been found to be related to use of formal agencies and programs (for a review, see Unger & Powell, 1980). For example, parents have been found to use informal social network ties extensively in searching for a child care provider (Powell & Eisenstadt, 1982). It appears that, when in need of professionally delivered services, individuals consult with familiar and trusted persons about the availability and quality of formal services.

Regarding parent education programs, Kessen et al. (1975) found that working-class parents who belonged to extensive family networks were more responsive to a home-based parent education curriculum than parents with restricted family networks. The study suggests that extensive family ties may provide parents with a secure, stable framework which facilitates acceptance and utilization of new information from change agents outside the family milieu (e.g., home visitors). It also supports findings of several other studies (see Unger & Powell, 1980) which suggest that restricted (or close-knit) social network ties operate as a social control mechanism to keep out external information which is discrepant with the beliefs of the family network.

One of the reasons there is a dearth of information about the processes of change in parent programs is that evaluators largely have ignored variations in parents' experiences in a program. The tendency has been to view the program as a unidimensional construct rather than as a set of variables; typically, the treatment is viewed as present or absent (Powell, 1983b). Recent evidence suggests considerable variation in parents' experiences in a parent program, however. A preliminary analysis of patterns of participation in a neighborhood-based parent support program suggests differences in terms of such factors as interpersonal ties with other participants, use of staff services, and involvement in special program activities. Moreover, the analysis showed that diverse participation patterns were related to parents' life conditions (i.e., economic hardship, type of social network ties). For instance, it was found that parents who participated in the program's special events (e.g., field trips) also were involved in other community organizations. It appears that a certain interest or skill level in understanding social systems facilitated participation in the program's "extracurricular" activities. These data suggest that parents respond in different ways to the same program setting, and in a manner consistent with past and present life circumstances (Powell, 1983a).

Most parents do not enter parent education programs as blank slates. The content domain is familiar territory. Parents approach a program with many experiences and ideas about the processes of parenting; indeed, one of the influences on parental behavior is one's own childhood experiences. Perhaps a major step toward recognition of this dynamic is to conceptualize parent education as a form of adult education (Dokecki et al., 1979). Adult learners need to accommodate new information and experiences with previous knowledge; discrepant information may be distorted to fit existing beliefs, for instance. In the education of adults, it is important for the learner to identify objectives and methods of learning. Time should be devoted to an exploration of a learner's previous experiences and knowledge regarding the topic (Knox, 1977). The lack of attention to the principles of adult education may account for the ineffectiveness of some parent education programs.

Recent research evidence points to the importance of parents' belief systems and conceptualizations of the child, suggesting that the effectiveness of parent education programs depends partly on methods (e.g., group discussion) which recognize these existing constructs. McGillicuddy-DeLisi, Sigel, & Johnson (1979) have carried out an investigation of parents' belief systems which is based partly on George Kelly's (1955) personal construct theory. Kelly has proposed that each individual formulates his or her own personal constructs based on experiences, and that the world is viewed through these constructs. New experiences (e.g., a parent program) may confirm or disconfirm previously evolved constructions. McGillicuddy-De-Lisi, et al. found that the constructs referred to by parents fall into patterns which resemble established theoretical perspectives of child development. While parents did not use psychological terms to represent their views, it was possible to classify parents according to maturational, Skinnerian, information-processing, and psychoanalytic models of human development. Also, Sutherland (1983) found participants in parent education programs to have well-developed "folk models" of childrearing which parallel traditional theories of child development.

It appears essential, then, for the design and delivery of parent education programs to be based on a recognition of the complexities of adult change processes. The socioecological conditions of parents' lives as well as parents' constructions of how children develop seem to be major factors which bear directly on the influence of program workers. Clearly, expert opinion is only one of many interrelated forces in a parent's world. Future research needs to examine carefully the interplay among the diverse determinants of parental attitudes and practices.

A CONCLUDING COMMENT

The questions about program effectiveness posed at the beginning of this chapter—"What is the most successful approach?" and "What really works?"—imply a limited view of how to enhance parents' roles and practices. Inherent in these questions is the idea that some approaches are better than others. Although many diverse approaches and strategies have been found to be effective, the search for the "very best" program model is likely to be futile. A more exciting, potentially worthwhile venture is to uncover the *conditions* under which programs are effective. This should be a high priority for the parent education field. This chapter has highlighted three areas of program functioning which appear to have a major influence on program effectiveness: professional roles, program incorporation of parental values, and conceptions of adult change processes. There are other salient program dimensions, as well as different ways to conceptualize the issues. It is hoped that this chapter's examination of selected program parts has pointed to a clear message about programs as a whole: the issue of program effectiveness entails significantly more than consideration of the curriculum.

Effective parent education is not a simple process. Program designers and operators need to make many critical decisions about the focus and methods of change. The premise of this chapter is that the improvement of program effectiveness begins with a careful scrutiny of the assumptions which form the basis of program structure and content. An exploration of basic program assumptions is likely to provide a framework for defining expectations of program activities, assessing the usefulness of particular practices, and considering alternative approaches. Not all beneficial aspects of a program begin with the question, "How?" There also is value in asking, "Why?"

REFERENCES

Bell, T. The child's right to have a trained parent. *Elementary School Guidance and Counseling,* 1975, *9,* 271.

Bronfenbrenner, U. *Is early intervention effective? A report on longitudinal evaluations of preschool programs* (Vol. 2). Washington, DC: Office of Child Development, Department of Health, Education and Welfare, 1974.

Bronfenbrenner, U. Who needs parent education? *Teachers College Record,* 1978, *79,* 767–787.

The childhood "industry": Conflicting advice. *The New York Times,* March 16, 1981.

Clarke-Stewart, A. Evaluating parental effects on child development. In A. Shulman (Ed.), *Review of research in education.* Itasca, IL: F. E. Peacock Publishers, 1978.

Cochran, M., & Woolever, F. Beyond the deficit model: The empowerment of parents through information and informal support. In I. Sigel & L. Laosa (Eds.), *Changing families.* New York: Plenum Publishing Corporation, 1983.

Cremin, L. Family-community linkages in American education: Some comments on the recent historiography. *Teachers College Record,* 1978, *79,* 683–704.

*Dokecki, P., Roberts, F., & Moroney, R. Families and professional psychology: Policy implications for training and service. Paper presented at the annual meeting of the American Psychological Association, New York City, September, 1979. (ERIC Document Reproduction Service No. ED 182 626)

Elardo, R., & Caldwell, B. Value imposition in early education: Fact or fancy? *Child Care Quarterly,* 1973, *2*(1), 6–13.

Fein, G. The informed parent. In S. Kilmer (Ed.), *Advances in early education and day care* (Vol. 1). Greenwich, CT: JAI Press, 1980.

*Goodson, B., & Hess, R. The effects of parent training programs on child performance and parent behavior. Unpublished manuscript, School of Education, Stanford University, Stanford, CA, 1976. (ERIC Document Reproduction Service No. 136 912)

Gottlieb, B. Social networks and social support. In B. Gottlieb (Ed.), *Social networks and social support.* Berkeley, CA: Sage Publications, 1981.

Hess, R., Price, G., Dickson, W., & Conroy, M. Different roles for mothers and teachers: Contrasting styles of child care. In S. Kilmer (Ed.), *Advances in early education and day care* (Vol. 2). Greenwich, CT: JAI Press, 1981.

Hughes, E. *The sociological eye: Selected papers.* Chicago, Aldine Publishing Co., 1971.

Joffe, C. *Friendly intruders: Child care professionals and family life.* Berkeley, CA: University of California Press, 1977.

*Katz, L. Contemporary perspectives on the roles of mothers and teachers. In L. Katz (Ed.), *Current topics in early childhood education,* (Vol. 3). Norwood, NJ: Ablex Publishing Corporation (ERIC Document Reproduction Service No. ED 196 511)

Kelly, G. *The psychology of personal constructs,* (Vol. 1). New York: W. W. Norton & Company, 1955.

Kessen, W. The American child and other cultural inventions. *American Psychologist,* 1979, *34*(10), 815–820.

*Kessen, W., Fein, G., Clarke-Stewart, A., & Starr, S. Variations in home-based infant education: Language, play and social development. Final report to the Office of Child Development, Department of Health, Education and Welfare. New Haven, CT: Yale University, August, 1975. (ERIC Document Reproduction Service No. ED 118 233)

Knox, A. *Adult development and learning.* San Francisco: Jossey-Bass, 1977.

Laosa, L. Parent education, cultural pluralism and public policy: The uncertain connection. In R. Haskins (Ed.), *Parent education and public policy.* Norwood, NJ: Ablex Publishing Corporation, 1983.

Lasch, C. *Haven in a heartless world: The family besieged.* New York: Basic Books, 1977.

Levenstein, P. Learning through (and from) mothers. *Childhood Education,* 1971, *48*(3), 130–134.

Lightfoot, S. *Worlds apart: Relationships between families and schools.* New York: Basic Books, 1978.

McGillicuddy-DeLisi, A., Sigel, I., & Johnson, J. The family as a system of mutual influences: Parental beliefs, distancing behaviors, and children's representational thinking. In M. Lewis & L. Rosenblum (Eds.), *The child and its family.* New York: Plenum Publishing Corporation, 1979.

*O'Keefe, R. A. What Head Start means to families. In L. Katz (Ed.), *Current topics in early childhood education* (Vol. 2). Norwood, NJ: Ablex Publishing Corporation, 1979. (ERIC Document Reproduction Service No. ED 180 596)

Powell, D. R. Family-environment relations and early child rearing: The role of social networks and neighborhoods. *Journal of Research and Development in Education,* 1979, *13*(1), 1–11.

Powell, D. R. From child to parent: Changing conceptions of early childhood intervention. *Annals of the American Academy of Political and Social Science,* 1982a, *416,* 135–144.

Powell, D. R. The role of research in the development of the child care profession. *Child Care Quarterly,* 1982b, *11,* 4–11.

Powell, D. R. Individual differences in participation in a parent-child support program. In I. Sigel & L. Laosa, *Changing families.* New York: Plenum Publishing Corporation, 1983a.

Powell, D. R. A neighborhood approach to parent support groups. *Journal of Community Psychology,* in press.

Powell, D. R. Evaluating parent education programs: Problems and prospects. *Studies in Educational Evaluation,* 1983b, *8,* 253–259.

Powell, D. R. & Eisenstadt, J. W. Parents' searches for child care and the design of information services. *Children and Youth Services Review,* 1982, *4,* 223–253.

Rheingold, H. To rear a child. *American Psychologist,* 1973, *28,* 42–46.

Schaefer, E. Parents as educators: Evidence from cross-sectional, longitudinal and intervention research. *Young Children,* 1972, *27*(4), 228–239.

Schlossman, S. Before Home Start: Notes toward a history of parent education in America, 1897–1929. *Harvard Educational Review,* 1976, *46*(3), 436–467.

Schlossman, S. The parent education game: The politics of child psychology in the 1970s. *Teachers College Record,* 1978, *79,* 788–808.

Sutherland, K. Parents' beliefs about child socialization: A study of parenting models. In I. Sigel & L. Laosa, *Changing families.* New York: Plenum Publishing Corporation, 1983.

Unger, D., & Powell, D. R. Supporting families under stress: The role of social networks. *Family Relations,* 1980, *29,* 566–574.

*United States Department of Health and Human Services. Head Start in the 1980s: Review and recommendations. Washington, DC: Office of Human Development Services, United States Department of Health and Human Services, September, 1980. (ERIC Document Reproduction Service No. 197 848)

Valentine, J., & Stark, E. The social context of parent involvement in Head Start. In E. Zigler & J. Valentine (Eds.), *Project Head Start: A legacy of the war on poverty.* New York: The Free Press, 1979.

Wandersman, L., Wandersman, A., & Kahn, S. Social support in the transition to parenthood. *Journal of Community Psychology,* 1980, *8*(4), 332–342.

Weikart, D., Epstein, A., Schweinhart, L., & Bond, J. *The Ypsilanti preschool curriculum demonstration project: Preschool years and longitudinal results.* Ypsilanti, MI: Monographs of the High/Scope Educational Research Foundation, 1978, No. 4.

White, B. L. Guidelines for parent education, 1977. Paper presented at a Working Conference on Parent Education, Charles Stewart Mott Foundation, September 29–30, 1977.

Yando, R., Seitz, V., & Zigler, E. *Intellectual and personality characteristics of children: Social class and ethnic group differences.* Hillsdale, NJ: Lawrence Erlbaum Associates, 1979.

Zigler, E., & Kagan, S. Child development knowledge and educational practice: Using what we know. In *Eighty-first Yearbook of the National Society for the Study of Education.* Chicago, IL: National Society for the Study of Education, 1982.

Zigler, E., & Berman, W. Discerning the future of early childhood intervention. *American Psychologist,* 1983, *38,* 894–906.

6

Latchkey Children

Thomas J. Long

The Catholic University of America

Lynnette Long

Loyola College of Maryland

More than half the nation's children have mothers who work away from home, the Bureau of Labor Statistics of the United States Department of Labor reported today. About 31.8 million children below age 18— 54% of the nation's total—had mothers in the labor force in March 1981. This number has risen steadily throughout the past decade, even though the size of the children's population has declined substantially.

(United States Department of Labor *News,* USDL 81–522,
November 15, 1981)

Two significant changes in social structure during the 1970s dramatically changed family patterns in the United States. These were a large increase in the proportion of mothers who work and increased numbers of children living in single-parent households. These two changes contributed to two related phenomena: the number of children living in poverty and the rapid rise of children left unattended, or "latchkey children."

WHAT IS MEANT BY "LATCHKEY CHILDREN"?

In the 18th century, the term "latchkey" denoted the implement used for gaining access to one's house—for lifting the door latch. During the late 19th and early 20th centuries, the term was sometimes applied to young single ladies who went about unchaperoned, thus requiring a key to gain access to their homes. The first clear print reference to American latchkey children, indicating young children left to shift for themselves while their parents worked, with the associated symbol of the housekey tied around the child's neck, appears to be in Zucker (1944). While the term was not new, Zucker referred to "latchkey" or "doorkey" children, or "8-hour orphans," as newly coined phrases in his article of that date.

In the context of this chapter, "latchkey children" generally refers to children who are left to take care of themselves—or for whom care arrangements are so loosely made as to be virtually ineffective. They may use group recreational programs, play in the street, stay home alone, or join a gang. Specifically, the term refers to children who are regularly left unattended or who are only attended by another underage child most days, when ill, during school holidays, snow days, teacher workshop days, and vacation periods, or whenever these children's schedules do not jibe with the usual schedules of their primary adult caregivers. Latchkey does not include children infrequently left alone for short periods of time while their adult caregiver runs an errand, picks up a sibling from an athletic event, visits a neighbor, or even goes out for an evening without otherwise providing adequate supervision.

The above definition of latchkey children can apply to 3- and 4-year-olds whose parents routinely and intentionally leave them unattended for some period of time most days. This situation occurs, though perhaps not frequently. (The United States Department of Labor reported in 1977, for example, that 20,000 3- to 6-years-olds were in self care.) The term can also apply to those 15- or 16-year-olds who are routinely left unattended in their own homes before or after school while their parents work or while their parents spend extended periods of time away from home (several weeks, for example). Situations like these occur with some regularity, and many adolescents rountinely find themselves unsupervised by their parents at all hours of the day and night.

The latchkey population of greatest current concern, however, is the 5- to 13-year-old group. In 1975, the federal government identified 1,575,000 such children of employed mothers as being in self-care (United States Department of Labor, 1977). Five- to 13-year-olds are those most frequently left to take care of themselves during periods in which their school schedules fail to overlap the work and work-related travel schedules of their parents.

Some readers might disagree with a latchkey definition that includes children in self-care who are routinely supervised by teenagers, believing 15-or 16-year-olds to be adequate caregivers not only for themselves, but also for younger children left in their charge. Nonetheless, growing concern exists about the risk to young children as the result of physical and sexual abuse perpetrated by underage but still older caretakers (Finkelhor, 1979; Rogers, 1982). This would lead one to wonder whether no care might be preferable to abusive care. However, we do not want to argue here whether adolescents can adequately respond to the demands of serving as substitute parents. Some can and some can't. Certainly a 15-year-old charged with the care of an 8-year-old can often provide a better care environment than no care at all. It is important to note, though, that most children left to care for each other are relatively close in age. It is more common to find a 12-year-old charged with the care of an 8-year-old than it is to find an older adolescent sibling providing the caregiving function for a younger child.

Nonrelated teenagers are often employed as babysitters. And, though data in this area is sparse, growing evidence indicates that children between the ages of 12 and 14 are given much more responsibility for younger children than in the past. A recent study (Medrich, 1982) of time use among a diverse sample of Oakland, California, youth showed that 66% of 11- to 14-year-olds care for younger siblings at some point in the week. Ten percent of these have daily childcare responsibilities, and 23% have responsibilities two to five days a week. Another study indicates that older elementary school-age children take considerable responsibility for younger children when a parent is not at home (Long & Long, 1982).

The thrust of this review, then, is to summarize what little is known about school-age latchkey children, and, it is hoped, to prompt more research into the area and to stimulate whatever solutions identified problems might demand.

How Many Latchkey Children Are There?

The exact number of latchkey children is uncertain, since the numbers reported are generally accepted as partial and the most recently available general study is itself dated (United States Department of Commerce, 1976). The fact that a current comprehensive and reliable tally of children enrolled in the various forms of child care is as yet unavailable is perhaps indicative of the low level of importance the nation places on the care of its children. But there are some encouraging signs.

The United States Department of Health and Human Services issued its seven-volume National Day Care Home Study in 1981 (Divine–Hawkins, Executive Summary). And the results of a study on school-age day care were released by the same agency in 1983 (Divine–Hawkins, Contract No. 105-81-C-011). Data for this study was collected in Minnesota and Virginia during the 1981–1982 school year through telephone interviews with a random sample of 1,000 households with children ages 5 through 14, in-person discussions with a subsample of 60 parents who responded to the telephone interview and their school-age children, providers of day care services and state and local officials involved in day care. These two study states were selected because of their prevalence of programs for school-age children, the rural–suburban–urban contrasts that existed, their female labor force participation rates, and the adequate numbers of families with school-age children in both states. Results of this study indicate that self-care or care by a sibling who was age 14 or under was the second most frequently used arrangement for school-age children, exceeded only by parental care. Twenty-seven percent of the Minnesota and 25% of the Virginia families with full-time working parents used this arrangement. School-based programs accounted for no more than five percent of the care arrangements used regularly in either state.

Simons and Bohen (1982) estimate that 5.2 million American children (age 13 and under) of parents employed full-time are without adult care or supervision for significant parts of each day. In 1976, the United States Department of Commerce Bureau of the Census reported that 18% of children ages 7 to 13 cared for themselves while their mothers worked full-time. It is hard to imagine that this percentage has declined since 1975. According to Lopata (1978), of full-time employed mothers with children ranging from ages 3 to 13, 12.9% report that their children care for themselves on a regular basis. In a study by McMurray and Kazanjian (1982) 19% of the families involved admitted that they had to leave their children unsupervised during all or part of the day, with over one-fifth of the parents beginning such practices when the children were 7 years old or younger. Admittedly, this population is unusual in that it was working poor, most of whom had lost eligibility for publically supported child care subsidies.

In a study carried out by Long and Long (1982) it was found that one of every three elementary school children in the Washington, D. C., school surveyed regularly engaged in some form of self-care. It is also true that among the nation's ten largest metropolitan areas, Washington's labor force has the highest proportion of working women (R. Smith, 1979). Moreover, interviews with children in selected schools in Washington's wealthiest suburbs indicated that between 11 and 12% of these children fit the definition of latchkey (Long & Long, 1983).

It is likely that the number of American children routinely left in self-care varies depending on the locale and the composition of the community. The high figure of one-third for some areas has been corroborated by a study by Hughes (1982). The Hughes study, conducted for the Association for Supportive Child Care, sampled major employers in Maricopa County, Arizona, to generate a list of employees with children under 12 years of age in which both parents or the single head of household was employed outside the home. Of the 144 employee families that participated, 62% were married couples and 38% were single heads of households. There were 207 children under 12 years of age in these families; 114 children were 5 years of age or under, while 93 were age 6 through 11. In 31% of the families with children ages 6 through 11, children cared for themselves on most weekdays.

In a survey of child care practices conducted by *Family Circle* magazine, 30% of mothers reported that their school-age children under 13 were left at home alone after school (as reported in Friedman, 1979). In a survey conducted by Louis Harris (1981) for General Mills, Inc., only 9% of the families surveyed making use of child-care arrangements besides parental care reported that their children cared for themselves. Unfortunately, this question was posed in such a way that children who took care of each other were generally not counted in the self-care category. Nicholas Zill (1983) reports from a study conducted in 1976 that, among his sample of 2,301 children age 4 through 11, fewer than 5% were latchkey.

Where the percentage of families with a working single parent is high, even the one-third figure might be too low. Our preference is to stay with the figure of approximately 6 million latchkey children 13 years of age or under, since this figure seems conservative. Regardless of discrepancies among findings, the bottom line is that, whatever the actual figure, a large number of children in America spend some portion of most days caring for themselves, and this number is growing.

Is Self-Care Really a Problem?

More than a year ago, Garbarino (1981) asked whether the latchkey child was a problem. He conceded that some latchkey children "feel rejected," were "prone to become involved in delinquent behavior," and were more likely to become "victims of accidents" and "sexual victimization by siblings and non-parental adults." But he also suggested that we don't know how many children suffer such adverse consequences and indeed asserted that latchkey children may find that their situations promote development because of the greater demands placed on them to act independently and responsibly.

Elkind (1981), however, contends that the pressure on children to grow up quickly produces unnecessary stress. Children respond to stress in a variety of ways, including developing anxiety that is not attached to a specific fear. This type of fear is often experienced as a result of separations, including the continuing though temporary separation occasioned by parents' jobs. Under stress, children often cope by overstructuring their environments. As reported by Elkind, this characteristic has been a trademark of low-income children, who often appear to attain independence early in response to living in single-parent families or in households in which all adults work outside the home, as well as in reaction to poverty. These situations demand growing up rapidly.

At present the pressure on children to act grown-up prematurely in order to satisfy family or parental needs has gained a strong foothold across a wide spectrum of American society. Single-parent or working-parents homes, once thought to be confined to the lower class, now are common to all levels of society. There is a possibility that premature life structuring among children will lead to lower achievement and increased social and emotional problems, as has apparently been the case among the children of the nation's working poor for decades. But then, not every child responds to situations that are normally stressful by crumbling, or burning out, or producing at less than potential (Pinas, 1979).

The practice of older children caring for younger ones is widespread in non-Western societies, where children typically take on responsibilities that range from complete and independent full-time care of children to child-care tasks under adult supervision (Rogoff, Sellers, Pirotta, Fox, & White, 1975; Weisner & Gallimore, 1977; Whiting & Edwards, 1973). But because mothers have been the primary caregivers in Western industrialized societies, little attention has been given to child care by children themselves. Psychologists are divided about the advisability of giving children cargiving responsibility for themselves or other children.

In the few school programs that have engaged junior high school students as aides in preschools, young adolescents are reported to be "still near enough to childhood to identify spontaneously with children's interests, feelings, and behavior" (Mallum, unpublished). We lack information, however, about how they handle child care in unsupervised situations. Research and theory on early adolescence, and on the transition into puberty, do not provide clear predictions about the ways in which early adolescents will perceive and handle child care. While there is general agreement that major biological, psychological, and social changes take place during the period from 11 to 14 years of age, this period has been viewed by some as highly stressful and disorienting (Erikson, 1968; Freud, 1958; Mead, 1970; Muuss, 1975) and by others as impressively stable and continuous (Bandura, 1964; Douvan & Adelson, 1966; Dusek & Flaherty, 1981; Hill, 1980; Rutter, 1980). Social or cognitive disorientation may take place; their implications for young adolescents' child care abilities have never been addressed.

The continuity and similarity that some writers have pointed out between preschool and early adolescent development (Feeney, 1980) could lead to a strengthened ability to identify with a younger child or to difficulties for the adolescent in separating his or her needs from the child's. Elkind's (1967) conception of adolescent egocentrism suggests that young adolescents' preoccupation with how others see them could create difficulty in understanding the younger child's viewpoint. Cobb's (1975) study confirms this problem.

Are latchkey children at risk? If so, at how much risk? In which areas are they at risk? Are there factors that lead to greater risk? Factors that mitigate risk? What are the long-term effects, whether positive or negative, of the latchkey experience? If self-care appears to produce risks that outweigh the opportunities it provides, what might be done to change this proportion? These and other questions need to be answered. Since the current magnitude of the latchkey phenomenon has been only quietly expressed during the past 30 years, little in the way of data directly applicable to these questions exists. And yet some information at least illustrative of the scope and complexity of the latchkey phenomenon has emerged.

THE CONTEXT OF LATCHKEY RESEARCH

The body of research literature that deals at least contextually with latchkey children has attempted to determine whether children are benefited or injured by living with a mother who works outside the home (Dellas, Gaier, & Emihovich, 1979; Duncan & Morgan, 1975; Etaugh, 1980; Feldman, 1980; Hoffman, 1979; Kammerman & Kahn, 1981; Lueck, Orr, & O'Connell, 1982; Moore, 1978; Nye & Hoffman, 1963; Price, 1979; Rallings & Nye, 1979; R. E. Smith, 1979; Taveggia & Thomas, 1974). The growing consensus of this research is that the adverse effects on children and on parent/child relationships, feared by many as a result of maternal employment, have not occurred.

The most recent *critical review* of the research on the relationship between maternal employment and the academic attitudes and performance of school-aged children appears to support this statement (Hoffman, 1980). Although Hoffman states that, "Most of the research relating maternal employment to academic measures of children are 'mini-studies', conducted by inexperienced researchers on a 'one-shot' basis." And she suggests support for continuing work on parent-child interaction and its effects on cognitive development.

The most recent and most extensive *studies* of the relationshilp of the family to school achievement, however, report that children from one-parent families, or children from two parent families whose mothers work, tend to have lower academic achievement (Ginsburg, Milne, Myers and Ellman, 1983 a & b) the results of these studies are significant because they are recent, are drawn from a large national data base and were produced by researchers with noteable scientific qualifications. Further, the results of these studies assume special importance because today's children are growing up in a substantially different family environment than children even a decade ago.

An article by Mathews dealing with the effect of mothers' out-of-home employment on children was published in 1934, but most published research about this problem did not begin to appear until about 1950. Of the articles published between 1950 and 1970, most used criterion variables dealing with intellectual performance, emotional and/or physical development, indicators of school achievement, measures of social behavior, or measures of children's ideas and/or attitudes (Banducci, 1967; Cartwright & Jeffreys, 1958; George & Thomas, 1967; Glueck & Glueck, 1957; Hand, 1957; Hartley, 1960; Hoffman, 1961; Jones, Lundsteen, & Michael, 1967;

McCord, McCord, & Thurber, 1963; Nelson, 1969; Nye, 1952; Nye, 1959; Nye & Hoffman, 1963; Stoltz, Hitchcock, & Adamson, 1959). Combined results of these studies generally showed no difference between the children of mothers who worked and mothers who did not work, although many scattered differences in results did appear. To date most research dealing with the impact of maternal employment on children has assumed the alternative of continuous child care, seldom considering whether or not the children were fending for themselves while their parents were working out-of-home.

Harris (1981) conducted a survey of American families for General Mills, Inc. The sample of 1,503 adult family members was drawn from the civilian population over age 18 residing in the contiguous United States. All interviews were conducted by telephone, using a procedure known as random-digit-dialing. Almost twice as many respondents thought that the effect of both parents working outside the home was negative as thought the effect was positive. The reason most often cited for this suspected negative effect on families concerned the belief that children needed stronger parental guidance, supervision, and discipline than those questioned thought could be provided when both parents in the household were employed. On the positive side, about nine family members in ten polled by Harris believed that when both parents worked, children had to become more self-reliant and independent. Eight of ten thought this was good.

The clash between the consensus of research writing and common opinion can lead one to wonder whether collective research wisdom is more accurate than collective common opinion, or whether family members are considering reality factors as yet unexamined by researchers. To put the Harris poll in perspective, work was not seen as the sole factor influencing attitudes toward current changes in child care. Certainly the perception of the deterioration in the overall quality of parenting is widespread. A majority of all groups polled by Harris (except for a sample drawn from a selected list of women's leaders and groups published by the White House in 1980 and for participants of the National Organization for Women's Legal Defense Fund Program) believed that even when parents stay at home, they don't give their children the time and attention needed. The majority of Harris's family members felt that when both parents work children were more likely to get into trouble and the parents were more likely to indulge their children to make up for the time spend apart. This same group, however, also felt that work and childrearing were generally compatible despite the time demands of work, if the quality of time spent with children was good. An equally positive opinion was that children benefit when mothers and fathers play an equal role in caring for them—an attitude shared by a growing number of researchers.

CURRENT LATCHKEY RESEARCH

Zucker's (1944) picture of wartime latchkey children, as described earlier in this chapter, somehow seems quite modern. His answer to the question of whether it was harmful for a mother to work was that it depended on if she could make adequate child-care arrangements. Without meticulously detailing the extent of the latchkey problem in 1944, Zucker clearly believed that war-bred latchkey children would become the problem adolescents of the 1950s and the maladjusted parents of the 1960s. Even his suggestions for ameliorating latchkey problems seem applicable today. But to what extent does the research illuminate the effect of the latchkey experience on children?

Cognitive Functioning and Adjustment

Woods (1968, 1972), following the lead of previous research, investigated developmental variables relating to achievement, intelligence, personal and social adjustment, health, family relationships, and school and community behavior in a group of fifth-grade black ghetto children from Philadelphia. Her primary purpose, however, was to determine whether those children who reported they had little or no maternal supervision during the summer and during periods of the school day when not in school differed from children who experienced almost continuous supervision.

Woods' findings were that while the teachers at school could not distinguish between supervised and unsupervised children, there were a number of significant differences between groups of girls with regard to academic achievement and school relations. Unsupervised girls, of which there were significantly more in this study than unsupervised boys, exhibited marked deficits in cognitive functioning and personality adjustment. In contrast, children who reported mature substitute supervision were more self-reliant.

Woods collected her data from children using a series of paper-and-pencil instruments. She also solicited written evaluations from teachers; checked school, local hospital, and police records for all her subjects; and interviewed 38 mothers. In addition to the deficits noted, Woods found positive relationships between mothers' attitudes toward their work and child-care roles, the quality of mother/child relationships and the children's achievement, intelligence, and personality. She surmised that maternal employment might be differentially associated with the development of children depending on the family's social class, but she did not test this hypothesis.

Following suggestions made by Woods, Gold and Andres (1978a) investigated the differing conceptions of sex roles in children of employed and unemployed mothers by social class. The subjects were 223 10-year-old

Canadian children who came from two-parent families with no history of parental death or divorce. All data collected were obtained on paper-and-pencil measures.

The areas of greatest interest to this discussion are the investigation's inquiry into social class differences and the supervisory arrangements parents made for their children. Gold and Andres (1978a) found that significantly more nonemployed mothers indicated that only they supervised their children in the evenings and on weekends, while employed mothers indicated that both parents supervised their children. This finding stands in contrast to results reported by Pedersen (1982) in which American fathers with unemployed wives spent significantly more time with their children upon return home from work than did fathers whose wives were also employed.

Of the 20 unsupervised children with employed mothers in the Gold and Andres (1978a) study (16% of the total number of children with employed mothers), 16 were boys, 11 from middle-class and five from working-class families. When researchers divided the sons of employed mothers into supervised and unsupervised groups for comparison, the unsupervised boys were consistently lower on all adjustment and academic achievement test scores, but none of these differences reached significance.

In a companion study of 14- to 16-year-old Canadian youths, Gold and Andres (1978b) focused on hypotheses similar to those in their study of 10-year-olds. Again of special interest to our discussion, approximately half of the employed and nonemployed mothers indicated that they did not supervise their children's free time. Supervised and unsupervised children were compared on sex-role concept measures, adjustment test scores, academic achievement, and intelligence scores. The unsupervised children had slightly lower adjustment and academic scores, but few of those differences reached significance.

Children's Fears

In a study by Zill (1983), boys and girls ages 7 through 11 were asked if they worried when they had to stay at home without any grownups to watch them. Thirty-two percent of the boys and 41% of the girls said yes. When the children were further asked which of several possibilities made them feel afraid, the most frequent issue identified was that somebody bad might get into their house (62% of the boys and 75% of the girls). The next most frequent issue seen as frightening was when their parents argued (48% of the boys and 56% of the girls). Girls also indicated that they were afraid of thunder and lightening (46%). Otherwise, less than one-third of either the boys or girls said they were frightened by any other item.

A study conducted and subsequently reported by Galambos and Garbarino (1982) at the annual convention of the American Psychological

Association attempted to answer questions relating to whether a lack of supervision affected school adjustment, academic achievement, orientation to the classroom, and fear of going outdoors alone in fifth- and seventh-grade students who were regularly unsupervised before or after school and who had mothers employed outside the home. Children in this group were compared with continuously supervised children of employed mothers and continuously supervised children of nonemployed mothers. All measures were of the paper-and-pencil type, some completed by the children and others completed by teachers who had known the children for at least three months.

No significant main effects or interactions were found for any supervision/maternal employment status group. The results suggest that latchkey children reared in a relatively safe rural environment perform no differently in school than other children, nor are they more fearful of being outside alone. Galambos and Garbarino suggest that community and neighborhood characteristics may influence how well the child is able to adjust to the latchkey situation. One possibility is that in neighborhoods perceived as safe, the latchkey child more likely will be allowed to play outside, a fact that perhaps leads to better adjustment than if the child is required to stay indoors.

Underreporting of Self-Care Arrangements

McMurray and Kazanjian (1982) carried out a study of how poor working families involved in New York City's public day care programs manage their family life and work responsibilities. Results were based on home interviews with 211 individuals. Of the respondents in this study, 70% were single parents, 94% were female, and 95% were from a racial minority. One hundred three of those interviewed were from a group of families whose children had been terminated from public day care services, 59 were from families whose children were still enrolled in such services, and 49 were from families whose children were on a waiting list for these services. Of all respondents, 56% were employed at the time the data was collected, 15% were looking for work, and 95% had worked at some time since the birth of their first child. Overall, this study focused on the most vulnerable segment of the population—urban working poor, single parents, minority individuals, and families headed by women.

For purposes of this review the most striking finding of the study was that only 58% of the families interviewed were using child care on a regular basis, a low percentage, while analysis of the data showed that only about 19% of the parents who were employed admitted that they made no arrangements for the care of children. McMurray and Kazanjian are sensitive to the underreporting of the latchkey phenomenon. By analyzing the number of hours of care reported and comparing that to the number of hours of employment in their sample, they estimate that more than half of the children in their study were regularly or occasionally left without supervision for part of the day while their parents worked.

In a study by Long and Long (1983) in which interviews with approximately 100 parents were conducted, it was evident that parents were reluctant to leave their children alone or to admit to having to resort to this arrangement. Some parents interviewed said that while they routinely left their children unattended, they would never admit this to their own parents and actually tried to keep the reality of their child's self-care as little known as possible.

One reason Long and Long found for underreporting, a reason also cited by McMurray and Kazanjian, is that parents who leave a 7-year-old in the care of a 10-year-old, for example, do not consider this to be leaving either child "alone." McMurray and Kazanjian report that the median age of children surveyed when first left alone was 9.8 years. Long and Long (1982) found that black children, when asked when they first began staying home alone, reported a median age of 8, if left by themselves, and 6, if left with some other underage child, usually a sibling.

It is interesting to note in the McMurray and Kazanjian study that almost one-quarter of the parents reporting that they left their children unattended reported also that they began this practice when their children were age 7 or younger; 10% indicated beginning self-care for children at age 3 or younger. By the time children reached age 12, as McMurray and Kazanjian indicate, 95% were staying by themselves. Further, when asked whether any of their children under 14 had responsibility for looking after younger brothers and sisters, almost 30% of the parents said yes. In the McMurray and Kazanjian study the median age at which children assumed responsibility for caring for a younger sibling was 10.6 years, some caring for siblings as young as 1 year old. These findings parallel the Long and Long (1982) study of minority children in Washington, D.C.

The Choice of Self-Care

In reporting how parents came to the decision to leave children alone, Mc-Murray and Kazanjian (1982) found that many factors played a part, including the parents' assessment of the age and maturity of the child, the parents' need to work, the availability of affordable and reliable child care, the child's preference, and certain other environmental factors.

In the results of the study reported by the U.S. Department of Health and Human Services (Divine-Hawkins, 1983) parents said that their greatest concern when selecting their children's care arrangements was that their children be adequately supervised. Parents in this study were also reported as indicating as important child-related factors: that their children could be with peers; that there were developmentally appropriate activities; that their children had freedom to do as they wanted; and that their children were safe and secure.

Long and Long (1983) found that parents did not carelessly choose self-care for their children simply because they wanted to work. The factors indicated by McMurray and Kazanjian were indeed considered by parents who opted for self-care, and those parents choosing self-care for their children usually did so with a great deal of concern (many said "guilt"), ambivalence, and uncertainty. Neither are most parents who employ a self-care arrangement for their children satisfied with this arrangement (McMurray and Kazanjian cite 46% satisfaction among their respondents). They express concern for their child's safety and social development, and worry about the negative impact of too much television viewing, despite the fact that they and their children are also proud of the responsibility and independence latchkey children often appear to exhibit.

THE LATCHKEY EXPERIENCE

As reflected in a series of studies conducted in the Washington, D.C., metropolitan area (Long & Long, 1982; Long & Long, 1983), including interviews with several hundred children, parents of latchkey children and former latchkey children from families that range from working poor to affluent, a constellation of common concerns and experiences has begun to emerge.

The first Long and Long (1982) study was carried out in an all-black parochial school in Washington, D.C. Data from this study compares most easily with data obtained by Woods (1972) and McMurray and Kazanjian (1982), though differences among all these studies occur. It is important to point out that children interviewed in the Long and Long study cannot be considered typical of children enrolled in the public schools of the city of Washington—not because of religious affiliation (in fact, the majority were not Catholic), but because their parents could afford to pay an additional 750 dollars a year tuition per child to have them enrolled in a parochial school. This fact is mentioned only to indicate that the latchkey phenomenon occurs across a fairly broad sweep of income levels in the black community.

In the Long and Long (1982) study, data was obtained by individually interviewing every latchkey child in first through sixth grades (30% of all children enrolled in these grades) following a structured protocol. This investigation appears to be the first reported attempt to obtain data directly from latchkey children. Unlike the Woods (1972) or McMurray and Kazanjian (1982) studies, the latchkey children in the Long and Long study were almost equally divided as to sex. Figures in the last investigation as to the number of children living with a single parent (44% of the group left alone and 40% of the group left with siblings) almost exactly parallel the national average for black children living with only one parent (United States Department of Health and Human Services, 1982).

Length of Unsupervised Time

The children in the Long and Long (1982) study were without adult supervision an average of 2 1/4 hours each weekday if home alone, 3 hours if home with siblings. McMurray and Kazanjian (1982) report that three-quarters of their latchkey parents left their children alone for between 1 and 3 hours, and nearly one-fifth left their children unsupervised for between 4 and 8 hours, apparently on a daily basis. Ruderman (1969), in a study conducted for the Child Welfare League of America, found that 36% of the children ages 9 to 11 of working mothers were alone for 1 hour each day and that 43% were left for up to 2 hours. The average of hours reported in all studies should be considered a minimum since it generally does not reflect parental delays in getting home or the full days children may be left unsupervised when ill or during holiday or vacation periods.

Keys

Most latchkey children carry or have access to a house key. In suburban and rural areas the key may be hidden on the premises or the house may be left unlocked, thus providing easy access for the child should a key be lost. In urban areas lost keys pose a real problem for children. Of the children in the Long and Long (1982) study, 38% said that if they lost their keys, they would wait outside until an adult arrived. Many urban children were quite concerned about the possibility of losing their keys, and key loss was not an uncommon experience.

Restricted Freedoms

Parents of urban children often restrict the freedom of their children for safety's sake. Long and Long (1982) found that 43% of the children at home alone and 33% of those at home only with siblings could not play outside. Eighty percent of the urban children who spent their latchkey time without any other person at home were told by their parents that they could not have friends visit while their parents were away. When siblings were at home together, however, only 60% of the boys and 30% of the girls were so restricted. When children in suburbia were studied, restrictions on outside play and having friends visit during the latchkey time were much relaxed (Long & Long, 1983). Freedom to engage in outside play seemed to be even more relaxed in a rural community (Galambos & Garbarino, 1982).

Since nearly all children with continuous adult supervision are allowed regular play contact with their peers during out-of-school hours (Long & Long, 1982), latchkey children probably suffer some social deficit when their ability to play with peers is severely restricted.

The Long and Long (1982, 1983) data seems to indicate that contextual variables make a difference in how latchkey children behave and how the experience affects them. These results support those issues raised by Galambos and Garbarino (1982). Suburban latchkey children seem to be accorded greater freedom to play outside and make use of public recreational facilities than do urban children in self-care. Children who live in neighborhoods considered to be safer seem to exhibit less fear than those living in more crime-ridden neighborhoods.

Children's Perceptions of Self-Care

Long and Long (1982, 1983) found that the number one complaint of latchkey children was loneliness or boredom. While it is not clear whether these same children might make the same complaint if they were under continuous adult supervision, those children who were so supervised did not make such a complaint to any significant degree.

The most startling finding in the Long and Long (1982) study was the elevated fear levels found among latchkey children. Fear levels were judged by five methods: (1) Did the child say he or she was afraid? (2) Did children use intense words to express fear, like "terrified" or "very frightened"? (3) Did children say they had recurring sleep disturbances? (4) Had children developed a plan of action for coping with expected fears? and (5) Did the interviewer rate the child as highly fearful as a result of impressions drawn from the interview in general?

Using these benchmarks and realizing that most children express some degree of fear at some time or another, investigators classed 30% of the latchkey children who were home alone and 20% of those routinely left at home with siblings but without continuous adult supervision as expressing unusually high levels of recurring fear. The most commonly expressed fear was that someone might break into the house, followed by fear of noises, of the dark, of rain, of thunder or lightening, or of animals barking or crying that might indicate the presence of some further danger. These elevated levels of fear were found, but with much less frequency when children in affluent, suburban settings were interviewed (Long & Long, 1983). These results might indicate that environmental factors, such as the customary or perceived safety of one's neighborhood, can play a distinct role in determining the impact of the latchkey experience.

Risks to Unattended Children

Children left alone are always at risk from natural disasters, as well as from those assaults perpetrated by individuals around them. Fire deaths, for example, are disproportionately high among the young. Children are curious to try what they see adults doing—using matches or cigarette lighters, for example. They are not always able to foresee the consequences of their acts and may be insubordinate and play with matches even though emphatically told not to do so. And too frequently children have not been trained in the rudiments of self-protection from fire or other emergency conditions.

Only Long and Long (1982, 1983) have investigated the number and nature of emergencies latchkey children experience, or the responses of latchkey children to such emergencies. In the 1982 study, the investigators found that fewer than 5% of the children interviewed had been involved in an emergency they considered serious. This low percentage might be accounted for by the fact that the average age of the children at the time they were interviewed was 8.5 for those left with siblings and 9.5 for those left alone. When former latchkey children (a population which averaged nearly 9 years in latchkey arrangements) were interviewed, more than half recalled at least one serious emergency in which they had been involved while unattended. A great deal of additional data on local and national levels is needed about the risks experienced by children left unattended. No comprehensive data exists, for example, that outlines abuse by siblings of children left alone together, even though Long and Long (1983) discovered that when siblings were left unattended together the majority complained that they fought and argued frequently. National figures report abuse by under-age siblings as abuse by mother/substitutes. This may account for the listing of 46% of sexual abuse cases, 72% of physical abuse cases, and 90% of all other maltreatment as attributable to mother/substitutes (United States Department of Health and Human Services, 1981).

The current role latchkey arrangements play in the abuse and neglect of children is an issue that needs serious research attention. In much the same way, we know little about the role lack of continuous adult supervision plays in juvenile delinquency. (This latter issue was poignantly illustrated in a report prepared by the Committee on School Age Child Care of the Arlington, Virginia, Health and Welfare Council [1969]). Although about 2% of all children in the United States are abused each year, the majority of latchkey children will probably not be abused, nor will the majority become known to the courts, or become severely injured, or die by accident (even though accidents are the leading cause of death in children). However, these concerns should be investigated in light of supervision arrangements in order to give some insight into the impact of the latchkey phenomenon on those issues that society views as having the most serious consequences for children.

Effects of Parent/Child Relationship

While the risks of leaving children unattended are real, one factor Long and Long (1982) found that considerably moderated the undesirable impact of the latchkey experience was the closeness of the relationship the child experienced with one or both parents. These results support findings by Woods (1972) that those children who enjoyed the best relationships with their mothers had the highest achievement, best personality adjustment, highest verbal and language IQs, and the best reading achievement. Even teachers responded most favorably to those children who had the best mother/child relationships at home.

Children in the Long and Long (1982) study appeared to perceive a closer parental relationship if their parents engaged in activities with them or expressed concern about their welfare, and if the parents responded when their aid was enlisted in resolving child conflicts. Children experiencing closer parent/child relationships also indicated that their parents told them that they loved them and/or acted loving toward them.

INTERVENTIONS AND SUGGESTIONS

Large and increasing numbers of children are being left alone while their parents work. This reluctantly used arrangement puts a special burden on children, many of whom have outgrown usually available full-day care. Latchkey children are left unsupervised before and/or after school hours, and at other periods during which their schedules fail to correspond with the times their parents are available for supervision. Many children are also pressed into service to supervise younger siblings. These children are filling the gap between parent care and other forms of child care that inadequately meet the needs of working parents.

Whether the lack of continuous supervision for our nation's children creates a problem and if so, of what magnitude, is a question not entirely settled. A growing amount of evidence seems to indicate that unsupervised subteens *are at risk* to a greater or lesser extent, depending on the context of their care arrangements (Wellborn, 1981). Even when assessments are made of the impact of poor or nonexistent supervision versus continuous adult supervision on such qualities as school achievement, school adjustment, and social behavior, results vary from no differences between groups to a negative impact on the unsupervised group. A great deal more research is needed to determine the full impact of self-care on children.

Survival Skills

Since children are being required to assume more responsibility for their own care and for the care of their siblings, and because the risks are high, there appears to be a strong need to give children better instruction in child development and survival skills. Two examples of such programs are described in *Survival Skills Training for Kids* (Pfafflin, 1982) and *I'm in Charge* (Swan, Briggs, & Kelso, 1982). *The Official Kids' Survival Kit* (Chaback & Fortunato, 1981), *In Charge* (Kyte, 1983) and *The Handbook For Latchkey Children And Their Parents* (Long and Long (1983) are other examples of responses to a perceived need for systematic information for children on how to be prepared to care for themselves while home alone. *On My Own,* a survival skills workbook that contains many do-it-yourself activities, written by Lynette Long, is scheduled for publication by Acropolis press, Washington, D.C., during 1984.

Moreover, because so many women are now in the labor force, parents cannot assume that a neighbor will be available should their child at home alone need immediate assistance. This situation demands that the usual sources of emergency assistance (police or fire and rescue groups, for example) be better prepared to deal with the emergency needs of unattended children. There is a growing need for alternative forms of assistance not only to help children cope with physical emergencies but also to help reduce loneliness, boredom, and fright. One such service is provided by the State College Branch of the American Association of University Women at the Pennsylvania State University (Guerney & Moore, 1982). This service, called "Phone Friend," makes a telephone hotline available in the area to provide empathic listening and responding, help in problem solving, and referral for children. During its first 5 months of operation, 369 calls were answered—87 from children who were lonely, 50 from those who were bored, and 41 from those who were scared. Calls in these three categories accounted for more responses than all other types of calls combined.

Flexible Childcare Services

In addition to teaching children survival skills and providing services to help them while they are alone, there appears to be a growing demand for increased before- and after-school care and a greater variety of care arrangements suited to the demands of school-age children. Some of these arrangements will have the effect of providing continuous adult supervision for children. The extended-day programs operated in the elementary schools of

Arlington and Fairfax Counties in Virginia are excellent examples of such programs. Others, such as neighborhood block mother programs or community recreation programs, will guarantee that at least one responsible adult will be home when children on the block need help. Such programs may also help break the monotony of the latchkey arrangement by providing regular community recreational activities that recognize the existence and needs of latchkey children, including provision for transporting children safely between such activities and their homes.

Many parents would make better use of already available community services if they knew these services existed. Improved information and referral services for parents are needed to identify not only public resources, but also private ones. Employers can be enlisted to help establish these child-care information and referral services. Several employers can jointly establish a child-care consortium, provide subsidized child-care projects through grants, or help generate parenting workshops. Flexible work hours for parents and provisions for employees to carry out assigned duties at home are only a few things employers can do to make parental fulfillment of childcare responsibilities easier. Those interested in what employers can and are doing to help should obtain a copy of the Executive Summary of the National Employer Supported Child Care Project (Divine-Hawkins & Collins, 1983).

Community organizations can also take leadership roles in bringing together a variety of community resources designed to relieve the problems of unattended children. For example, an intergenerational model designed by Thomas Long for Young Volunteers in Action, a federal agency in Washington, D. C., showed how senior citizens could effectively be paired with juvenile volunteers to provide care for young children at an annual cost of about $600 per child. Existing homes for the elderly can expand their care concepts to involve the elderly in care activities for otherwise unattended youngsters. And community organizations, such as the YMCA, can expand their already sizeable network of after-school programs to accommodate a growing number of needy children. One excellent source of assistance is the School-age Child Care Project located at Wellesley College, Wellesley, Massachusetts. Michelle Seligson and her colleagues offer a wide range of technical assistance, especially for those who want help establishing a school-based extended day program. It is important to note in this regard that no one model or plan will satisfy the needs of all children or all families in every community. Each community will likely require a number of approaches to adequately respond to family needs for child-care.

The issue of children in self-care is a complex one, not readily answered by a single solution. Even parents' decisions on the amount and type of child-care arrangements used are complex (Moore, 1982), including household structure, wage earners' employment status and annual income, cost of care, distance of care from home, and the necessity for regular or flexible care arrangements. Further, choices of care arrangements are mediated by race and ethnicity, educational level of parents, geographical region, and type of community in which the family lives. As a consequence, any community that wishes to help in supplying adequate child-care services must recognize the complexity of influences that affect the choices parents make and provide a variety of supportive services from which parents may choose, depending how they assess their own family situations.

Ambivalent Responses To Self-Care

The impact of the lack of a clear indication as to the positive or negative effects of self-care on children is dramatically underlined in data obtained by Long and Long (1983) and that reported by the U.S. Department of Health and Human Services (Divine-Hawkins, 1983). In these studies parents generally respond that they would feel comfortable leaving a child at home without adult supervision at an older age than when children in these studies actually began this practice. Children in self-care also reported that they would feel comfortable without adult supervision at a later age than that at which they were actually left unattended. The disparity between values and practice is particularly pronounced for children under age 8.

On the other hand a large percentage of adults, 90–95% in the U.S. Department of Health and Human Services study (Divine-Hawkins, 1983), reported that there were advantages to the latchkey arrangement including increased independence and learning new survival skills. And few parents actually using self-care expressed dissatisfaction with their own arrangements. In this study the overwhelming majority of parents (86–99%) said that the self-care arrangement met their needs. And more than half the parents who had children in self-care said that this arrangement allowed them to do things they would not otherwise be able to do such as go to work or date.

While the majority of parents did not directly report dissatisfaction with self-care by their school-age children, however, half the adults responding did mention at least one worry. Accidents topped the list of concerns and the largest percentage of problems that developed were related to accidents. Certain concerns that receive a great deal of popular attention, such as sexual activity, drug use, or other criminal behavior, account for a very low percentage of reported worries (0–5%). A result supported by a majority of more than 200,000 readers of *Better Homes and Gardens:* "What's Happening to American Families?" (Keating, 1983).

Perhaps these ambivalent responses arise because parents are caught between their own values and the practicalities of a world in which most adults are employed outside the home and that there is not sufficient affordable child care available. Actually families with all adults working full-time outside the home report difficulties with their school-age care arrangements more frequently than other types of families. This suggests that, at least for this population, existing modes of child care should be made more accessible, more age-appropriate programs should be developed, school-based before-and-after school programs should be expanded in size and number, employers should become more involved in providing child care assistance and children should be better instructed in those skills necessary to maintain themselves when adult supervision is lacking. In the long run, however, the nation will have to discover even more acceptable means than now exist for providing for the care and maintenance of its children during all those hours their parents work.

REFERENCES

Banducci, R. The effect of mother's employment on the achievement, aspirations and expectations of the child. *Personnel and Guidance Journal,* 1967, *46,* 263–267.

Bandura, A. The stormy decade: Fact or fiction? *Psychology in the Schools,* 1964, *1,* 224–231.

Cartwright, A., & Jeffreys, M. Married women who work: Their own and their children's children's health. *British Journal of Preventive and Social Medicine,* 1958, *12,* 159–171.

Chaback, E., & Fortunato, P. *The Official Kids' Survival Kit.* Boston: Little Brown & Company, 1981

Cobb, C. How adolescents see their role in a fieldsite. *Voice for Children,* National Council for Day Care and Child Development, 1975, *8* (6).

Committee on School Age Child Care (Arlington, Virginia, Health and Welfare Council). *The choice is ours: A report on the latch key child.* Arlington County, VA, March 27, 1969.

Dellas, M., Gaier, E. L., & Emihovich, C. A. Maternal employment and selected behaviors and attitudes of pre-adolescents and adolescents. *Adolescence,* 1979, *14* (55), 579–589.

Divine-Hawkins, P. *Family day care in the United States* (7 vols.). Washington, DC: United States Department of Health and Human Services, 1981.

Divine-Hawkins, P. *School-Age Day Care Study: Executive Summary* and *Final Report* (2 vols.) Washington, DC: Department of Health and Human Services, 1983.

Divine-Hawkins, P., & Collins, R. C. Employer Supported Child Care: Investing in Human Resources, Washington, D. C.: Department of Health and Human Services, 1983

Douvan, E., & Adelson, J. *The adolescent experience.* New York: John Wiley & Sons, 1966.

Duncan, G. J., & Morgan, J. W. (Eds.). *Five thousand American families—Patterns of economic progress.* Ann Arbor, MI: University of Michigan Institute for Social Research, 1975.

Dusek, J., & Flaherty, J. The development of the self-concept during the adolescent years. *Monographs of the Society for Research in Child Development,* 1981, *46,* (9), No. 191.

Elkind, D. Egocentrism in adolescence. *Child Development,* 1967, *38,* 1025–1034.

Elkind, D. *The hurried child.* Reading, MA: Addison-Wesley Publishing Co., 1981.

Erikson, E. H. *Identity, youth and crisis.* New York: W. W. Norton & Company, 1968.

Etaugh, J. E. Effects of non-maternal care on children. *American Psychologist,* 1980, *35,* 309–319.

Feeney, S. *Schools for young adolescents: Adapting the early childhood model.* Chapel Hill, NC: University of North Carolina, 1980.

Feldman, R. Working mothers: Employed nurses and their children's anxiety levels. *Occupational Health Nursing,* 1978, *26,* 16–19.

Finkelhor, D. *Sexually victimized children.* New York: The Free Press, 1979.

Freud, A. *Psychoanalytic study of the child.* New York: International Universities Press, 1958.

*Friedman, D. C. *Community solutions for childcare.* Washington, DC: United States Department of Labor, Women's Bureau, 1979. (ERIC Document Reproduction Service No. ED 182 030)

*Galambos, N. L., & Garbarino, J. *Identifying the missing links in the study of latchkey children.* Paper presented at the annual convention of the American Psychological Association, Washington, DC, August, 1982. (ERIC Document Reproduction Service No. to be assigned)

Garbarino, J. "Latchkey" children: How much of a problem? *The Education Digest,* February 1981, 14–16.

George, E. E., & Thomas, M. A comparative study of children of employed and unemployed mothers. *Psychology Studies,* 1967, *12,* 32–38.

Ginsburg, A., Milne, A., Myers, D., & Ellman, F. Single Parents, Working Mothers and The Educational Achievement of Elementary School Age Children. A revision of a paper presented at the annual meeting of the American Educational Research Association, New York, March 21, 1982. Washington, DC: U.S. Department of Education, 1983a.

Ginsburg, A., Myers, D., Milne, A., & Ellman, F. Single Parents, Working Mothers and The Educational Achievement of Secondary School Age Children. An extensive revision of a paper presented at the annual meeting of the American Educational Research Association, Montreal, Canada, April, 1983. Washington, DC: U.S. Department of Education, 1983b.

Glueck, S., & Glueck, E. Working mothers and delinquency. *Mental Hygiene,* 1957, *41,* 327–352.

Gold, D., & Andres, D. Comparisons of adolescent children with employed and non-employed mothers. *Merrill-Palmer Quarterly,* 1978, *24*(4), 243–254. (a)

Gold, D., & Andres, D. Developmental comparisons between ten-year-old children with employed and non-employed mothers. *Child Development,* 1978, *49*(1), 75–84. (b)

Guerney, L., & Moore, L. *A prevention-oriented community service for latchkey children: An after-school telephone line.* Paper presented at the annual convention of the American Psychological Association, Washington, DC, August, 1982.

Hand, H. B. Working mothers and maladjusted children. *Journal of Educational Psychology,* 1957, *30,* 245–246.

*Harris, Louis. *Families at work: Strengths and strains.* Minneapolis, MN: The General Mills American Family Report, 1981. (ERIC Document Reproduction Service No. ED 212 370)

Hartley, R. E. Children's concepts of male and female roles. *Merrill-Palmer Quarterly,* 1960, *6,* 83–91.

Hill, J. P. *Understanding early adolescence: A framework.* Chapel Hill, N.C.: Early Adolescence, University of North Carolina, 1980.

Hoffman, L. W. Mothers' enjoyment of work and effects on the child. *Child Development.* 1961, *32,* 187–197.

Hoffman, L. W. Maternal employment: 1979. *American Psychologist,* 1979, *34*(10), 859–865.

Hoffman, L. W. The effects of maternal employment on the academic attitudes and performance of school-age children. A paper presented for Families as Educators Team, Washington, DC: National Institute of Education, 1980.

Hughes, C. D. *Children of working parents: Where are they?* Phoenix, AZ: Association for Supportive Child Care, 1982.

Jones, J. B., Jundsteen, S. W., & Michael, W. G. The relationship of the professional employment status of mothers to reading achievement of sixth-grade children. *California Journal of Educational Research,* 1967, *18,* 102–108.

Kamerman, S. B., & Kahn, A. J. *Child care, family benefits, and working parents: A Study in comparative policy.* New York: Columbia University Press, 1981.

Keating, K. "What's Happening to American Families?" *Better Homes and Gardens,* August, 1983, *61,* (8), 15–33.

Kyte, K. *In charge: A complete handbook for kids with working parents.* New York: Alfred A. Knopf, 1983.

Long, L. *On my own.* Washington, DC: Acropolis Press, in press.

*Long, T. J., & Long, L. *Latchkey children: The child's view of self care,* 1982. (ERIC Document Reproduction Service No. ED 211 229)

Long, T. J., & Long, L. *The handbook for latchkey children and their parents.* New York: Arbor House, 1983.

Lopata, H. (Ed.) *Family factbook.* Chicago: Center for the Comparative Study of Social Roles, Marquis Academic Media, 1978.

Lueck, M., Orr, A. C., & O'Connell. *Trends in child care arrangements of working mothers.* Unpublished manuscript, United States Bureau of the Census, Population Division, 1982.

Mallum, M. A case for the involvement of secondary school students in early childhood programs. Unpublished paper, The National Commission on Resources for Youth, Inc.

Mathews, S. W. The effect of mothers' out-of-home employment on children's ideas and attitudes. *Journal of Applied Psychology,* 1934, *18,* 116–136.

McCord, J., McCord, W., & Thurber, E. Effects of maternal employment on lower class boys. *Journal of Abnormal and Social Psychology,* 1963, *67,* 177–182.

McMurray, G., & Kazanjian, D. *Day care and the working poor: The struggle for self-sufficiency.* New York: Community Service Society, 1982.

Mead, M. *Culture and commitment: A study of the generation gap.* New York: Doubleday & Co., 1970.

Medrich, E. *Children's time study.* Berkeley, CA: University of California Press, 1982.

Moore, J. C. Parents' choice of day care services. *Annals of the American Academy of Political and Social Science,* May 1982, *461,* 125–134.

Moore, S. G. Working mothers and their children. *Young Children,* 1978, *34*(1), 77–84.

Muuss, R. E. *Theories of adolescence.* New York: Random House, 1975.

Nelson, D. C. A study of school achievement among adolescent children with working and non-working mothers. *Journal of Educational Research,* 1969, *62,* 456–458.

Nye, F. I. Adolescent-parent adjustment: Age, sex, sibling number, broken homes and employed mother as variables. *Journal of Marriage and the Family,* 1952, *14,* 327–332.

Nye, F. I. Maternal employment and the adjustment of adolescent children, *Marriage and Family Living,* 1959, *21,* 240–244.

Nye, F. I., & Hoffman, L. W. *The employed mother in America.* Chicago: Rand McNally & Co., 1963.

Pederson, F. A. Presentation to the members of the Interagency Panel for Early Childhood Research and Development, Washington, DC, April 20, 1982.

Peterson, E. T. The impact of maternal employment on the mother-daughter relationship. Marriage and Family Living, 1961, *23,* 355–361.

Pfafflin, N. *Survival skills for kids.* Blacksburg, VA: Virginia Polytechnic Institute and State University, 1982.

Pinas, M. Superkids. *Psychology Today,* January 1979, 52–63.

Price, J. *How to have a child and keep your job.* New York: St. Martin's Press, 1979.

Rallings, E. M., & Nye, F. I. Wife-mother employment, family, and society. In W. R. Burr et al. (Eds.), *Contemporary theories about the family* (Vol. 1). New York: MacMillan Publishing Co., 1979.

Rogers, C. (Sexual Abuse Unit of Children's Hospital, Washington DC.) Personal communication, November 10, 1982.

Rogoff, B., Sellers, M., Pirotta, S., Fox, N., & White, S. The age of assignment of roles and responsibilities to children: A cross-cultural study. *Human Development,* 1975, *18,* 353–369.

Rouman, J. School children's problems as related to parental factors. *Journal of Educational Research,* 1956, *50,* 105–112.

Roy, P. Maternal employment and adolescent roles: Rural-urban differentials. *Journal of Marriage and the Family,* 1961, *23,* 340–349.

*Ruderman, F. H. *Child care and working mothers: A study of arrangements made for the daytime care of children.* New York: Child Welfare League of America, 1969. (ERIC Document Reproduction Service No. 045 175)

Rutter, M. *Changing youth in a changing society: Patterns of adolescent development and disorder.* Cambridge, MA: Harvard University Press, 1980.

Scott, D. C. Do working mothers' children suffer? *New Society,* 1965, *151,* 8–9.

Siegel, A. E., Stoltz, L. M., Hitchcock, E. Q., & Adamson, J. Dependence and independence in the children of working mothers. *Child Development,* 1959, *30,* 533–546.

Simons, J., & Bohen, H. *Employed parents and their children: A data book.* Washington, DC: Children's Defense Fund, 1982.

*Smith, R. *Women in the labor force in 1990: Some new data series.* Washington, DC: The Urban Institute, 1979. (ERIC Document Reproduction Service No. 185 417)

Smith, R. E. (Ed.). *The subtle revolution: Women at work.* Washington, DC: The Urban Institute, 1979.

Swan, H., Briggs, W. M., & Kelso, M. *I'm in charge: A self-care course for parents and children.* Olathe, KS: The Johnson County Mental Health Center, 1982.

Taveggia, T. C., & Thomas, E. M. Latchkey children. *Pacific Sociological Review,* 1974, *17*(1), 27–34.

*United States Department of Commerce, Bureau of the Census. *Daytime care of children: October 1974 and February 1975.* Current Population Reports Series P-20, No. 298, 1976. (ERIC Document Reproduction Service No. ED 130 792)

*United States Department of Health and Human Services. *National study of the incidence and severity of child abuse and neglect: Study findings.* Washington, DC: DHHS Publication No. (OHDS) 81-30325, September 1981.

United States Department of Health and Human Services. *Office for families fact sheet.* Washington, DC: Administration for Children, Youth, and Families, 1982.

*United States Department of Labor. *Working mothers and their children.* Washington, DC: Employment Standards Administration, Women's Bureau, 1977. (ERIC Document Reproduction Service No. ED 149 862)

Weisner, T. S., & Gallimore, R. My brother's keeper: Child and sibling caretaking. *Current Anthropology,* 1977, *18* (2), 169–190.

Wellborn, S. When school kids come home to an emply house. *U.S. News and World Report,* September 14, 1981, pp. 42, 47.

Whiting, B., & Edwards, C. A cross-cultural analysis of sex differences in the behavior of children aged three through eleven. *Journal of Social Psychology,* 1973, *91,* 171–188.

Woods, M. B. The unsupervised child of the working mother. (Doctoral dissertation, Bryn Mawr College, 1968) (University Microfilms No. 69-9058)

Woods, M. B. The unsupervised child of the working mother. *Developmental Psychology,* 1972, *6,* 14–25.

Zill, N. *American children: Happy, healthy, and insecure.* New York: Doubleday/Anchor Press, 1983.

Zucker, H. L. Working parents and latchkey children. *The Annals of the American Academy of Political and Social Sciences,* November 1944, *236,* 43–50.

7

The Challenge of Employer-Supported Child Care: Meeting Parent Needs

Dana E. Friedman

Work and Family Information Center
The Conference Board, New York

INTRODUCTION

The challenge of making the business sector a part of the child care landscape is in recognizing mutual self-interest. During these hard economic times, both business and child care struggle for survival. And for both employers and child care providers, a critical element of that survival is the capacity to respond to the changing and diverse needs of parents. The solutions to child-care problems will not be determined only by the dreams of early childhood educators, nor by the agendas of corporate managers—the contributions of both must be fashioned by parent needs and preferences.[1]

---

[1] Much of the information presented in this chapter derives from original research gathered through visits and telephone conversations conducted over a period of 4 years, during which time the author attended nearly 70 conferences on the subject of employer-supported child care. Among Dr. Friedman's most recent publications on the subject are the following: *Strategies for expanding employer supports to working parents* (New York: Carnegie Corporation of New York, 1983), *State and local government strategies to encourage employer-supported child care* (New York: Center for Public Advocacy Research, 1982), *Management by parent objectives: A case study establishing the feasibility of employer-sponsored child care and other family supports* (Doctoral dissertation, Harvard University, 1982), and *Designing a feasibility study: A starting point for considering new management initiatives for working parents* (paper presented at the Conference on New Management Initiatives for Working Parents, Boston, April 1-2, 1981).

An Historical Overview

When one considers early childhood education as a matter of policy, its purpose and purview go beyond the care and education of our nation's pre-schoolers. Historically, government involvement in child care includes a patchwork of programs focused primarily on broader social and economic concerns. During the Depression, the Federal Emergency Relief Administration provided funds for day care to soften economic hardships and create jobs for the unemployed. During World War II, thousands of centers were established through funds provided by the Lanham Act to encourage female employment within war-related industries. During the 1960s, Head Start was created to break the "cycle of poverty." And throughout the 1970s, there were five unsuccessful attempts to pass comprehensive child care legislation. Each effort failed, in part because of political confrontation or moral ambiguities which in and of themselves had little to do with child care.

Now, with the prospect of private sector support, it is imperative that advocates learn from the mistakes made in the public sector. As with public policy, it is likely that private policies will embrace early childhood education for reasons that go beyond the best interests of the child. And as has been shown in the past, corporate America will likely be motivated to support child care when it can be shown to have positive effects on what management is concerned about—recruitment, retention, and productivity. For example, during the United States Civil War, some employers opened temporary child-care centers to enable women to help manufacture gunpowder and tend to the injured, and at the turn of the twentieth century, when factories needed cheap labor, the industrial day care nursery was provided in order to exploit working mothers. As with the United States Civil War, World War I again saw some employers opening temporary child-care centers to meet worker shortages (Feinstein, 1979). World War II gave rise to another round of employer-sponsored centers, only this time there was support from the federal government. In 1940, Congress passed the Lanham Act, and a year later it passed amendments that encouraged the creation of community-based child-care programs in defense plants to help the war effort. Among the most famous of these centers were the two family-centered child-care programs at the Kaiser Shipyards in Portland, Oregon.

After the war, many women returned home and the work force swelled with returning servicemen. Industry's interest in day care remained inactive until the 1960s. In 1967, federal legislation created the opportunity for rapid tax amortization of constructed buildings used to serve employees' children. The increased demand for child care, caused by the increasing labor-force participation of women, prompted widespread interest in day care as a potentially profitable investment. However, since profit in day care is difficult to attain, especially when the centers are underutilized, a number of companies (Curlee Clothing, KLH, Avco Printing, C & P Telephone, and Westinghouse, to name a few) suffered significant losses. Fifteen of the 18 on-site centers opened between 1964 and 1972 closed.[2] (For additional information on center operation, see Besner, 1971, and Welfare Research, Inc., 1980.)

Current Interest in Employer Support

An estimate provided by the National Employer Supported Child Care Project in Pasadena, California, suggests that in 1982, approximately 415 employers are responding to their employees' child-care needs. Best estimates are that 80 corporate work-site day care centers exist at the time of this writing. There may be as many as 1,000 employers providing some form of child care support. The largest industrial group today providing on-site day care services to employees is hospitals. Facing a nationwide nursing shortage, nearly 300 hospitals are providing some sort of child-care services to encourage recruitment and retention.

What characterizes recent interest in exploring corporate sponsorship is the variety of *alternatives* to work-site child care. (Table 1 indicates the number and variety of these programs.) Not only are companies learning from the lessons of earlier center closings, but they are also recognizing the inappropriateness of center-based care given the adequacy of existing community-based programs, the preferences of parents, and the special needs of children. Parents may not need additional child care services at the work place as much as they may need assistance finding, selecting, or paying for child care already available in the community. Another concern for parents may be their need for time in balancing the responsibilities of home and work.

Whether business will support child care and how it will choose to do so will be based on a unique blend of management agendas, community resources, and parent needs. Those management agendas may override con-

---

[2] In *Day care services: Industry's involvement,* Besner has identified 11 on-site day care centers. These centers include Avco Economic Systems (Dorchester, MA), Bro-Dart Industries (Williamsport, PA), Control Data Corporation (Minneapolis, MN), Curlee Clothing (Mayfield, KY), KLH Research and Development Corporation (Cambridge, MA), Mr. Apparel, Inc. (High Point, NC), Skyland Textile Company (Morgantown, NC), Tioga Sportswear (Fall River, MA), Tyson Foods, Inc. (Springdale, AR), Vanderbilt Shirt Factory (Asherville, NC), and Winter Garden Freezing Company (Bells, TN).

A 1980 study by Welfare Research, Inc., *On-site day care: The state of the art and models development,* identified an additional seven centers in operation between 1960 and 1974. These included Forney Engineering (Dallas, TX), Jefferson Mills (Williamstown, NC), Joshua Tree Manufacturing (Gardena, CA), Levi Strauss (Star City, KS), PhotoCorporation of America (Matthews, NC), Security National Bank (Walnut Creek, CA), and Stride Rite Shoes (Boston, MA). As of 1982, only three of these 18 centers have remained open and operating as originally sponsored—Forney Engineering, PhotoCorporation of America, and Stride Rite.

TABLE 1 Forms of Child Care Assistance
Provided by Various Employer Groups*

Assistance	Number of Companies Sponsoring Programs				
	Industry	Health Care	Government	Union	TOTAL
Child Care Centers	43	151	14	4	212
Information and Referral	20	17	0	0	37
Vouchers	10	7	0	0	17
Family Day Care	0	7	0	0	7
Parent Education	23	0	0	0	23
Support for Community-based Child Care	78	11	2	0	91
Other	23	2	1	2	28
TOTAL	197	195	17	6	415

* Data provided by the National Employer Supported Child Care Project, 363 E. Villa, Pasadena, CA 91103.

sideration of community resources. In order to approach corporations with any degree of success while retaining a commitment to quality of services for children, early childhood educators need to understand the pressures on business to respond to working parents.

PRESSURES ON EMPLOYERS TO SUPPORT CHILD CARE

There are a variety of internal and external pressures on employers to attend to family needs. For one, families are less able to rely on themselves for the daily care of their children than was once the case. This situation would seem largely due to the increase of mothers in the work force, stimulated by the women's movement and/or economic necessity. There is also a trend for families to have fewer children, which means there are fewer older siblings to take care of younger children. In addition, relatives are less able to take on this responsibility due to family mobility or their own need to work. The cumulative effect of these changes is that families are increasingly turning to the community for child-care support.

The same economic forces creating the two-wage earner family have also resulted in government cutbacks to various child care programs, thus eroding the capacity of community-based services to meet parent needs. In other words, the supply of services is declining at a time when the demand is increasing. These changes in family and service capacity are creating two sources of external pressure on employers to play a role in meeting the needs of working parents: (a) parents who, with no recourse, may bring their unmet problems to the workplace, and (b) those involved in community-based services who, faced with a struggle for their own survival, look at the business community in the hope of tapping a new source of revenue.

There is a third source of external pressure on the business community—more nebulous in its origins, but no less forceful in its impact. What seems to be evolving is a business enterprise no longer able to define itself solely as an economic unit. In the past, criticism of business focused on the practices of underpaying workers, overcharging customers, and fixing prices. Today, the corporation is held responsible for everything from air pollution to executive stress. Whether these charges are justified is not the issue; the concept they imply is important, however. A corporation is no longer responsible for simply making a profit or producing goods, but for simultaneously contributing to the solution of extremely complex ecological, moral, political, racial, sexual, and social problems (Toffler, 1981). Further changes in industry and worker values create internal pressures on employers to respond to the needs of working parents. Business today is dealing with a new breed of workers who are becoming increasingly concerned about the quality of their lives and more willing to express those concerns (Yankelovich, 1981).

Another pressure, this one internal, is the changing nature of industry itself. High technology firms and the growth of services characterize our post-industrial society. Businesses involved in these concerns are replacing the classical industries of Toffler's (1981) "second wave": coal, rail, textiles, steel, auto, and rubber. When the shift within industry began in the 1950s, old industrial regions like New England's Merrimac Valley started to decline. Now, places like Route 128 outside Boston and Silicon Valley in California have zoomed into prominence. And it is interesting to note that the areas now providing the home for today's growth industries are precisely where we find the most activity in employer supports to working parents. These newer industries, which are generally experiencing a demand for labor, are responding by offering employees the attraction of family benefits. An increasing concern about productivity has also led to the belief among many employers that attention to family concerns may help worker performance.

THE RATIONALE FOR EMPLOYER SUPPORT

Many child care providers recognize the need to justify the provision of child care on the basis of corporate self-interest—that is, the extent to which child care will solve management's problems by aiding recruitment, increasing productivity, or by reducing turnover, absenteeism, or tardiness. While common sense would appear to support the notion that management will gain from the provision of services, there is very little empirical evidence to suggest that this is true. The assumption that provision of child care improves productivity was made most poignantly in the movie *9 to 5*, in which a corporation providing flexible schedules, part-time work, and a day care center to its employees apparently increased productivity by 40%. Unfortunately, the research findings supporting a causal relationship between provision of child care assistance and the amelioration of management woes is hardly more substantial than the Hollywood version.

The anecdotal evidence from existing programs is overwhelmingly supportive of the use of child care as a management tool. According to Perry's 1978 survey of 305 on-site centers (including those in companies, hospitals, and unions), a great number of managers responding believed their programs accomplished a variety of benefits (reported in Fishel, Balodis, & Klaus, 1982—see Table 2). The fact that managers believe provision of child care services improves overall operations was confirmed by a study conducted by Welfare Research, Inc. (1980). However, investigators in this study spoke to managers and based their findings on impressions and not empirical evidence.

TABLE 2   On-Site Day Care Center Reports of Employer Benefits*

Benefits Reported	Percent of Employer Response
Increased ability to attract new employees	88
Lowered absenteeism	72
Improved attitude toward employer	65
Improved attitude toward work	55
Created Favorable publicity	60
Lowered job turnover	57
Improved community relations	36

* From *Appalachian Regional Commission Employer-Supported Day Care Study: Final Report* (1982), prepared by Leo Fishel, Inese Balodis, and David Klaus. (Reprinted by permission by Appalachian Regional Commission, 1666 Connecticut Ave., NW, Washington, DC 20035.)

Intermedics, the sponsor of the largest near-site day care center in Freeport, Texas, found a 1% yearly reduction in turnover, which yielded a gain of 3,700 work hours annually. Photo Corporation of America estimates that their on-site center saves them $40,000 a year as a result of reduced turnover (*Child Care Resource Service Newsletter,* 1981). These estimates were not the result of a scientific study, however, To date, only one company has attempted an experimental study of productivity gains resulting from the provision of a child-care program. The Northside Child Development Center in Minneapolis, sponsored by a consortium of businesses and spearheaded by Control Data, studied 90 employees over a 20-month period. Thirty mothers with children in the day care program were matched to a sample of 30 mothers who did not have children in the program, and to another 30 employees who had no children or who had grown children. The average monthly rate of absenteeism for the group of mothers provided day care was 4.40, as compared to 6.02 for nonparticipants (the two control groups combined). The average monthly turnover rate was 1.77 for day care mothers and 6.3 for those not in the day care program. Both these findings were statistically significant. (For a report of the study, see Milkovich & Gomez, 1976).

Empirical evidence supporting the bottom-line value of company-sponsored family supports is scanty due to a lack of research, a lack of models on which to base research, and the difficulty in establishing a cause and effect relationship between provision of child care and subsequent reductions in management problems. Many of the companies providing child care also have flextime (or flexible work schedules), as well as an interesting array of other innovative benefits and work policies. How can one control for these other factors when trying to measure the true effects of day care? We need more longitudinal research including control groups, pretests, and post tests. In the meantime, it is wise not to over promise what child care is capable of achieving, lest we disappoint employers.

The assumption that a demand for labor and a concern for increased productivity are the primary forces motivating employers to support working parents suggests that the provision of day care is an issue of corporate self-interest, where a return on an investment is expected. Corporate social responsibility, which is charitable giving, is not implied. An interesting point to note is that even if actual funding for a child-care initiative comes from corporate contributions designed to fulfill social responsibilities, it is likely that some element of self-interest is being served. The interface between corporate self-interest and social responsibility is most clearly seen in the success of the Corporate Child Development Fund for Texas. The fund, which began in 1979, raises money from city-based corporations to sponsor day care programs in rural parts of the state. In most cases, the funds are given to programs in the communities where the donating company has a plant site. The center is used by all residents, but company employees also have access to it. Consequently, there is some return to the company on their investment and self-interest has been served through corporate giving.

Acknowledging the rationale for corporate involvement may be the most important change required by early childhood educators in their efforts to obtain employer support. The fact that children are our nation's greatest resource is perhaps not the most convincing argument for bottom-line oriented business managers.

EMPLOYER OPTIONS FOR SUPPORTING CHILD CARE NEEDS

Since management has ultimate control of decision making in the quest for corporate support of child care, it is their needs and expectations which must be satisfied. However, corporate self-interest can be satisfied only if the parents' needs are also met. Consider an employer who, having attempted to boost staff morale by providing a free lunch of chicken and ribs, is faced with the realization that the staff is vegetarian. If it is useless to the employee, ultimately it is useless to the employer.

Employer responses to the needs of working parents from around the United States indicate four basic categories of parent needs: (1) the need for *services* where the community supply is lacking, (2) the need for *information* about services in the community that provide child care or general parenting help, (3) the need for *financial assistance* in purchasing community services, and (4) the need for *time* to help balance the dual responsibilities of family and work. Both the parent needs and employer responses are based on the strengths and weaknesses of existing community resources—programs are fashioned as much by parent needs and management agendas as they are by community needs.

Response to Parents' Need for Service

For many, initial thoughts about employer-sponsored child care turn to a work-site day care center. However, the success of these programs is mixed, in part due to the fact that parents may need or prefer services of another type, such as family day care, before- and after-school care, or care for sick children.

Preschool care alternatives.   If parents commute to the work site, they may not want to travel on public transportation during rush hour with their preschoolers. The Unco Survey, conducted by Rodes and Moore (1975), found that parents prefer their children to be cared for in their home neighborhoods and that they also prefer more informal arrangements, such as family day care, especially for children under 3 years of age.

If a center is to be built, it may be established on-site and run by the company, by a nonprofit organization, or by a profit-making center or chain of centers. Also, when a firm does not have enough employees who prefer an on-site center, the company might organize a group of firms in the area to jointly support child-care services for the employed parents of all the firms. In Washington, DC, for example, five television and radio stations have each made $7,000 loans to establish a center for their employees. The center is housed in a nearby church convenient to all employees.

School-age child care.   Another set of parent needs and employer responses exists regarding the school-age child. Child-care problems related to school-age children occur because school may begin after parents start work and end before they finish. The after-school programs provided by public schools often do not provide the kind of structured activities needed by 5- to 12-year-old children. Appropriate before- and after-school programs may be needed either in cooperation with the schools or elsewhere in the community. The School-Age Child Care Project of the Wellesley Center for Research on Women, located at Wellesley College in Massachusetts, has identified approximately 150 school districts providing after-school services, but very few of these programs have received any corporate support. Working parents also have particular difficulties when school is not in session. An unusual response developed by Fel Pro Inc. in Skokie, Illinois, is a day camp which employees' children can attend during the summer.

Caring for sick children. It is difficult enough to arrange child care on a regular basis, but when emergencies arise, such as the child becoming ill, working parents often have few options except to stay home and miss work. Although most states require day care centers to have quiet, semi-isolated rest areas for children, if a child's illness is contagious, it is deemed best that he or she not remain near other children. However, an alternative approach being tried in Minneapolis and Berkeley is for a company to contract with a local agency to send health care workers into the child's home. This arrangement may be more convenient for the parents, more comfortable for the child, and more beneficial for other children than group care solutions.[3] But, as day care directors will attest, if the child is too sick to come to the center, the parent usually wants to remain with the child.

An effective solution to sick-child care may involve changing personnel policies so that employees would be permitted to use sick leave for the illness of a member of the immediate family or would be allocated a specified number of "personal days" for attending to family matters. A study by the Catalyst Career and Family Center (1981) indicated that 29% of companies in the United States provide employees with days off when their children are ill.

Response to Parents' Need for Information

According to Zigler, cited in a study conducted by Project Connections (1980), "A major problem with day care is the lack of centralized information to help parents locate existing day care services" (p. 2). Dwindling resources usually lead to pressures for a more efficient use of existing resources. An obvious mechanism for reducing overlap and maximizing limited resources is a central clearinghouse in the community which collects and disseminates information about the supply of and demand for child-care services.

Problems in locating child care have been recognized by other researchers as well (Keniston, 1977; National Academy of Sciences, 1976), by policy analysts (Kamerman & Kahn, 1978, 1979), and by parents who responded to the Unco Survey (Rodes & Moore, 1975). The parents surveyed indicated that the support service they would most like to see provided by the govern-

---

[3] Wheezles and Sneezles in Berkeley, California, and Child Care Services, Inc. of Minneapolis, Minnesota, are two groups providing health care workers in children's homes so that the parent can go to work. These groups charge on an hourly basis, a practice prohibitive to the parent unless partially funded by a difficult-to-obtain corporate subsidy.

ment was "a referral system where parents could get information about screened and qualified people and agencies to provide child care" (part II, p. 32).

Information and referral (I & R) services, supported by employers, have the potential for providing employees with access to well-planned and coordinated child-care systems that include a variety of choices for care at high levels of quality. While I & R services may be provided through Title XX without regard to income, only a few states have opted to make such services available for child care. A 3-year study of child-care I & R by Project Connections (1980) estimates that there are 6,390 organizations in the United States providing some child-care I & R services. However, only 4.1% of these agencies receive financial assistance from industry.

Employers can supply I & R services through a variety of means. As a 1-year pilot project, the Gillette Company of Boston has implemented for their employees a telephone hotline to the local Child Care Resource Center, a Boston-area I & R agency. A firm might also internalize I & R services by hiring an individual to provide child-care information. Such services could be housed in the personnel department, as occurs at Steelcase, Inc. in Grand Rapids, Michigan, or be provided through an employee assistance program (EAP). Designed primarily for counseling chemically dependent employees, EAPs cover an estimated 6.2 million workers in the private sector (Brasch, 1980). Honeywell, Inc. in Minneapolis initially used their EAP for child care I & R services, and EAP counselors were also able to address other family-related problems affecting employees. In addition, some companies provide for parents' child care information needs by holding parent education seminars at the workplace. The Texas Institute for Families in Houston, for example, has conducted "Noontime Seminars" in more than 20 companies throughout the state. These hour-long brown-bag seminars are offered at the workplace and cover a range of parent/child topics. The Center for Parenting Studies at Wheelock College in Boston also conducts noontime seminars at some downtown Boston banks, as do a growing number of mental health and family therapy organizations.

The appeal of I & R and parent education to companies relates to the fact that such progams allow data to be collected about parent needs without the administration of a survey. Employers fear that surveys will create the expectation that the company will provide a "solution" to parents' child care problems before the decision to do so has been made. Information and counseling services enable the company to respond to needs with a relatively low-cost program, at the same time collecting data far richer than can be obtained from a questionnaire.

Response to Parents' Need for Financial Assistance

Parents are sometimes unable to afford the child care arrangement of their choice once they have located it. As a result, children may be placed in care that is inappropriate for their needs or inconvenient for their parents. A high level of guilt is typically reported by women who leave their children under someone else's care during the day (Rodes & Moore, 1975; Whitbread, 1979), and dissatisfaction with child care arrangements may cause even greater strain for the parent. The subsidization of child care, enabling the purchase of quality care, may reduce such parental stress.

Child care cost.   The cost of child care depends upon a number of factors: type of child care used, fees charged by the provider, number of hours care is used, number and ages of children, and economic status of the parent and the neighborhood. The Unco Survey (Rodes & Moore, 1975) explains that child care costs and standards are more influenced by micro-community standards than the market for goods; in other words, child care in a low income neighborhood will cost less than that provided in a more affluent community. The survey concludes that people pay what they can afford, and as Morgan (1980) notes, generally, the higher the income, the higher the price paid for child care. Based on Department of Labor projections, Ruopp (cited in Morgan, 1980) contends that day care costs range between 9 to 11% of the total family budget and remain the fourth largest budget item for the family, after food, housing, and taxes.

Voucher systems.   Problems associated with the cost of child care can be eased for parents by the employer's offering to pay for a portion of the cost. In a flexible benefits plan or salary reduction program, employees trade off other benefits or a portion of their salary for child care assistance. A voucher system, on the other hand, requires a total employer contribution for reimbursement of a portion of their child care expenses. Polaroid is one of a handful of companies currently offering a voucher system. In operation since 1972, Polaroid's program pays a percentage of the cost of care on a sliding scale for employees with incomes of less than $25,000 a year. The percentage of reimbursement remains the same regardless of the cost of care selected. The Ford Foundation in New York has a similar program, while Measurex Corporation of Cupertino, California, offers a $100 per month stipend to employees as an incentive to return more quickly from maternity leave.

Financial assistance may help parents defray a portion of the cost of care and may also encourage the expansion and improvement of child care services in the community as providers compete for the new market of paying clients. The cost of child care may also be eased by the corporate purchase of child-care slots in local community programs.

Employer Responses to Parents' Need for Time

If all needs for information, money, and services are being met, parents' overriding concern may then become the need for more time with their families, or for more conveniently arranged time. Analysis of the 1977 Quality of Employment Survey by Pleck (1979) indicates that

> about 35% of workers with spouses and/or children report that their job and family life 'interfere' with each other, either somewhat or a lot. Interference occurs significantly more frequently among parents than among nonparents (p. 482).

An employer decision to offer employees more discretion over their working hours may relieve some of these "interferences." Flextime, for example, allows employees to choose the time they arrive at work and the time they leave, as long as they accumulate the prescribed number of hours per day or week. There is usually a core time during which all employees must be present and flexible periods of time when employees exercise choice. Other alternatives to standard work hours may occur through part-time work, job sharing, or work at home (also called "flexiplace").

A study by Harris (1981) for General Mills, Inc., indicated that 51% of professional women surveyed from a United States sample preferred working part-time. Smith (1979) notes that part-time work most clearly offers additional hours for family involvement. Between 1965 and 1977, the number of part-time workers increased nearly three times as rapidly as the number of full-time workers. Most of the increase was among women. By 1977, women held nearly 70% of the part-time jobs. Smith sees this as a consequence of the number of working mothers with young children.

An option that has not been tested on a widespread basis, but which is promising in terms of its flexibility for working parents, is work at home. It appears that high technology may be moving us back to a form of cottage industry. Continental Bank of Chicago, for example, is presently conducting an experiment which involves the installation of word processors in employees' homes and the transmission of information over sophisticated communications equipment.

These options, relating to the need for more time, call for radical changes in the traditional structure of work and in traditional management practices. While child-care providers may not possess the expertise to advise corporations about alternative work scheduling, it is essential that employers remain open to the possibility that more flexibility in their employees' work hours may be the most helpful solution.

STRATEGIES FOR EXPANDING CHILD CARE THROUGH EMPLOYER INVOLVEMENT

While it is critical that parent need to be the focus of efforts to stimulate a corporate response, attention to parent needs is also imperative for the survival of child care. It appears that parents will play an increasingly influential role in determining the kinds of child care services that survive during the present difficult economic period in the United States.

The only federal legislation from which providers might directly benefit in the next few years is expansion of the child-care tax credit. (Less beneficial directly to preschool providers are legislative proposals to expand school-age child-care services and information and referral programs.) While "supply-side" economics is fashionably applied elsewhere, the term "demand-side" economics is more appropriate for child care.[4] The tax credit does not directly increase the supply of child care, but rather gives available funding to parents to purchase the child care of their choice. Where federal monies are available for direct funding as in the case of Title XX programs, states may administer the flow of dollars through consumer voucher systems. Like the tax credit, this mechanism favors parent choice. In the Boston, Massachusetts area, the Child Care Resource Center is responsible for $1 million of the state's tax levy funds. Parents come to the center to learn about their child care choices. They then pay a portion of the cost of care for choosing a participating program, and the Resource Center reimburses the provider for the remainder. All of Florida's public child care is funded through a vouchering program. Families, Inc. located in Austin, Texas, has also set up such a system for the expenditure of employer dollars.

Some employers seem more willing to consider voucher plans than on-site centers. For large companies with a diverse parent population, perhaps located in several sites around the country, the creation of one day care program will obviously not serve the needs of all concerned. Subsidies to employees through a voucher system may help a greater number of employees as well as favor parent choice. Parents receiving a subsidy are not limited to the particular form of care chosen by their employer; they may purchase care close to home if they prefer or choose between family day care or center-based care. If parents are able to pay for child care but cannot find their preferred form of care, the underlying theory of our free enterprise system suggests that there will be a new growth of services to meet the new demand —that is what supply-side and demand-side economics are all about.

Child Care Community Response

If these patterns emerge as predicted here, the child care community, as it is presently established, may be unprepared to respond appropriately to the demand. First, there is the practical problem of start-up funds. More debilitating, however, is that fact that early childhood educators know little about parent choice. Studies of child-care comsumers have been few. To a certain

---

[4] In "supply-side" economics, the focus is placed on stimulating the supply of services available to those who need (or demand) such services; funding of programs is a "supply-side" activity. Putting dollars into the hands of those (e.g., parents) who demand the services is a "demand-side" activity.

extent, child care providers do not recognize the fact that they serve the whole family. While companies may be remiss in not having family profiles of their employees, one may well ask how many child care programs have a work profile on the parents of the children they serve.

While early childhood educators seem ready to acknowledge their role as it relates to children, they seem less ready to acknowledge that they serve parent needs as well—possibly because, to accept the latter, they must simulaneously accept the custodial role they play in society. The connotation of a custodial role is that educators are merely "babysitters," a function not requiring the commitment of professional skills. But in fact the derivation of custodial is "custody." For most parents the initial reason for seeking child care services is that they need to place their children in someone else's custody because they must work out of economic necessity. This is not to say that they do not seek or appreciate the developmental services that can indeed enrich the social, emotional, and intellectual lives of their children. But for most parents, the impetus for seeking child care services would seem to be their need for custodial care. In fact, it is *only* the custodial function of child care that public policy has addressed, for it is this function that justifies the investment in child care on the part of both government and the business community.

As explained earlier, government invests in child care because they want parents to go to work, thus reducing welfare dependency. Business considers child care support so they can recruit parents to work or help those already working to work better. Both these sectors view child care as an important investment because they need working parents to reduce deficits and increase profits. Quality in child care has almost always been an afterthought. Safety and health are to be protected without question, but developmental care is a luxury. This lack of attention to quality on the part of benefactors is a direct indication that child care is viewed more as a support to parents than as a contribution to the lives of children.

The unwillingness of child care providers to consider their role in meeting parents' needs for child care as being equally important as their role in meeting children's needs is one cause of their ineffectiveness in convincing government and business of the importance of child care. The three parties have not found the common ground on which to base a discussion.

Child-care Consultants Fever

The current emergence of corporate child care consultants who focus exclusively on on-site centers highlights the misguided nature of child care advocacy. The burgeoning of the child care consultant role characterizes the reaction to the prospect of corporate involvement in child care. Most would-be "consultants," so named because very few have any company contracts, have as their primary area of expertise the planning and running of a day care center. Their pursuit of on-site centers is based on three erroneous assumptions: (a) that business wants to build day care centers, (b) that parents want their children in them, and (c) that the community is incapable of providing needed services. Where on-site care works, it works well, but as discussed earlier, day care centers may not satisfy either management agendas or parent needs. One danger of trying to sell on-site care is that, while those promoting the concept may be effective sales people, their programs may fail. At the beginning stages of a movement, these failures not only impede progress but may move us back a few steps. Because early efforts are so few in number, they are more visible and hence more influential. Corporations look to other businesses experiences, and failures will be seriously considered. Thus, early failures hurt everyone in the field.

The second danger of consultants' marketing on-site care is that it may ultimately undermine the existing child care system, crafted over a period of two decades. Why should a company start an on-site center when the terrific Title XX center up the block is about to close for lack of funds? Even if the community program is not of high quality, why not improve it with the infusion of corporate dollars? The most significant danger of an inappropriate peddling of on-site care is that it may neglect parent preference. Those whose only expertise is in the establishment of day care centers are acting more out of self-interest than are the corporations which hope to solve their management problems with day care. It is only with attention to the variety of ways in which parent needs can be addressed that we may find the common ground on which to negotiate with employers and ultimately serve children. In short, a look at the alternatives to on-site day care centers is not only more responsive to parent and child needs, it is also more attractive to the employer.

The increase in number of consultants is to a large degree understandable. There is the hope that corporate contracts will provide them with the respect, money, and professionalism that elude them as directors and teachers in child care programs. One of the largest problems in retaining very dedicated and talented day care directors is the short career ladder they climb. Is there life after directing? And what kind? Consulting to business about the child care needs of employees appears to be the pot of gold at the end of the child-care rainbow.

Of course, many consultants who move beyond their experience as early childhood educators deserve the respect and income they seek. These consultants travel to various companies and communities to learn about the successes and failures of employer-supported child care. They attend conferences, make contacts, establish networks, and open themselves to new ways of thinking about the issues. Some have hired a team of management consultants, benefits specialists, and personnel and tax experts who complement their own child-care skills. They have recognized the complexity of the marketing choices and ultimately of the choices that must be made in properly advising employers. They recognize that by working with other child-care groups they may derive benefits for themselves in the long run. They understand that competitive consulting and information sharing are not mutually exclusive activities. And they remain respectful of parent choice and the existing child-care community. If any consultants succeed, they will be those with this kind of sophistication. For the next few years, however, everyone must contend with obstacles in the economy and the market.

THE FUTURE

With whatever crystal ball policy analysts are equipped, I am prepared to say that within the next 3 to 5 years, employer supports to working parents will increase dramatically in number and variety. Those practices currently in place suggest only the realm of possibility. Unfortunately, the ability of the business community to respond to the immediate survival needs of child-care programs is diminished by a variety of forces.

Obstacles to Employer-supported Care

The economy.   Growth in employer-supported child care is seriously hampered by the recession. The current economic climate does not lend itself to experimentation with programs that are potentially costly. Until there are many more companies with experience providing child care supports or there is data substantiating the economic wisdom of each support, many companies will place child care on a back burner. The lack of research on the extent to which provision of child-care support can ameliorate management problems by reducing turnover and absenteeism or by improving productivity and recruitment efforts is another serious obstacle to the immediate growth in the number of companies supporting child care.

Equity.   In addition to the economic climate and the general lack of research, a third obstacle is posed by the issue of equity. Employers are concerned that if parent employees receive a child-care benefit, their nonparent employees will demand a benefit of equal value. However, companies with child-care programs suggest that to date this has not been a problem. In fact, employers already providing family supports contend that they receive from all their employees considerably more positive than negative feedback on the provision of family benefits. (For those with on-site centers, *all* employees derive pleasure from watching little "Pac Men" and "E.T.'s" march through the office on Halloween. It humanizes the workplace.) Also, inequities already exist in benefit plans. For example, single employees do not receive equal value in pension plans because of spouse-only benefits.

One way of avoiding discrimination is to adopt a system of flexible benefits in which employees choose the benefits most appropriate to their needs. More and more companies are coming to realize that most benefit packages were designed for the male breadwinner with a spouse and children at home—a design inappropriate for all but 4.8% of American families, according to Bureau of Labor Statistics.[5] Only a few companies have implemented flexible benefits (only some including child care), and these have met with mixed success. Such a system is difficult to administer because companies usually have to manage thousands of individual benefit packages.

In the 50-odd companies with flexible benefits, a core set of benefits is offered, covering basic benefit areas: retirement, medical, disability, life insurance, and vacations. "Flexible credits" are given to employees based on salary and tenure to augment their benefits package as desired. A young single parent whose time with children is more valuable than increased retirement benefits may thus apply credits to vacation days. An older employee will probably choose more retirement.

Benefits specialists predict more wide-scale adoption of flexible benefits as more experimentation occurs. Child care is likely to become one of those benefit choices because of passage of the Dependent Care Assistance Plan (DCAP) as part of the 1981 Economic Recovery Act. Now part of the Internal Revenue Service code, Section 129 of the DCAP makes corporate expenditures for child care (and care for elderly parents and handicapped dependents) not taxable to employee or employer. This plan makes child care very easy to insert into a flexible benefits program. A variation of the flexible benefits approach, the Salary Reduction Plan, may also result in more care, although it has not yet been approved by the Internal Revenue Service. Under this plan the employee may reduce his or her salary by a certain amount and receive the difference as pre-tax dollars which can be used for child care. Notably, this plan may be of little help to low-income parents, who cannot afford a reduced salary.

Equity becomes an obstacle at another level: namely, equity within the corporate system between company headquarters and local home offices. Headquarter offices do not wish to antagonize local offices and hesitate offering child care unless it is made available to all. At the same time, local offices claim they want to move ahead with supports to families, but feel constrained by headquarters. This same control issue arises between parent companies and their subsidiaries. A data processing firm in Massachusetts, for example, was ready to build an on-site center, but was stopped by the parent company. A Chicago subsidiary, on the other hand, went against the wishes of its parent company, by starting a day care center without official sanction.

---

[5] The Bureau of Labor Statistics, March 1981, has indicated that there are 2.9 million married couple families with only the husband working and with two children. This number equals 4.8% of all families and 9% of families with children.

The solution to this equity problem may entail a willingness on the part of the headquarter/parent company to establish broad policy while allowing the local branches to design their own programs according to headquarter/parent company guidelines. For instance, the broad policy might be that only licensed child-care facilities could be used and that a child-care subsidy may not exceed a set monetary limit. The local site is then able to reflect the specific needs of its employee population and the resources in the community to determine the most appropriate form of subsidy.

An interesting irony surrounding the equity issue is that the problem does not occur when subsidiaries of a United States based company are located overseas. In these instances, the overseas subsidiaries offer the same services to their employees that national companies do in those countries. For instance, Levi Strauss in Argentina and IBM in Italy both sponsor day care centers. In some cases when foreign employees of such companies relocate in the United States, their firms give them the cash value of the child-care benefit they received in their home country. While headquarter offices are able to acknowledge and accept the differences in cultures overseas, they apparently cannot see the importance of varying cultures in different parts of America (i.e., that the needs in the headquarter community may differ from those in a subsidiary site elsewhere in the country).

Values.   Yet another obstacle to the growth of corporate involvement is more elusive and difficult to change: our value system. In a time of rapid social change, a level of uncertainty accompanies decision making. And because someone must make decisions, there must be personal discretion. As Kanter (1977) observes in her examination of corporate practice, discretion raises not technical but human and social questions or values. The issue of child care does not personally touch most decision makers in our society, and at a deeper level there may even exist an ambivalence about women working, about child care, and about corporate involvement in family life. These issues should be acknowledged, for they help shape the education and consciousness-raising that must be sustained if any of these obstacles are to be removed.

Child-care market.   Finally, we must consider the obstacle presented by the quality of the existing child-care market, for which we are soliciting corporate support. If service providers hope to persuade companies to purchase their services or help employees pay for them, those services must be of such quality that employers have confidence in their ability to satisfy workers. For some, the notion of corporate involvement is posed as the panacea for child-care program woes. In truth, however, the poor quality of many child-care services may impede corporate commitment rather than inspire involvement. To elaborate, if child care is to fulfill the purpose for which it was intended (let us assume for the moment, a reduction in absenteeism), then it must be of high quality. A poor-quality program is very unstable and likely to close at any time with little warning. If parents are left to find other care, then the company has not eased the burden on the parent or on itself. Therefore, efforts made to involve corporations should be accompanied by efforts to expand and improve the existing market of services.

The strategic use of evaluation research can be critical here. In a study conducted at High/Scope (Schweinhart, 1981), results indicated that economic savings can accrue for a community when child care is provided. However, implicit in the findings of the study was the suggestion that such effects of child care are positive only when the program is of a high quality. The National Association for the Education of Young Children (NAEYC) is attempting to address the quality issue more directly. Recently, NAEYC announced plans to serve as an accrediting agency for day care centers, both nonprofit and proprietary (Bowman, 1982). The association's "seal of approval" could be an important contribution.

The Prognosis

Despite current problems, my faith in the continuous emergence of employer-supported child care is based on a variety of factors. First, there is likely to be some improvement in the economy. This will enable companies to move from the research stage into implementation. Second, benefits specialists predict that the institution of flexible benefits may be 3 to 5 years down the road. The equity issue is a real concern and flexible benefits effectively eliminate it. The non-taxability of child care for employee and employer through the Dependent Care Assistance Plan makes child care an uncomplicated addition to flexible benefits program. It is likely that employer support of child care will burgeon simultaneously with flexible benefits programs.

Third, in 3 years time, a number of companies will have had their programs in place long enough to generate decent evaluation research. The experiences of other companies and the data to substantiate program effectiveness will provide convincing evidence to those who were willing to take fewer risks in earlier years. There is, of course, the possibility that these efforts toward family support will not prove efficacious. In that case, there would have to be a reassessment of the merits upon which to rest family benefits.

In the near future, the federal and state governments will perhaps have defined more clearly their roles in shaping the emergence of employer support for child care, removing barriers and constructing incentives in the process. Furthermore, those service providers still in existence in 3 to 5 years will have experienced the phenomenon of "survival of the fittest." Program closings, mergers, and more professional management styles will characterize the social services during this period. Technology may augment the capacity to monitor supply and demand with such innovations as computerized information and referral. In 5 years time, then, the child-care market could well be in a better position to sell its services to the business community.

Unions will have made progress in recruitment among women, technical, and white-collar workers. These employees are in industries experiencing a demand for labor and looking for innovative ways to recruit labor in short supply. This means that unions, currently benign in their child-care efforts, may begin to exert more pressure on management to offer child care assistance. This pressure may be instigated by workers in the baby-boom generation, who, because of their sheer numbers, will be employed in jobs without opportunities for advancement. Caught in what is called the "pyramid squeeze," employers may have to respond by providing new, attractive fringe benefits to compensate for the loss in expected job mobility. Child care may well be included in this effort.

The values that permeate our culture and affect our views of the world will take many years to change. However, we can begin a process of education that may help bring about a level of awareness regarding the family-work interface. The next step is understanding, then commitment. For the present, I believe we are in an education phase. Employers need to understand the impact of work on family life and to be shown the reciprocal effects of family concerns on work. Service providers need to be educated about the workings of corporate decision making and the most effective ways of influencing it. Yet, while more widespread adoption of child care benefits is a few years away, the business community will still be faced with an increased demand by employees for child care services. One thing seems certain: If an employer role in service delivery and family benefits is to emerge successfully, it must proceed incrementally.

IMPLICATIONS OF EMPLOYER-SUPPORTED CHILD CARE

Potentially negative consequences of employer involvement also need to be addressed if we are to effectively shape the emergence of the employer role in child-care and family-supported services. When we talk about employer supports to working parents, we are talking about a self-interested, profit-oriented institution having a greater say in the lives of families. Are we therefore promoting a "cradle to grave" benefits situation, raising a society dependent on the private dole? And if we use tax deductions as incentives to business to provide child care, have we really increased the amount of revenues available for child care, or have we merely shifted the onus of responsibility from the public to the private sector?

Lessons from the public sector suggest that many of our current problems are the result of our earlier problem solving. Problem solving is often a hydraulic process in which solutions to one problem merely displace the problem to another level. Even with the best of intentions, it is possible that provision of child care as an employee benefit may thwart efforts to raise wages to more equitable levels, particularly for women. Similarly, while part-time work may be preferred and advocated by many, part-time workers earn less. It may also mean less financial security if prorated benefits do not accompany wages.

Not all employers can or will respond to the needs of their parents employees. Many parents work in small companies; they may work in dying industries, or they may be unemployed. Further, what responsibility does the business community have for parents not in their employ? Is it possible that the parents who benefit from corporate involvement will be those in the middle- and upper-income brackets? Given that demand for labor is a driving force, and that labor in short supply is generally skilled and highly paid, it seems possible that less-skilled parents will be left to rely on decreasing, publicly supported programs.

It would help if it could be shown that corporate self-interest can be served by helping *all* parents in the community with child care. To the extent that more members of society are contributing meaningully to the economy rather than receiving welfare, the private sector will benefit. If an economically healthy community helps business, then there is a long range pay-off to companies investing in the child-care component of economic and community development efforts. However, American management has traditionally focused on the short-term payoffs. Suggestions for preventive efforts, such as child care, often fall on deaf ears.

Certain employer-supported child care initiatives raise some fundamental questions concerning the value of childrearing in our society. The $100 per month subsidy offered by Measurex to persuade employees to return sooner from maternity leave is a case in point. Whereas in Sweden and most other industrialized nations a family allowance is designed to help mothers stay home with their children (Kamerman & Kahn, 1979), in the United States we appear to be encouraging their earlier separation.

Perhaps the most serious of all potential consequences of employer-supported child care initiatives concerns an inference that may be made about the quality of work performed by working parents. If the feasibility of child care is best justified in terms of its ability to improve productivity and solve management problems, then that justification has within it the assumption that, without the employer's child care assistance, parents are not as effective workers and perhaps should not be hired. Even in a tight labor market, such attitudes may not always prevent the hiring of parents, but they might affect the way parents are treated once on the job. Also, the mandating of child care as a fringe benefit, as the Florida legislature has considered doing, would, in effect, make it more expensive to hire parents.

An overambitious policy such as this might open the door to widespread discrimination against working parents (particularly women, who are the most likely to seek child care).

Although presenting child care as a panacea for all of management's problems provides a convincing case for its provision, such an argument can be dangerous. Child care has long been advocated as a means of reducing poverty, helping children succeed in school, and preventing a later life of crime and delinquency. But Grey (cited in Ryan, [1976]) points out with regard to Head Start programs that

> An effective early intervention program for a preschool child, be it ever so good, cannot possibly be viewed as a form of innoculation whereby the child is immunized forever afterward to the effects of an inadequate home and a school inappropriate to his needs. (p. 136)

Similarly, child care cannot be expected to innoculate an employee against boredom or lackluster performance in a job that is inherently boring and lackluster. Nor can it immunize an employee against the effects of poor working conditions and a management system inappropriate to his or her own needs.

Government policies have not been particularly family- or child-focused. Similar patterns are emerging in corporate personnel policies relating to families. Without a concern for the child, there is a chance of skimping on quality—an action with possible negative, long term consequences. Further, the quality of child-care programs is largely determined by the quality of the staff, and the staff of child-care programs are notoriously underpaid and overworked (Whitebook, Howes, Darrah, & Friedman, 1982). A discussion of the benefits and work conditions of employees in corporate America cannot ignore employees engaged themselves in child care programs. Given that approximately 60 to 80% of the cost of operating a center is absorbed by staff (Abt Associates, 1977), it is difficult to make a profit in child care without cutting back on salaries. If a company, well-intentioned about meeting its employees' child-care needs, recommends an inexpensive or underfunded program, a company may, in the process of serving its own employees, exploit the employees of the child-care program and contribute to the reduced quality of child-care service. Without a concern for the quality of the child-care programs in which employees' children are placed, there may be no overall easing of parental concern.

These consequences cannot be overlooked during the initial phases of an employer presence in family support services. Because this presence is relatively new, there is a great need for careful planning and analysis. The rationales and foundations established today for employer involvement will have lasting effects on later developments. As Amory Houghton (cited in Baden & Friedman, 1981), Chair of the Board of Corning Glass, has said, "One percent of all companies want to be first and 99 percent want to be second'' (p. 23). What motivates that 1% is very important to the 99% who follow.

Those of us in the field have the opportunity to shape the emergence of an employer role in child care. It is a formidable task requiring considerable rethinking to assure that a high quality of care is preserved and that parent preference is respected. It is also one of the most creative and exciting tasks ever placed before the child-care community. We need only heed the lessons learned in the public sector. When we asked for universal comprehensive child care, we achieved nothing. Perhaps an incremental approach will work in the private sector. As Lindblom (1968), a scholar of the policy process, observes:

> Policymaking is typically a never-ending process of successive steps in which continual nibbling may be a substitute for a good bite. (p. 25)

Bon appétit.

REFERENCES

Abt Associates. *Day care centers in the United States.* Washington, DC: Department of Health, Education, and Welfare, Administration for Children, Youth, and Families, 1977.

Baden, C., & Friedman, D. *New management initiatives for working parents: Report of a conference.* Boston: Wheelock College, 1981.

*Besner, A. *Day care services: Industry's involvement* (Bulletin 296). Washington, DC: Department of Labor, Women's Bureau, 1971. (ERIC Document Reproduction Service No. ED 056 757)

Bowman, B. Recognition for quality in centers for young children. *Young Children,* January 1982, *37*(2), 33–34.

Brasch, P. A helping hand from the boss. *Parade,* June 8, 1980, 6.

Catalyst Career and Family Center. *Corporations and two-career families: Directions for the future.* New York: Catalyst Career and Family Center, 1981.

Child Care Resource Service Newsletter, April 1981, *1*(4), 3.

Feinstein, K. W. (Ed.). *Working women and families* (Vol. 4), Beverly Hills, CA: Sage Publications, 1979.

Fishel, Balodis, & Klaus. *Appalachian Regional Commission Employer-Supported Day Care Study: Final report.* Washington, DC: Appalachian Regional Commission, 1982.

Harris, L. *Families at work: Strengths and strains,* Minneapolis, MN: The General Mills American Family Report, 1981.

Kamerman, S. B., & Kahn, A. *Family Policy.* New York: Columbia University Press, 1978.

Kamerman, S. B., & Kahn, A. The day care debate: A wider view. *The Public Interest,* Winter 1979, 76–93.

Kanter, R. M. *Men and women of the corporation.* New York: Basic Books, 1977.

Keniston, K. *All our children.* New York: Harcourt Brace Jovanovich, 1977.

Lindblom, C. *The policy making process* (2nd ed.) Englewood Cliffs, NJ: Prentice-Hall, 1968.

Milkovich, G. T., & Gomez, L. R. Day care and selected employee work behaviors. *Academy of Management Journal,* March 1976, 111–113.

Morgan, G. *Studies of day care from a consumer perspective.* Unpublished manuscript, 1980. (Available from the author, Wheelock College, Boston, MA.)

National Academy of Sciences. *Toward a national policy for children and families.* Washington, DC: National Research Council, Advisory Committee on Child Development, 1976.

*Perry, K. S., & Moore, G. T. *Employers and child care: Establishing services through the workplace.* Pamphlet 23. Washington, DC: Department of Labor, Women's Bureau, 1981. (ERIC Document Reproduction Service No. ED 198 950)

Pleck, J. Men's family work: Three perspectives and some new data. *The Family Coordinator,* October 1979, 481–488.

Project Connections. *A study of child care information and referral services, Phase I.* Cambridge, MA: American Institute of Research, 1980.

*Rodes, T., & Moore, J. *National child care consumer study.* (Vol. 1: Basic tabulations). Washington, DC: Department of Health, Education, and Welfare, Office of Child Development, 1975. (ERIC Document Reproduction No. ED 131 933)

Ryan, S. Overview. In S. Ryan (Ed.), *A report of longitudinal evaluations of preschool programs* (Vol. 1). Washington, DC: Department of Health, Education, and Welfare, 1976.

Schweinhart, L. Research report: High quality early childhood programs for low-income families pay for themselves. Ypsilanti, MI: High/Scope Educational Research Foundation, 1981.

Smith, R. (Ed.). *The subtle revolution.* Washington, DC: The Urban Institute, 1979.

Toffler, A. *The third wave.* New York: Bantam, 1981.

*Welfare Research, Inc. *On-site day care: The state of the art and models development.* Albany, NY: Welfare Research, Inc., 1980. (ERIC Document Reproduction Service No. ED 208 977)

Whitbread, J. Who's taking care of the children? *Family Circle,* February 20, 1979, 9.

*Whitebook, M., Howes, C., Darrah, R., & Friedman, J. Caring for the caregivers: Staff burnout in child care. In L. Katz, C. Watkins, P. Wagemaker, & M. Spencer (Eds.), *Current topics in early childhood education* (Vol. 4). Norwood, NJ: Ablex Publishing Corporation, 1982. (ERIC Reproduction Service No. ED 188 764)

Yankelovich, D. *New rules.* New York: Random House, 1981.

8

Factors Affecting Policies in Early Childhood Education: An Australian Case*

Jacqueline J. Goodnow and Ailsa Burns

Macquarie University, North Ryde, Australia

INTRODUCTION

Early childhood educators and advocates are often faced with the task of trying to make sense of federal and state policies. This involvement may come from the wish to understand events or from the hope of designing a change in policy and having it implemented. For either goal—understanding or introducing change—Takanishi (1977) has argued for an historical perspective, especially one which attempts both to describe and to analyze the social context in which change or an attempt at change occurs. How to analyze the social context, however, is by no means obvious. A major purpose of the present paper is to suggest some ways of doing so.

Takanishi's (1977) argument for a more analytic social history is part of her account of shifts in federal involvement in early education from 1933 to 1973, within the USA. The history offered here covers a briefer period (1970 to 1980) and a different country—Australia. During this time in Australia, federal policies veered from providing restricted preschool and day care programs, to a plan for universal preschool and expanded day care, and then returned to a position close to the original one. Similar changes in federal policies have been noted by Takanishi for the United States and by Tizard (1976) for England. We wish to use the Australian events as a way of asking a question that could apply in any country: What factors are involved in policy variations?

Broadly speaking, there are two routes towards answering that question. One is to look at policy variations across countries. Chazan (1978), for

---

* We are much indebted to Deborah Brennan for pre-publication access to her material.

189

instance, provides a set of descriptions of early childhood policies in a number of countries in which provisions for preschool and/or day care range from being almost completely absent to being close to universal. The second route is to look at policy variations within a country. These historical accounts may be long-term and cover a range of services for children (Ariès, 1962; Kessen, 1979; Rosenkrantz, 1978; White, Day, Freeman, Hartman, & Messenger, 1973, provide examples). Or they may concentrate on a shorter time span, on recent events, and on early childhood programs, as Takanishi (1977) has done and as we propose doing. This second route provides a sharper focus. It also has the particular advantage of allowing us to work from several sources: written documents, verbal reports, and our own memory of events.

Selecting a route or general method, however, is only part of the story. Takanishi (1977) has argued strongly for a social history that is not purely descriptive, and with this we would agree. In particular, we wish to start by taking up three of her arguments: (a) that the account must describe the social context (p. 160), (b) that it must consider "social, political, and economic conditions" (p. 155), and (c) that there "must be room for the impact of different ideologies, strongly held assumptions about childhood, the family, and the role government should play in the lives of young children" (p. 160).

Ideologies and Their Impact

Ideologies and their impact provide the first major factor we wish to examine. We use the term "ideologies" to cover the ideas people hold both about the way things are and the way they ought to be: in more formal terms, both the cognitive and normative aspects of knowledge or of consciousness (Berger, Berger, & Kellner, 1974). In our history these ideas appear to have several forms of impact. They provide a basis for feelings, in the sense that when expectations are met, people have a sense that everything is in order. When they are not met, the result is a sense of alarm and a conviction that a problem exists where it did not before. More subtly, ideologies provide the categories or divisions in terms of which people think: distinctions, for example, between "care" and "education," "mothers" and "working mothers," private" and "public" areas of responsibility. Of particular importance is the concept of "need," either in terms of a total group (e.g., all children) or in terms of a subgroup who have "special needs." Ideologies provide, as well as the terms of an appeal, the basis of an argument or an attempt to persuade. Finally, they provide the basis for friction, for a failure not only to cooperate effectively but even to understand what another party is attempting to do.

Interested Parties and Their Resources

The second major factor we wish to point to consists of interested parties and their resources. A cast of characters is a standard part of any history. Attention to resources is less standard. We have taken the concept of resources primarily from sociological studies of interactions within the family, studies that ask who holds what resources, and what the expected pattern is for an equitable exchange of resources: my physical, financial, or moral support, for instance, in exchange for your deference, fidelity, affection, or commitment to bringing up the children (cf. Scanzoni & Scanzoni, 1976). We have found the concept helpful in analyzing the impact of changes in family patterns (Burns & Goodnow, 1978; Goodnow & Burns, 1980). We find it again useful in this look at shifts in federal policy. No account of federal policy, for instance, can ignore the resource of money. We have found it equally necessary to consider a less obvious resource, namely the presence of procedures, channels, or "machineries" that can be brought into action whenever an issue arises.

With these two general factors sketched out, let us turn to the specific events and see how they both illustrate the general factors and point to further conditions affecting the making and unmaking of policy.

EVENT 1: 1970

During an election year, then Prime Minister Gorton (of the Liberal-Country Party, the more conservative of Australia's two main political parties) announced that the government intended to establish a network of "preschool-cum-childminding centers."

This announcement was a major shift in policy. Despite pressure from a variety of groups during the 1920s, the federal government had stuck to its policy of defining education as a *state* rather than federal responsibility, except at the tertiary or postsecondary level. (In Australia, all universities are federally funded.) At this tertiary level, the government had been moving towards more direct involvement in the training of teachers and caregivers for children below the age of 5, stepping a little beyond its existing commitment to teacher training for primary and secondary schools. This funding, however, was for teacher training and not directly for children's services. Up to 1970, direct support for children's services had been largely limited to the period during World War II, when many young mothers moved to war work. The Federal Ministry of Health then set up a system of subsidized creches, or day care centers. Subsidy lapsed after the end of the war, as it did in the USA (Takanishi, 1977).

Why should the new federal policy be so surprising? And how did it come about? For these questions, we need to consider the social context and the impact of some particular lines of evidence and argument.

The Social Context

The Australian scene was and is marked by a set of distinctions and values that structure all discussion and thought about services for young children.

Forms of service.   A sharp distinction is drawn between "preschool" (or "kindergarten") and "day care." Preschools offer short sessions (usually 2½ hours) to children age 3 years of more. Day care centers are open for up to 12 hours a day, and some accept children younger than a year. Buildings for either type of service are typically separate from each other and from other elementary schools. The state of Queensland, as Ashby (1980) has noted in an earlier volume of this series, is an exception. There the two types of service have been covered for some time by one association (Kindergarten and Creche Association); in recent years, the shift has been to attach most preschools to primary schools under the control of the Queensland Department of Education.

This distinction between preschool and day care echoes Takanishi's (1977) description of the situation in the United States:

> Historically, within American society...the nursery school was to pro-
> vide an educational program for children of the middle and upper
> classes; the day care centers, run by social welfare agencies, were to pro-
> vide all day "custodial" care for children who fitted within identified
> categories of "problems" (p. 141).

As Takanishi points out, no hard and fast distinction exists in reality between preschool and day care. It is a distinction, however, that is still deeply
imbedded in Australian arguments about services for young children. A
conceptual distinction might have little impact or be easy to undo if it were
not supported by other factors. In the Australian case, this distinction has
been supported by differences in the history, clientele, forms of training,
and professional associations of the two types of service. Historically, day
care centers in Australia have always been oriented towards women who
earned money outside the home. The assumption—and until recent times
the reality—was that the major reason for women taking such work was
economic necessity.

In contrast, kindergartens had a more checkered history. Originally,
they had been established for the benefit of the poor, with an eye to improving the quality of motherhood and of care within the home. The kindergarten was to serve as a model, assisted by middle-class kindergarten teachers,
who would make "home visits." After World War II, however, middle-

class parents began to set up kindergartens for their *own* children. The change has been related to the diminished number of other adults in the house (both paid domestic help and extended family), the relative isolation of young mothers in new suburbs, and a change in mothers' expectations, both about their own development and their responsibility to provide preschool experience for their children's optimal development (Burns, 1978; Spearritt, 1974). These kindergartens were still, however, perceived as an addition to family care, with the latter covering the major part of the day.

Along with the difference in clientele went a difference in staff training. Separate training colleges were established in most states. The state of New South Wales (Australia's most populous state), for instance, has the Kindergarten Teachers College and the Nursery Teachers College. In 1982, the two were merged—by federal fiat—into a single Institute of Early Childhood, with a single director.) Not surprisingly, teachers also belonged to different professional associations. It was not until the late 1970s that a single Association for Early Childhood was established, combining members of the two main groups.

Do such distinctions matter? Two immediate effects may be noted at this point. At the professional level, the distinction between "care" and "education" led to a lack of communication and trust between the two groups, making them a less effective lobby than they might have been. At the funding level, the lack of overlap escalated the cost of developing services for children. What was being asked for was the separate development of services, buildings, and training colleges. Any effort at expansion would have to come to terms with a double drain. This was not a major problem as long as the double line was privately financed (from fees, philanthropic sources, and drives to raise funds from the general public). Once resources were sought from a single federal purse, however, cost became a factor and duplication a source of concern. The distinction between preschool and day care had to be faced and, as we shall see, the two-system approach ended, if at all possible.

Values and labels.   Allied to the two forms of service is a set of values and labels. Preschool supervisors usually describe their role as "educational," applying the term "custodial" to other forms of care (day care, after-school care, or emergency care). Few people can be as indignant as the preschool teacher who sees his or her service being treated as custodial by mothers seeking to be "free" of their children. (Mothers who arrive dressed for tennis or golf are spoken of with special scorn.)

The critical underlying values, however, are those related to the expected role of the family, especially of the mother, and linked to the concept of young children as being especially vulnerable and of early experience as critical and probably irreversible in its effects. The pervasive belief was that men had paid work, while women kept houses and raised children, exclusively and single-handedly. In the words of two middle-class women interviewed by Burns in 1978: "I deplore the idea of women seeking baby-minding help when it is not absolutely necessary"; and "I wouldn't think of going to work while my children are young, no matter what I needed."

Such values were in themselves part of a wider social context. They reflect a time period (from 1946 to 1970) that one family historian in the United States (Glick, 1975) has called the most "familistic" on record. Within Australia, marriage became all but universal, and the number of marriages which remained childless shrank to about 10% (Borrie, 1975). John Bowlby's (1969) writings on "maternal deprivation" were widely read and used to substantiate the view that even brief separations from the mother (as opposed to the traumatic separations of hospitalization or the "stimulus deprivation" of sterile institutional care) caused irreparable harm. The critical period of early childhood development soon came to extend beyond the infant and toddler stage. One reputable film from the United States, popular in early childhood circles, had the daunting title *If at First You Don't Succeed, You Don't Succeed.* In this era, the concepts of "later is easier" and of "second chances" were definitely not in vogue.

Once again, an aspect of ideology might be easy to undo if it were not supported by other factors. In the present case, the stress on mothers being at home also fitted well with economic traditions. Government, business, and trade unions in Australia have all long shared the conviction that the unpaid work of women makes possible the paid work of men (Ryan & Rowse, 1975). Since 1907, that conviction has been embodied in the legal judgment that a man's wage should be calculated as a "family wage," covering the support of a dependent wife and children.

Do such values matter? Again, as Takanishi (1977) argues, we need not only to describe the prevailing ideas about children and families but also to ask about their impact. One immediate impact is on the kinds of argument one can present for an expansion of services. Advocates of preschools, for instance, have an advantage in a context where most people think of pre-schools as benefiting all children. The appeal can be framed in terms of children in general, with the underlying implication that the children who benefit are the children of the worthy middle-class, the group that both makes and responds to the appeal. Advocates of expanded day care are often in a more difficult position. They may operate in a context where day care is regarded as possibly damaging and where mothers wanting day care may be defined as indifferent to the best interests of even their own children. The clientele of day care centers can be denied support on the grounds that they are "undeserving," a classic maneuver in the denial or contraction of support (Goodnow, 1981). The people to be helped are "problem" families or "women who don't want to be women." As we shall see, the day care group needed to find a way out of the "small" and "undeserving" categories, as well as a way of arguing that they were not a deviant minority and that their cause was just.

Responsibilities of the private and public sectors.   At any time children may be regarded as part of an "eternal triangle" with the family and the state as the other two points (Goodnow & Burns, 1980). What shifts from one time to another is the division of labor and responsibility among the three parties, together with "access routes." There are times, for example, when the responsibility for children is regarded as almost exclusively the family's. The state steps in only in cases where the parent can be defined as clearly incompetent or markedly abusive. Assistance from the state to children is funnelled through the family (child endowment, paid directly to the mother, is an example). At other times, the state plays a more active role, and may intervene more readily, allowing children or minors direct access to services (e.g., to legal representation or to advice and assistance on contraception), without the parents' knowledge or even against the parents' wishes. The variations appear to reflect shifts in the state's perceived needs (e.g., for a population or a work force of a certain size), the state's resources, and the extent to which adopting or denying an obligation is perceived as an acceptable part of a political platform.

In the United States (Takanishi, 1977) and in the United Kingdom (Tizard, 1976), federal or state acceptance of responsibility for children of preprimary school age has consistently been reluctant, sporadic, confined to setting up "model" or "demonstration" programs that others are encouraged to continue, responsive largely to crises, and accompanied by a great deal of cautionary rhetoric. Australia fits the same tradition. Until the 1960s, almost all services for children under school age were privately financed. Support came partly from fees, but also from charity drives and the donations of both money and labor. The training colleges were also privately financed. Students paid fees and helped raise funds. In effect, the services were part of a philanthropic and self-help tradition.

The first clear break came during the period from 1968 to 1971, when the federal government began to provide grants to cover a major part of the building costs for training colleges in the early childhood area. This appeared to pave the way, but was still very distant from the announcement in 1970 of a plan to fund services directly through the establishment of "preschool and childminding centers."

We have sketched out so far three major features of the social context prior to 1970: (a) a distinction between "care" and "education"; (b) a set of values and labels, especially those related to the definition of early experience as critical and to the mother's role in the home; and (c) a distinction between "private" and "public" responsibility, with a federal government reluctant to extend its responsibility beyond the established school system.

Given such distinction and traditions, how did change come about? Several forms of evidence and argument appear to have set the stage, again revolving around the major factors of ideology, and interested parties and their resources.

Arguments for Change

Limited resources of the private sector.   Whether the form of service was preschool or day care, increasing professionalization was bringing a shift in resources and in costs. The drive for professional credentials is worth noting in itself. In any field of work, professionalization means higher wages, and a spiralling demand for higher and higher credentials. In the area of early childhood services, Joffe (1977) argues that a further factor is important. People wish to regard themselves as "experts" or as teachers. To use an Australian term, they prefer to describe themselves as "trained," in contrast to the untrained majority. Establishing such status, however, is especially difficult for people who teach or care for young children. Their jobs are often seen by the general public as being no different from what any well-intentioned mother with a little experience could do. The link to motherhood may even be made explicit in the arguments for training, as in the 1911 prospectus from the Sydney Kindergarten Teachers' College, which described teacher training as a way "to keep alive and develop more of the potential of motherhood" (p. 2). Where the "potential of motherhood" ends and the status of "trained teacher" or "expert caregiver" begins may be a boundary that, by its fuzziness, prompts teachers to search with special vigor for documentable ways of distinguishing between "us" and "them."

In the push for a clearer professional status, personnel argued for longer training, higher wages, and less reliance on volunteer help. The cost of care spiralled, both for the volunteers raising funds and for the families using services. The overall result was a need to turn more and more to other sources of funding. This was, in fact, the precise course taken in the late 1960s by the Children's Action Group (a group with a preschool base) who lobbied first the reluctant state government of New South Wales and then the federal government for financial support (Spearritt, 1974). For both governments, reasons were needed to justify their support, other than those based on financial difficulty. These reasons came in the form of there being a need that should be met, and of that need affecting large numbers of children.

An insufficient number of preschools.   In any modern society, an appeal to numbers is often a legitimizing argument (Berger, Berger, & Kellner, 1974). The early childhood area is no exception. Some significant numbers in the present case came from a 1970 survey by the Australian Council for

Educational Research on the proportions of eligible children attending pre-schools. The figures varied from state to state but were typically low: 52% in the Australian Capital Territory (an area similar in size to Washington, DC, with funds from federal sources); 29% in Victoria; 17% in South Australia; 13% in Queensland, Western Australia, and Tasmania; and 3% in the largest state, New South Wales.

The assumptions behind this survey and its use are of interest. The argument starts from the assumption that preschools are valuable either as a form of education in their own right or as a preparation for later formal schooling. Children need preschool education. To the extent that it is not provided, a loss of benefit exists. To the extent that it is provided to some children but not others, the loss of benefit is unequal. All such argument would be irrelevant, however, if the prevailing ideology did not contain the concept that children's needs should be met and that the level of inequality within the population should be a source of concern. As Takanishi (1977) notes, there is an in-built tension in societies that believe in both economic and political liberalism; people should be free to accumulate individual wealth and status, but the resulting gaps violate a sense of fairness and can provide a spark for reform.

Limited resources of the family.   Even if preschool education were not regarded as an asset and unequally available, evidence was accumulating that other aspects of children's needs were not being met in the expected way. The family picture was changing from the image of "father at work, mother at home."

Again, some of the prominent evidence consisted of numbers, especially numbers showing that many mothers in the paid labor force had preschool children. The evidence came from surveys in the late 1960s undertaken by the Women's Bureau within the Department of Labour and National Service, and from a Child Care Survey carried out in 1969 by the Commonwealth Bureau of Census and Statistics. These results shattered the illusion that few women, especially women with preschool children, were working outside the home. The 1969 survey was conducted as a result of pressure from the Australian Pre-School Association. Its results showed that some 270,000 preschool children had working mothers, and, of these, only an estimated 6% were in preschool centers. The majority were cared for by private minders, friends, or relatives.

Unsatisfactory care outside the home.   Burns and her colleagues (Burns, Fegan, Sparkes, & Thompson, 1975) found a majority of women working in the electrical trades dissatisfied with the arrangements they had to make for their children and in favor of a subsidized, "official" system. In addition, cases were reported of children being left unattended at home or in the care of a person least able to be employed in the usual labor force. Some of these cases were officially noted (e.g., a 1970 report by the Mental

Health Association of New South Wales, recommending preschool centers attached to factories). Some appeared in newspaper reports of household accidents. Many were noted in conversation among people involved in the early childhood field. These latter cases seemed to be almost invariably stories about "Mediterranean" families (of Turkish, Greek, or Italian background), and the goal of assimilating these people into the mainstream of Australian society provided another rationale for departing from the usual pattern of upholding care at home by mothers. (There could, for instance, have been an attempt at large-scale family support, or parent education, or campaigns persuading mothers not to work.) At the least, these case studies were an uncomfortable challenge to the Australian conscience, a conscience based on the conviction that young children deserve at least a "reasonable start in life," that Australia is "a lucky country," and that Australians are by and large fair. Since the case studies could be easily presented by the media and understood by all, a climate of some need could be established.

A Change in the Interested Parties

So far, we have been dealing with arguments for change, many of them presented by people associated with half-day preschools. (The Pre-School Association has a long tradition of support from upper middle-class women interested in philanthropy, including one woman whose family played a major role in Australian media—newspapers, radio, and television. As in other countries, children before school age are often the concern of "first ladies" but seldom of presidents.)

However, the set of interested parties was becoming more diverse. The labor market was expanding, and new workers were needed. Brennan (1982), for instance, notes a 1971 study carried out jointly by the Australian Clothing Manufacturers and the Department of Labour and National Service. Its conclusion was that increasing numbers of women would be needed for the expanding economy, and it recommended, as one inducement toward their return to work, the establishment of subsidized child-care centers. As both Tizard (1976) and Takanishi (1977) note, the expected need for women in the labor force overrides the belief in the necessity for young children to be cared for exclusively by mothers at home. Rosenkrantz (1978) makes a similar point with regard to ideas about the capacity of children—if employed at labor—to endure the usual conditions of paid work. The concept of physical and psychological unsuitability of children to work, she comments, coincided with a decreased need for them in the work force.

The number of women interested in paid work outside the home was also growing. Three groups of women were beginning to emerge, to whom the image of "men at work, women and young children at home" was unreasonable and often uncomfortable. One was a small group of well-educated women who wished to work. This group was to become larger, although even in 1974 Burns' survey of a middle-class group showed many women with strong professional qualifications (such as lawyers, doctors, and dentists) who regarded childrearing as a full-time role. The second group was larger; it consisted of new immigrant families who often combined the features of little ready money, a strong interest in upward mobility, little initial skill in English, unrecognized credentials, little knowledge of or ability to use what few community resources existed, and a background where a dependent, non-earning wife was not the norm. Within this group, both spouses often sought paid work, by necessity and/or choice. The third group—cutting across all others—consisted of a rising number of one-parent families, made up almost completely of women raising children without the presence or the adequate financial support of a male partner. For this group, the dominant ideology of "women at home" could not be observed and often rang hollow.

Overall, we have at this point factors for change on two sides. We have a federal government influenced by reports of a need for women in the labor force and by arguments that a gap exists between an image of reasonable concern for children and the existing services. We also have a set of interested parties pointing to specific ways in which the gap might begin to be closed. Action proceeded relatively slowly, however. In fact, it did not keep pace with further change in the interested parties, those parties' resources, or the type of argument presented for particular forms of assistance to young children and their families.

EVENT 2: 1972

In 1972, the Liberal-Country Party government passed the Child Care Act, which enabled the federal government to make capital grants (for building) and recurrent grants (for running costs) to nonprofit organizations providing child care. Funding was far from sufficient to allow unlimited support, however, a factor that brings up a recurring question in the provision of any selective service: How shall funding priority be established?

This question is both a thorn in the side of any funding agency and a boon in any analysis of the rationale or the ideology underlying policies. It has been answered at times in terms of the labor market, as in Tizard's (1976) report of special provisions in England in the 1960s for the children of nurses and teachers who were returning to work. In the Australian case, priority was established largely on a self-help basis: the government would fund in response to submissions by local groups rather than by designating priority areas, or, at this stage, by giving any blanket priority to individuals with "special needs."

The Child Care Act was passed with frequent reference in the course of parliamentary debate to the incipient dangers. As one senator who was later to become Minister for Social Welfare remarked, it was to be hoped that a sense of "parental responsibility" would dissuade parents of a child younger than 3 or 4 years of age from using the centers, unless the child had a single parent or a parent who was sick or incapacitated (cited by Brennan, 1982).

By now, however, the audience had begun to shift. The Women's Electoral Lobby was formed in 1972, aimed at uniting women from a variety of backgrounds. In addition, women's liberation groups were gathering strength. Both groups argued for a shift in the target of concern, to the quality of life for women. Both groups offered a challenge to the dominant ideology on two counts, namely that women should be exclusively at home (and were happiest there) and that day care was necessarily harmful to children. (As in the USA, research was felt to be needed to establish that the quality of care—at home or in a center—was the critical component.) Both groups also sought an alternative ideology. Often heard, for instance, was an argument by Margaret Mead: "We now expect the family to achieve alone what no other society has expected of such a small unit: in fact, we call on one or two adults to achieve alone what the whole clan used to do" (cited by McCaughey & Sebastian, 1977, p. 5). Since it was obviously neither fair nor reasonable—nor even possible—for small families to take up all this slack, the state should provide. In effect, all mothers and parents were now presented as "needy" or "deserving," by virtue of the nature of contemporary society.

Tizard (1976) reports a similar shift within England from arguments that were originally entirely child-centered to arguments that also took account of the needs of adults. His own position certainly illustrates both arguments, with a stress on the latter. He points out that "some programmes, and some nursery milieux, *have* been shown to have a remarkably powerful effect upon children's competencies" (Tizard, 1976, p. 153). At the same time, he gives the greater weight, in arguing for an expansion of services, to parents' interests and needs. The parents he stresses especially are the mothers of young children:

> A number of epidemiological studies indicate very clearly that, as compared with other women, and with women of older children, the majority of mothers of young children can in a real sense be regarded as disadvantaged. They are more likely to be poorer and worse housed and to have fewer services available to them. . . . Very many. . .suffer from severe psychological strain. (Tizard, 1976, p. 151)

Such widespread need provides, then, the basis for Tizard's advocacy of widely available services, as against selective services for cases of special need.

Arguments about the inevitable or "no-fault" needs of women with young children are an attempt to change the terms in which people think, especially to detach negative labels from women interested in their children receiving care and education outside the home. What the new lobbying groups needed, however, was a "machinery"—a way to have such views embodied in policy and action. They found it in the two-party system during an election year. The Australian Labour Party (ALP) was out of power but gaining support. It was seeking ways to attract the votes of women, since Australian women—like those in other countries—had typically been less inclined to vote Labour than men had been. Groups such as the Women's Electoral Lobby were designed to cut across political affiliations, but their interest in social change suggested a potential swing vote toward Labour, a party with a platform of social reform. Finally, the ALP was seeking ways to put into concrete form its general policy of social reform. And the man nominated to be the ALP Minister for Education if the election were won, Beazley, was well aware of the reports from Head Start and of Head Start's intended use as a means of bringing about social change. Beazley was also the member of Parliament who proposed an amendment to the Liberal Party's Child Care Act, urging the government to "establish Child Care Centers to meet the needs of working mothers" (cited by Brennan, 1982). In effect, he offered both rationales for expansion: advantages both for children and for women. The way was clear for at least a change of plan in policy.

EVENT 3: A NEW PARTY PLATFORM

During the election year of 1972, Labour's promise was (a) to make a year of preschool education available to every Australian child, and (b) to establish centers for child care. The policy was double-headed ("education" and "care"). So also was the rationale, legitimizing the initiative.

The first part of the rationale concerned advantages for children. The general theme of the ALP platform was a commitment to greater social equality. Equality of education was part of that theme (as both a means and an end). Preschool was "the area of greatest inequality of education" (speech by the Prime Minister-to-be E. G. Whitlam, Blacktown Civic Centre, November 13, 1972). It was also the route to equality: "the most important single weapon in promoting equality and in overcoming social, economic and language inequalities" (Commonwealth Parliamentary Debates, cited by Brennan, 1982, p. 13).

The second part of the rationale concerned the needs of women. Brennan (1982) cites Whitlam's policy speech:

> A woman's choice between making motherhood her sole career and following another career in conjunction with motherhood depends upon

the availability of proper child care facilities. The Pre-Schools Commission will be responsible for developing these facilities in conjunction with preschool centres, beginning in areas where the need is most acute. (p. 14)

The ALP won the election. Within ten weeks after taking office, the party set up a Pre-Schools Committee charged with implementing a double policy: (a) by the end of a 6-year period, the opportunity should exist for all children to have a year of preschool education, and (b) child-care centers should be provided to "meet the needs of children of working parents and underprivileged families" (*Committee's Terms of Reference*, cited by Brennan, 1982, p. 16).

At this point, there emerged most clearly two recurring problems in policies for early education. One is that resources are seldom equal to the initial promises or to the goal of equality. If the service is intended from the start to be selective (in this case geared towards the "disadvantaged"), we face the issue firmly stated by Tizard (1976):

The term disadvantaged is used...with many meanings....and different definitions of the term give rise to very different estimates of the proportions of families whose children are disadvantaged enough to warrant priority in nursery placement (p. 149).

Furthermore, it is difficult to claim that one definition has "more validity than others" (Tizard, 1976, p. 149). If we give priority to mothers in paid work, then

what of the young children of mothers who are psychiatrically depressed or anxious....Or children of single-parent families...? Or children in large families? In grossly overcrowded households? In low-income families? In households where the language in the home is not English? Or handicapped children? Or children who have nowhere to play? (Tizard, 1976, p. 150).

The same issues apply if we intend a service to be eventually nonselective (e.g., by the end of 6 years, free preschool education for all children) but must start selectively.

The second problem is one of implementation, especially when the interested parties do not have the same vested interests. The party platform had been designed to meet the needs of two relatively opposed interest groups: those interested in preschools and those interested in child care centers. Also interested were members of the bureaucracy waiting to see if the responsibility for the new expansion would be placed under "health," "welfare," or "education." These interest groups may be combined by fiat, or legislation, as proposed in the United States in 1971. However, "legislative language and child welfare standards do not necessarily ensure such a merger will take place in the delivery of services" (Takanishi, 1977, p. 153).

In the present case, the Pre-School Committee's task set off to a stormy start, marked by concern over the appointment of Joan Fry as chair. Joan Fry had been head of the Sydney Day Nursery School Teachers' Association. As such, she was regarded as suspect by the kindergarten associations (i.e., she represented "care" rather than "education"). She was also regarded as suspect by a number of women's groups, who thought she was likely to relate child-care centers to issues of poverty rather than to rights for women. The same groups were also concerned that the committee's six educators, one psychologist, and one professor of child health would be biased towards children's education and children's needs, with little concern for the wider needs of women and families.

Once again, these concerns needed to be effectively expressed. Two routes provided this expression: (a) Prime Minister Whitlam had appointed not only a Pre-school Committee but also a Women's Advisor (Elizabeth Reid). In effect, there were two routes to Whitlam's ear. (b) The New South Wales Branch of the Labour Women's Organization actively lobbied for a change in policy statements at the annual ALP conference in July 1973. These statements would effectively "frame" the political content for the Fry Committee. The goal of the new policy was "to provide community support for women to participate more fully in society" (ALP Platform, p. 17). The route to such a goal was to be a set of comprehensive child-care services that would be government sponsored, established on a "priority needs basis," and community-based (i.e., responsive to varying community preferences for various forms of care and involving the local community in the establishment and running of its own services).

EVENT 4: REPORTS AND ACTION

We shall briefly summarize a series of events that still evokes high feeling among many of those involved and affected. The Pre-School Committee, under the direction of Joan Fry, produced a report. It was widely criticized (in some respects, its terms of reference no longer applied and, in ironic fashion, the support it gave to "preschool education" rather than "child-care centers" was felt to be too strong). The report was eventually tabled and no action was taken. The committee was later disbanded, but before that reports were called for from two further groups: one from the Department of Social Welfare (*not* Education) and one from the Priority Review Staff, a political policy group. These two groups were relatively compatible.

The Social Welfare Commission produced a report in July 1974. In general, this report matched the 1973 restatement of party policy. Its more specific features were the following:

1. A challenge to the assumption that traditional preschool education would reduce inequality (a challenge fed by research questioning the effects of Head Start, but which also legitimated and gave a lower priority in funding to services that operated only for part of a day).

2. An argument for mixtures of services (preschool, long-day care, after-school care, occasional care, emergency care) that should extend to the shared use of buildings (i.e., services should be "integrated").

3. An argument for choice of any mixture to be made at a community level.

4. A recognition that communities could only choose what they knew about, and a proposal of appointments to communities of "catalysts" to promote both knowledge and services.

5. An endorsement of research on services such as family day care, to determine whether its popularity among government agencies was based on its low cost rather than its effectiveness.

6. An endorsement of personnel other than people trained for preschool. The field, it was argued, could use people trained to be child-care workers rather than nursery school or preschool teachers (this third and briefer form of training was recommended by the Fry Committee and is now available in a number of Technical Colleges, modelled after the United States pattern of Child Development Associates). The field could also make use of more social workers, psychiatrists, and pediatricians. (The Commission had relatively little representation from preschool organizations; the background of its chairperson was a combination of social work, administration, and sociology.)

7. An attempt to define "need" by a Needs Rating Scale devised from a factor analysis of selected variables from the 1971 Census.

The Priority Review staff produced a report agreeing with the concepts of the Social Welfare Commission but questioning the wisdom of leaving implemention in the hands of local government. It also recommended that the administration of the program be shifted to a special minister, responsible directly to the Prime Minister (in effect, away from the Department of Education).

These three reports were accepted and built into policy statements in 1974. The goal was to be free preschool education, subsidized child care with parents contributing according to their means, and the encouragement of industry to establish child-care centers. The program, it was argued, would break down the distinction between care and education.

The ALP won the 1974 election and established an interim committee for a children's commission. Despite the goal of widespread forms of care, the largest proportion of money went into traditional preschool centers (staff and buildings). The ALP had retained the system of response to community submissions and, to a very large extent, the percentage of money spent on preschools reflected the presence within preschool associations of available "machineries": procedures and people were already on hand to allow the swift submission of proposals and the swift spending of money.

A permanent children's commission did not result. In a series of events that again still evokes high feeling and that would seem mysterious to people accustomed to other forms of government, the Labour government was formally dismissed from office in November 1975, and an election was called. The election in 1975 saw a return of the Liberal-Country Party. The new Prime Minister, Fraser, took a more conservative step and established the Office of Child Care within the Department of Social Security, under the direction of Marie Coleman. The emphasis was back to the selective provision of child care on a needs basis, to no further expansion of preschool services, and to a stress on state rather than federal responsibility for the "regulation, licensing and provision of family and child welfare and early childhood education services" (Office of Child Care, 1979, p. 3). The strength of the push to integrate services also declined at this level. In a twist of fate, the push towards integration in the early childhood area has come from the Department of Education and from federal involvement in the complete funding of training colleges for teachers of young children (from 0 to 8 years, or from 2 to 8 years). Funding (covering both staff and building costs) has been included in the general contraction of funds for all forms of teacher training. The federal government would like to merge all training institutions that once felt (many of the staff in fact still do feel) that their strongest feature was the uniqueness of the training they offered. As Takanishi (1977) suggests, the "real" history in the merging of such different professional groups, covering their "relationships with and perceptions of each other, and the conditions under which cooperation did occur...is still to be written" (p. 153).

DISCUSSION

We have used a history of Australian events to illustrate some ways of analyzing variations in policies for young children, and to sort out some of the factors that appear to lie behind these variations. The factors noted, we propose, are equally applicable to other countries and other times.

What we have specifically proposed is a merger of two factors that are often considered separately. One factor has been termed "ideologies." It covers the values people adopt, the categories within which they think, and the kinds of evidence or argument they find convincing. The second factor may be termed "the resources of interested parties." These interested parties may be the people seeking change or the people who need to be persuaded. Their resources may be financial. In the history we have described, however, the important resources for people seeking change are of a different type, with one major resource being the presence of "machineries" or procedures by which one may bring acceptable evidence to the attention of people who are ready to listen and/or who wish to use it as support for a position to which they are already converted.

These two factors turn out to intersect in a number of ways and to be linked as well to economic conditions. It will accordingly be appropriate for us to end by underlining one particular point of intersection that emerged in our history and that seems in major need of clarification. This is the notion of allocating "resources according to need." (We shall set aside the question of how to separate "the needy" from "the deserving.")

Again and again in the history of early childhood education, the question arises of what need means to various people and of how it can be measured. It has been defined in at least two major ways, in terms of people (the "handicapped," etc.) and in terms of geographical areas (Britain's "priority areas," for example). In the one case, the individual is the client; in the other "the community" (Smith, 1979). Neither definition has been completely acceptable to all. Within Australia, for example, the Social Welfare Commission requested that two sociologists (Vinson and Homel) develop a way of designating areas as being at varying degrees of "risk" (i.e., likely to involve problems for children and families). Vinson and Homel (1976) did so, combining indicators such as the incidence of truancy, delinquency, admissions to general or psychiatric hospitals, unemployment, protection court orders, and child-care (maintenance) orders. The report was placed in Parliament but not used.

Instead, the continuing basis for defining need has been individuals. Children who are handicapped, isolated, or in one-parent families are regarded as in need and as having priority in access to preschools or child care centers. Some parents in Australia have begun to challenge the assumption that to be a member of these groups automatically means that one has a problem or is in need. Nonetheless, definition by individuals seems to be politically more attractive and easier to explain than definition by area. In a situation where policy analysts (Townsend, 1979) are themselves no longer completely enthusiastic about area definitions, individuals are likely to remain the major referent. The nature of the definition and the criteria for placing one need above another, however, require a great deal more thinking through.

Need is our last example of a term that overlaps two major types of factor: one concentrating on "meanings" or "ideologies," the other concentrating on "the resources of interested parties." Our overall hope has been to demonstrate that combining attention to both types of factor helps us move towards two goals. One is the goal of making less bewildering the array of policies we may encounter firsthand in the area of early childhood education. The other is the broad goal set for us by Takanishi (1977): specifically, finding ways to write an analytic history that helps us understand both past and present.

REFERENCES

ALP platform statement. Sydney, Australia: Australian Labor Party Documents, 1973.

Ariès, P. *Centuries of childhood.* London: Jonathan Cape, 1962.

*Ashby, G. F. Preschool education in Queensland, Australia—A systems approach. In L. Katz, C. Watkins, M. Quest, & M. Spencer (Eds.), *Current topics in early childhood education* (Vol. 3). Norwood, NJ: Ablex Publishing Corporation, 1980.

Berger, P. L., Berger, B., & Kellner, H. *The homeless mind.* Harmondsworth, UK: Penguin Books, 1974.

Borrie, W. D. (Ed.). *Population and Australia: A demographic analysis and projection.* Canberra, Australia: Australian Government Publication Service, 1975.

Bowlby, J. *Attachment and loss* (Vols. 1 and 2). New York: Basic Books, 1969.

Brennan, D. *Out of the frying pan. . . Federal reports on preschool and child care services.* Unpublished manuscript, School of History, Philosophy, and Politics, Macquarie University, Australia, 1982.

Burns, A. Australian attitudes to child care. In A. Graycar (Ed.), *Perspectives on Australian social policy.* South Melbourne, Australia: MacMillan Company of Australia, 1978.

Burns, A., Fegan, M., Sparkes, A., & Thompson, P. *Working mothers and their children: The Electrical Trades Union study.* Sydney, Australia: Macquarie University Publications, 1975.

Burns, A., & Goodnow, J. J. *Children and families in Australia: Contemporary issues and problems.* Sydney, Australia: Allen & Unwin, 1978.

Chazan, M. (Ed.). *International research in early childhood education.* Windsor, UK: National Foundation for Educational Research, 1978.

Glick, P. A demographer looks at American families. *Journal of Marriage and the Family,* 1975, *37*(1), 15–26.

Goodnow, J. J. *Some aspects of social policy in Australia and beyond.* Minneapolis, MN: University of Minnesota Press, 1981.

Goodnow, J. J., & Burns, A. Children and society. In R. Brown (Ed.), *Children Australia.* Sydney, Australia: Allen & Unwin, 1980.

Joffe, C. *Friendly intruders: Childcare professionals and family life.* Berkeley, CA: University of California Press, 1977.

Kessen, W. The American child and other inventions. *American Psychologist,* 1979, *34,* 815–820.

McCaughey, W., & Sebastian, P. *Community child care.* Melbourne, Australia: Greenhouse Publications, 1977.

Mental Health Association of New South Wales. *Pre-school centres in industry.* Sydney, Australia: Mental Health Association of New South Wales, 1970.

Office of Child Care, Department of Social Security. *Information kit.* Canberra, Australia: Australian Government Publication Service, 1979.

Rosenkrantz, B. C. Reflections on 19th century conceptions of childhood. In E. M. R. Lomax, J. Kagan, & B. C. Rosenkrantz (Eds.), *Science and patterns of child care*. San Francisco, CA: W. H. Freeman & Co. Publishers, 1978.

Ryan, P., & Rowse, T. Women, arbitration and the family. In A. Curthoys, S. Eade, & P. Spearritt (Eds.), *Women at work*. Canberra, Australia: Australian Society for the Study of Labor History, 1975.

Scanzoni, L., & Scanzoni, J. *Men, women and change: A sociology of marriage and the family*. New York: McGraw-Hill Book Company, 1976.

Smith, D. M. *Where the grass is greener: Geographical perspectives on inequality*. London: Croom Helm, 1979.

Spearritt, P. The preschool: A case study. In D. Jecks (Ed.), *Influences in Australian education*. Perth, Australia: Carroll's Book Company, 1974.

Sydney Kindergarten Teachers College. *Prospectus for students*. Sydney, Australia: Kindergarten Teachers College, 1911.

*Takanishi, R. Federal involvement in early childhood education (1933–1973): The need for historical perspectives. In L. Katz, M. Glockner, S. Goodman, & M. Spencer (Eds.), *Current topics in early childhood education* (Vol. 1). Norwood, NJ: Ablex Publishing Corporation, 1977. (ERIC Document Reproduction Service No. ED 097 969)

Tizard, J. Nursery needs and choices. In J. Bruner & A. Garton (Eds.), *Human growth and development*. Oxford, UK: Oxford University Press, 1976.

Townsend, P. *Poverty in the United Kingdom*. Harmondsworth, UK: Penguin Books, 1979.

Vinson, T., & Homel, R. *Indicators of community well-being*. Canberra, Australia: Department of Social Security, 1976.

*White, S., Day, M. L., Freeman, P. K., Hartman, S. A., & Messenger, F. D. Federal programs for young children (Vol. 1). *Goals and standards of public programs for children*. Washington, DC: US Government Printing Office, 1973. (ERIC Document Reproduction Service No. ED 092 230)

9

The Education of Preprimary Teachers*

Lilian G. Katz

University of Illinois, Urbana
Director, ERIC Clearinghouse on Elementary
and Early Childhood Education

INTRODUCTION

Although specialists in the field of preprimary education differ on many aspects of goals and methods, they generally agree that the competence and attitudes of teachers are major determinants of program effectiveness.[1] In spite of this agreement, few empirical studies of teaching have been reported, and virtually no research on teacher preparation and education has been accumulated.

From the general literature on preprimary education, it appears that the majority of people teaching children under 5 years of age (in some countries, under 6 years) have had no preservice education at all, and most have had only sporadic workshops or short courses. The proportion of trained to untrained personnel is not simply a function of the level of industrialization of a given country, nor is it simply related to per capita income or average educational attainment. Complex historical, political, and economic forces seem to be at work (cf. Goodnow & Burns, "Factors Affecting Policies in Early Childhood Education: An Australian Case," in this volume). One of the few fairly reliable generalizations about the field of preprimary education and its teachers is that the younger the child being taught, the less train-

---

* An earlier version of this chapter is forthcoming in T. Husen and T. N. Postlethwaite (Eds.), *International Encyclopedia of Education: Research and Studies* (London: Pergammon Press, in press).

[1] The term "preprimary" is used here to refer to what takes place in group settings for children who are below the age of entry into formal primary or elementary school classes.

ing the teacher is likely to have, the less status and prestige enjoyed, the fewer qualifications are required, the lower the wages, and the longer the hours of work.

UNIQUE CHARACTERISTICS OF THE FIELD

In many respects, the education of preprimary teachers shares some of the same problems as the education of primary and secondary teachers. However, education for preprimary instructors has some unique problems stemming from the nature of the field. These latter characteristics are discussed first, followed by consideration of the similarities between education for preprimary teachers and other groups.

In regions where preservice education is available for preprimary personnel, it is offered in many different institutions reflecting the wide variety of settings in which such personnel are employed. Some training is available in social work or social welfare departments, or in institutions sponsored by social work agencies (Husen & Postlethwaite, in press). Other training is offered in nursing or medical agencies or in highly specialized institutions such as Montessori institutes, teacher-training colleges, home economics departments of colleges or secondary schools, vocational or technical secondary schools, or human or child development divisions of psychology departments in colleges or universities.

Role Ambiguity

The diversity of training programs reflects the range of employment settings. Preprimary teachers work in nursery schools, creches, kindergartens, and day care centers, to name a few examples, all of which operate for different lengths of the day and serve a variety of age groups. This exacerbates a longstanding problem in determining appropriate goals and content for those training programs and education courses that are available.

Variations in Program Goals

Questions concerning what proportion of training time should be allocated to educational or health issues (and within these concerns, the issues of how much emphasis should be given to theoretical versus pedagogical studies or to the development of techniques for working with parents) are constant sources of discussion in the field (Katz, 1977). Almost all reports and proposals concerning the education of preprimary teachers emphasize the acquisition of skills and knowledge for building strong ties with parents and for helping parents to improve their childrearing. In addition, working closely with other professionals in related fields such as medicine, social work, nutrition, and primary education is seen as desirable (National Seminar, 1978). In the case of developing countries such as India, for example, many teachers are expected to recruit the mothers and children into the program as well as teach childrearing, hygiene, crafts, home management, and sanitation (Grant, 1982; Pakjam, 1978).

Low Wages

Another special characteristic of the preprimary field is the extent to which education programs are staffed by volunteers, in some cases because of the lack of funds with which to pay staff, but in others in order to create an informal, family-like atmosphere. In still other programs the motive underlying the use of volunteers is to strengthen relations between the home and the preschool or to help mothers learn to work with children by voluntary participation in the preschool (*Playgroups,* in press; Singer, 1979). These volunteer groups tend to undermine professional associations' and teacher trainers' arguments that teachers of young children need special skills and knowledge, acquired through advanced training.

Aside from the relatively large role played by volunteers, preprimary education seems to be caught in a vicious cycle: In the absence of training and qualifications, many preprimary teachers have few skills and are therefore very poorly paid; because of the poor pay, people who do have skills will not seek employment in preprimary education. Because employers lack sophisticated skills or training, clients, as well as sponsoring agencies, are unwilling to increase pay. In addition to the poor skills/low pay cycle, it is a fact that the younger the child in the setting, the lower the child/adult ratio. This means that when pay is increased, the costs of a program increase dramatically without corresponding increases in the number of children assigned to an individual teacher (Woodhead, 1979). Furthermore, rigorous or lengthy training is unlikely to attract candidates when the ultimate pay scale is so low. Nevertheless, some attempts to break this cycle with new training initiatives and with the introduction of "professional" standards and qualifications have been reported.

GENERAL ISSUES IN TEACHER EDUCATION
AND PREPRIMARY EDUCATION

Lack of Criteria for Good Teaching

Education of teachers for all levels of schooling suffers from the absence of agreed-upon criteria of effectiveness—definitions of or consensus upon what constitutes "good" teaching (Medley, 1982). The teacher education field is so diverse in terms of philosophy, curriculum styles, ages of children served, length of the teaching day, scope of functions of teachers, and so forth that such a consensus is unlikely to be achieved on a field-wide basis. And, since conventional academic achievement is rarely of central concern to preprimary staff, standardized achievement test scores are unlikely to be accepted as appropriate or meaningful measures of teachers' effectiveness from which inferences about the worth of training can be made.

Impact of Training

Another problem preprimary education shares with all other levels of schooling is that, even in those regions where teacher training is available, doubts about its impact on ultimate teacher performance are widespread (Raths & Katz, 1982). Some of these doubts are cast in terms of the relatively greater impact of the experiences provided during the preservice training. Other doubts are expressed by both trainees themselves and the practitioners who receive them after training has been completed. The latter critics assert that, from their "objective" view, training offered in preservice programs is too theoretical and idealistic. The candidates themselves claim that the training they receive is not sufficiently relevant or useful. It is possible that both these views are justified and appropriate, but without agreed-upon criterion measures it is difficult to empirically test them.

The "Feed-forward" Problem

One of the major difficulties in designing and assessing the impact of preservice training programs is the so-called "feed-forward" problem (Katz, Raths, Mohanty, Kurachi, & Irving, 1981)—namely, the problem stemming from the fact that preservice training consists largely of giving students answers to questions they have not yet asked, or of providing students with methods for dealing with eventualities rather than actualities. The phenomenon includes resistance from the student at the time of exposure to instruction and, later, protestations that the same instruction had not been provided, should have been provided, or should have been provided in stronger doses. Thus, for example, the advice that students should be more fully trained in Piagetian psychology and methods may seem reasonable to a teacher enjoying success in her fifth year on the job, but may seem irrelevant to a candidate struggling with the forthcoming challenges of managing 30 reluctant preschoolers.

This feed-forward problem, no doubt generic to anticipatory professional training in all professions, becomes an issue mainly when the training staff expects trainees to appreciate the relevance and usefulness of the training exercises and components provided for them at the time they are occurring. This hypothesized feed-forward situation implies that upon later reflection, students' feelings, attitudes, beliefs, opinions, and evaluations with respect to a given experience obtained earlier during their training may change, although candidates are unlikely to believe so. Thus, for example, students might be enrolled in a course in children's literature which requires them to read and annotate 100 children's books, and may resent the exercise at the time. However, it may be that during their actual employment at a later time, graduates will re-evaluate that set of experiences, thinking, "I hated it then, but now I'm glad they made me go through with it." Or, conversely, the graduate may look back on an enjoyed exercise and dismiss it as irrelevant.

In terms of the feed-forward problem it may be useful to look at teacher education in terms of three time periods:

Period I: Prospective   Opinions, feelings, beliefs *before* training
Period II: Introspective   Opinions, feelings, beliefs *during* training
Period III: Retrospective   Opinions, feelings, beliefs *after* training

Periods I and II may be characterized by the conviction that one knows how one is going to feel during the next periods. Opinions, feelings, and beliefs may be positive or negative about the anticipated or actual experiences during both periods, or they may be mixed. The experiences of Period II cannot be changed during Period III, but the evaluations of them may change or fluctuate during Period III. An example taken from another field is a study of the graduates of a business school, all of whom shared the same curriculum (Neel, 1978). Graduates were asked after 3 years, 7 to 10 years, and 12 to 15 years how the curriculum might have been better or improved. Graduates with 3 years on the job emphasized increasing the "how to" elements of the curriculum; graduates with 7 to 10 years of experience suggested additional courses in human relations, psychology and sociology, and how to get along in organizations. Graduates with 12 to 15 years experience stressed the need for additional courses in philosophy, religious studies, and literature. Though graduates might not have accepted predictions that they might have such opinions in the future, Neel points out that

> It was quite obvious that the more experienced business professionals were more interested than the younger men in reassessing who they were as individuals and at what place they had arrived in their lives as well as their careers. (p. 7)

In a sense, then, it is in the nature of things that students cannot know how they will feel about a given experience at a later point in time. The actual experiences obtained during the training never change; only the meanings and the evaluations given them may change in the light of subsequent teaching experiences. It should be noted that the meanings (including feel-

ings, attitudes, beliefs, opinions, and evaluations) associated with the experiences obtained during training may be correct or incorrect, positive or
negative, at the time they occur as well as in retrospect.

Another issue associated with the feed-forward paradigm is whether
such retrospective changes in the meanings and values assigned to earlier experiences are systematic, and if so, what is the system? If the hypothesis is
empirically confirmed, it could imply that teacher education must be designed and rationalized on bases other than the extent to which students
accept or like what is offered (at the time they experience it) or whether they
can even grasp the relevance of its components. Ideal bases for rationalizing
the design or content of teacher education should at least include theories of
adult learning and of professional or occupational socialization. However,
it appears that the pattern and structure of training programs are determined
more by tradition, economic exigencies, and common sense than by such
theoretical formulations. Confirmation of the feed-forward hypothesis
would require longitudinal studies of several cohorts of candidates from
their training through several years of employment.

Problems of Content

Early childhood teacher training and training for other levels of schooling
share concerns about the appropriateness and sufficiency of the content of
the training courses. Invariably, course revisions involve additions of new
specialities and experiences, giving rise to steady increases in the length of
training required. Questions such as, "What proportion of the required
work should be studied in how much depth?" arise constantly. However, it
is not clear what criteria, theories, or rules for decision making should be
used to answer these kinds of content questions.

From the scattered reports available, the education of preprimary
teachers appears to be following a trend noted in education for teaching at
the upper levels—namely, toward longer periods of training and greater emphasis on theoretical or "foundation" subjects. One of the best known
specialized preprimary training programs, nursery nurses training in the
United Kingdom, has undergone great changes in the last 10 years. In 1974
the 2-year course was changed so that the traditional three-fifths time allocated to practice and two-fifths to theoretical or academic work were reversed. In addition, the required age for entry was raised from 16 to 18 years.
Many of the specialized nursery nurse training institutions and programs
raised their general academic entrance requirements as well, and certifying
examinations have been upgraded substantially. These changes reflect increases in the knowledge base (particularly in the area of child development
and parent/child relations), the complexity of childrearing and education in
general, and strong pressures within the field for greater professionalization
(Batten, 1981).

A developmental perspective. Considerable interest has been shown in addressing these questions in terms of developmental stages trainees are thought to undergo. Katz (1972) proposed that in the case of preschool teachers, most of whom had little or no preservice training, the aspects and components of teaching with which they need assistance change as experience accrues.

Four stages of preschool teacher development have been hypothesized as occurring in sequence, although the duration of each stage may vary among individuals. The first of the four hypothesized stages is called *survival*. This stage is characterized by the trainee or teacher being preoccupied with management and control of the group of children, keeping them reasonably busy and content, having the children accept authority and accede to demands, and being liked by them. A second stage, called *consolidation*, is defined as a period that begins when the trainee or teacher has mastered control and management of the whole group and can provide suitable activities to which the children respond favorably. Now the trainee or teacher becomes concerned about individual children whose behavior is different from that of most of the others, who appear to be atypical to the teacher, or who are not learning or responding as well as the teacher would like.

A third stage, called *renewal,* beginning perhaps after 4 or 5 years of teaching, is characterized by a subjective feeling of becoming stale or weary of the same routines—tired of reading the same stories, singing the same songs, celebrating the same festivals, and perhaps finding that daily work with young children has become intellectually under-stimulating. Teachers in this stage typically ask for fresh ideas and techniques, new materials and methods, and enjoy and welcome opportunities to exchange ideas with colleagues in workshops. A fourth stage, called *maturity*, reached earlier by some than by others, includes the teacher's acquisition of self-renewal strategies but is marked further by the tendency to ask deeper and broader questions about the nature of education and its relationship to social, historical, philosophical, or ethical issues in teaching, and so forth. The latter stage has been difficult to validate, since many preschool personnel move up into directorships or other ancillary or administrative positions if they stay in the field as long as 5 years.

Implications for teacher training program content. The application of developmental stage constructs to preprimary teacher education can have three benefits. First, trainees and teachers can be shown that their own survival struggles at the beginning of their careers is "in the nature of things" and can thus put their lack of assurance and occasional fumbling into perspective, achieving greater patience with their own learning processes. Second, teacher education courses can be designed in such a way as to concentrate on providing at least minimal survival skills for trainees, but could do so in such a way as to strengthen trainees' dispositions to be resourceful and to go on learning after the basic survival stage is over. That is to say, one could offer trainees very practical "how to" exercises and equip them with activities to carry out during their initial teaching experiences (perhaps enough for the first 2 or 3 months of teaching). Such activities and projects could help trainees get started; as soon as they feel comfortable with these "survival kit" activities in the real life setting with the children, they can begin to develop their own activities and style, making plans for classroom activities over the longer period. The third and related value of looking at teacher education from a developmental perspective is that courses could begin with the very practical "how to" aspects of teaching and end with the theoretical subjects (e.g., psychology, philosophy, etc.), thus reversing the typical sequence.

It may also be useful to reconsider the best time period during training at which to provide the observational experiences that are usually given strong emphasis in the training of preprimary and primary teachers. If there is any validity at all to the application of the developmental stage metaphor to teacher training, it suggests that exercises in the observation of children may be more fruitful if taken after having had some actual classroom experiences with children, rather than before, as is customary. Young, inexperienced students generally find observation of children unrewarding, if not boring. There are no known studies of the extent to which exercises in observation of children affect subsequent teaching skills, yet these exercises remain an almost sacred component of many training courses. Perhaps candidates' restlessness with classroom observation exercises also fits into the feed-forward hypothesis in that retrospectively, graduates will acknowledge their value. However, no empirical data addressed to this issue have been found.

Field experiences. Teacher training or field experience appears to be the most highly recommended component of preservice training for teacher education, though the amount of practice provided in education courses varies widely. Arrangements for field experiences also differ from country to country. Some countries require practical or field experiences in a suitable or approved setting before admission to a formal certificate or diploma course (e.g., Sweden). Others feature practical experience similar to an internship throughout the period of training (e.g., nursery nurses' training in the United Kingdom). Still others provide as many as 3 years of academic work prior to field practice (e.g., courses for social pedagogues in the Federal Republic of Germany—cf. Austin, 1976). Empirical studies of the effects of different amounts of practice are few and inconclusive (Davis, 1975).

In an interesting series of studies of selected characteristics of students and their field placements for practice teaching, Becher and Ade (1982) reported data suggesting that students relatively low in self-confidence perform better in practice teaching when matched with a cooperating teacher who is relatively weak or "underwhelming." Apparently such students' self-confidence is further eroded when matched with a cooperating teacher who appears to be full of assurance and who makes teaching "look easy." Becher and Ade's research suggests that attempts to match students' characteristics (such as self-assurance) with those of the personnel in the field placement could increase the effectiveness of the practice teaching or field experiences provided in training.

The relative merits of imposing the practical or field experience requirements earlier rather than later in the training course are also under scrutiny. Early field experience is assumed to have the advantage of giving trainees better opportunities to try on the future teaching role and therefore to be better able to make an informed career choice. Some believe it makes theoretical studies more meaningful and useful, since the practical and theoretical components occur simultaneously. However, one investigation of students in training for elementary teaching has indicated that the early field experience overwhelmed the students and that their more theoretical courses, rather than assuming greater relevance, became distractions from the urgent and salient realities of coping with the field setting (Luttrell, Bane, & Mason, 1981). The results of another study also failed to confirm the assumed benefits of early field experience (Shorter, 1975).

The qualities of practice and setting. Another major issue in need of empirical investigation is the frequent complaint of insufficient opportunities for students to observe "good" practices. Questions concerning both the timing and amount of practice become virtually irrelevant if the community lacks settings in which trainees can observe such practices. In poor conditions the truism that "practice makes perfect" leads to a situation in which "bad practice makes perfectly bad." It can be argued that trainees do learn from imperfect or "bad" practices in field placements. However, just what is learned is not clear.

Students in preservice education programs are also known to complain that the field settings in which they practice require them to engage in pedagogical practices that their trainers and supervisors deplore or reject. The "bad field setting" predicament implies that the supervisors or tutors have special responsibilities to help trainees interpret and understand the realities of the field settings as well as to cultivate their capacity to adjust to those realities while simultaneously preparing to be able to ultimately progress beyond them. The apparent gulf between educators of teachers and practitioners in field settings has not been studied empirically, but is reflected in the general literature in education (cf. Katz, 1977). Such discrepancies between the idealized practices advocated by the staff of teacher education institutions and the actual professional practices in the field are no doubt generic to professional education in all areas.

At the other extreme of the field experience spectrum, some training courses may provide practice only in idealized laboratory settings, which may be different from more typical extra-campus settings. The more "artificial" training environment may encourage graduates to learn skills which are actually maladaptive to field settings outside the university situation. However, helping trainees to become aware of a range of alternative practices and field conditions by using films, slides, videotapes, and other materials may minimize the distorting effects of constant exposure to "bad" practices or to highly idealized settings. In addition, simulation exercises, role playing, microteaching, and the use of specially prepared slides or videotapes showing critical incidents in teaching, together with responses to specially prepared questions about the incidents presented, may help students to transcend local practices (Medley, 1982).

RECENT DEVELOPMENTS IN IN-SERVICE EDUCATION

Inasmuch as most preprimary personnel have little or no preservice education, various approaches to the education of those already employed merit particular attention. Two types of in-service education for preprimary personnel are outlined below, and a brief summary of an extensive in-service education project is outlined.

The Advisory Approach to In-service Education

The first method of in-service education is known as the "advisory approach" (Katz, 1974); employed in Great Britain, parts of Australia, and sporadically in the United States, this method grew from the earlier use of school inspectors (Bolam, 1982). In the early 1970s, Queensland became the first Australian state to adopt a policy of statewide access to preschool education. This very large state was divided into nine regions, and advisors were assigned to provide technical assistance to preschool classes within the regions, some of which are isolated geographically. Many of the preschool teachers in country schools are very young, fresh from their training college courses taken in the larger cities of the state. These teachers are assigned to "country service" for at least the first 2 years of their teaching careers. Preschool advisors, appointed by the State's Department of Education and chosen from practicing preschool teachers, serve for 3 years, after which they return to preschool classroom teaching. These advisors are expected to make regular visits to all preschool classes within their regions, to provide moral as well as technical support, and to conduct workshops on particular teaching or curriculum issues. Many of them also provide services through resource or teachers' centers in the region. These preschool advisors have no inspection or sanctioning authority; their role is limited to providing support and encouragement to practitioners.

The Enabler Model

A variant of the advisory approach is the Enabler Model of in-service training (Katz, 1972), developed especially for the in-service education of Head Start teachers in the United States and subsequently adapted for the support of day care staff (Holt, n.d.). This variant of the advisory approach may be useful in regions just beginning to develop their preprimary resources.

The objectives of the model are to help the local communities served by the Head Start program to define and achieve their own goals, to offer advice in such a way as to enable local leaders and participants in the program to develop their own strengths and to solve problems on their own, and to assist local staff and participants to build relationships with their own local resources and agencies. Qualifications of consultants engaged to perform in the Enabler Model include extensive experience in early childhood education and related fields, special skills in working with parents of diverse backgrounds, and demonstrated ability to be sensitive to the community's strengths and resources (Holt, n.d.).

The model is conceived in terms of two phases: "initiation" and "maintenance." During the initiation phase, the "enabler" is expected to meet with all community groups involved in the programs (staff, volunteers, social, medical and nutritional workers, primary school liaisons, and so forth). During formal and informal discussion with each group and among groups, the enabler encourages and facilitates the expression of community members' preferences, stressing the goals and purposes the members themselves want to achieve. During the second, or maintenance, phase of the model, the enabler's role is to provide support for smooth operation of the program. During this phase the enabler's functions include supplying information, serving as a link between all segments of the wider community involved in the welfare of the preschool children in the program, interpreting the program in terms of its own agreed-upon goals, serving as a source of support and encouragement, assessing staff strengths, occasionally demonstrating skills and techniques, and serving as a neutralizer of conflict (Katz, 1979).

Although no controlled empirical studies have been reported of the application of the Enabler Model or other variants of the advisory approach to preprimary in-service education, the following points have emerged from several years of experience. First, advisors or enablers have had to resist the temptation to give advice too early in the development of their relationship with the program or community to be served. Problems arising from giving advice too early are not a matter of the correctness of the advice, but of allowing enough trust between the advisor and advisees to be developed so that the advice can be interpreted as an offer to help, rather than as criticism from an outside expert.

Second, advisors who live in the community being advised have the advantage of greater understanding of local concerns and preferences, but they have the great disadvantage of being in too close and continual contact with the participants to be able to have a detached, respectful, and realistic overview of participants' contributions to the day-to-day quality of the program offered to children.

Third, it appears that, depending on the distances between preprimary settings, a maximum number of programs to be served by any one advisor or enabler might be between six and ten. This makes the advisory approach to in-service education very expensive, since the qualifications for advisors are at the highest level available in the educational system and salaries tend to reflect this. In addition, the enabler's work is by definition itinerant and incurs costs of travel and accommodation in most regions. Studies of the relative cost-benefit ratios of the advisory approach as compared to other forms of in-service training (e.g., courses, workshops, secondments, or release time for selected staff), which take into account the ultimate long-term benefits to the preprimary field in a given location, are greatly needed.

Finally, the advisory approach, as illustrated by the Enabler Model, seems to be worth considering seriously in planning in-service education for less developed countries. The Enabler Model—defined as a "non-model" by some—puts strong emphasis on the values and goals of the locale to be served. Its principles encourage sensitivity to the teachers' readiness to try alternative solutions to the pedagogical, social, and material problems they face within their own working environments. Additionally, assistance is directed toward a response to the realities of the actual situations at hand. Thus, rather than approaching the local program with a predetermined curriculum model, the enabler is expected to take into account the local material resources, customs, and preferences, as well as the readiness of the available staff to try alternative practices and experiment with different approaches. The introduction of a curriculum or a set of teaching strategies which might over-tax the local personnel and material resources, no matter how well-supported by empirical data gathered elsewhere, can only lead to a sense of failure which in turn might "backlash" into a hardened position insisting on the rightness of the previous customary practices thought to be in need of amelioration.

In order to implement the principles of the advisory approach or Enabler Model within in-service education, the advisors must have had extensive experience and possess a variety of interpersonal as well as pedagogical skills, making the cost of the program a serious consideration. However, if the advice and assistance given is of optimum quality, the long-term payoff can be expected to be greater than that accrued from less expensive one-shot workshops or short courses. Empirical tests of such predictions would be useful for the planning committees in less developed countries.

The Child Development Associate

By far the most radical departure from conventional training of preprimary personnel is the Child Development Associate (CDA) project, introduced in the United States in 1972. This project has deliberately attempted to upgrade the quality of teaching in Head Start classes. A Child Development Associate is defined as a person able to meet the specific needs of children in a preprimary setting by addressing their physical, social, emotional, and intellectual growth; by establishing and maintaining an appropriate child care and learning environment; and by promoting good relations with the parents they serve.

At the time the CDA program was conceived, competency or performance-based teacher education and certification was enjoying great popularity and credibility in the United States, especially among state and federal education agencies; the CDA project was heavily influenced by this trend. To date, the United States federal government has invested more than 50 million dollars in its development, testing, and application, indicating the importance given to strengthening the competence of Head Start personnel especially and other preprimary personnel generally. In the 10 years of CDA's existence, approximately 11,000 individuals have been credentialed, virtually all of whom were already employed in Head Start or similar programs at the time they undertook the training and completed the credentialing process (Klein & Lombardi, in press).

The CDA system consists of several interrelated segments. The central one is the set of CDA competencies which all candidates must demonstrate *in situ* in order to be awarded the CDA credential. The second major segment is CDA training, which must follow guidelines specified by the federal government in addition to being focused on preparing candidates to demonstrate their competencies. The third major segment is the CDA Assessment and Credential Award System.

CDA competencies.   One of the unique features of CDA training is the specification of teaching competencies, developed by specially assembled preschool professionals and endorsed by the major preschool professional organizations. These competencies cover six broad goals of preprimary teaching, emphasizing such areas as teacher responsibility for health and safety, stimulation of physical and intellectual development, strengthening self-concept, encouraging group participation skills, expediting cooperation between home and school, and performing other supplementary responsibilities. Each of the competency goals is further subdivided to yield a total of 13 so-called "functional areas." In addition, nine "personal capacities" are listed as essential features of the CDA requirements. These include being sensitive to children's feelings, listening and adapting language to suit children and families, being protective of children's individuality, and so forth. The competencies, functional areas, and personal capacities form the basis upon which CDA training programs are designed, although the precise links between demonstrable teaching skill and training curricula or content are difficult to ascertain.

Training. Though no specific restrictions are placed on the manner in which training programs address the competencies, functional areas, or personal capacities, the following training criteria are recommended:

1. The training must be based on the CDA competencies and should lead to their acquisition.
2. Valid credit should be offered for CDA training.
3. Fifty percent or more of the intern's total training time must be spent in supervised field work.
4. Academic and field experiences must be integrated.
5. Training must be individualized according to each intern's strengths and needs with respect to acquisition of the CDA competencies.
6. Training must be flexibly scheduled so that length of training time and exit from the training program depend on each intern's acquisition of the CDA competencies. (Vincent & Hamby, 1981, p. 12)

Flexibility in length of training per individual is deliberately encouraged in order to take into account the wide range of experience, education, and ability in Head Start personnel. To be eligible for assessment for the credential, candidates must be 18 or over and must have had at least 600 hours of experience working with children ages 3 through 5 years; that experience must also be attained in a group setting within the 5 years preceding application for the credential (Human Development Services, 1982). No data reporting the actual range of length of training have been reported.

These guidelines and criteria have been developed in such a way that any institution with relevant experience and appropriate personnel may provide training for CDA credential candidates, adapting their own teacher training curricula in any ways they wish to ensure the candidates' aquisition of the prescribed competencies. Since the training and the credentialing segments of the CDA program are completely separate, no institutions are specifically or officially "entitled" by the government or the state to offer training or to award credentials, and no institutions or organizations are excluded from providing training. The original planners of the CDA specifically wished to make training and the subsequent credential available in a wide variety of institutions at various levels of postsecondary education. However, to date most CDA training has been subsidized by the United States government, which thereby exercises some control over the implementation of the training guidelines and criteria.

The Credential Assessment and Award system. By far the most unique aspect of the CDA system is its Credential Assessment and Award system (Ward & CDA Staff, 1976), which continues to undergo development, extension, testing, and refinement. The process begins when an applicant for candidacy has been accepted "into the credential award system." As indicated above, the applicant must be at least 18 years old and have had at least 600 hours of experience with children within the preceding 5 years. Once the applicant formally becomes a CDA credential candidate, he or she selects a field trainer (often an experienced member of the staff) and an individual to represent the pupils' parents as well as the community. The trainers must be approved by the Bank Street CDA National Credentialing Program, a national office which carries responsibility for the assessment and credentialing processes. The assessment of competence is carried out by a Local Assessment Team (LAT) consisting of the candidate, the trainer, a parent/community representative, and a representative of the CDA National Credentialing Program in Washington, D. C. These four people gather information relevant to all aspects of the CDA competencies and include consideration of a portfolio prepared by the candidate which serves as a repository of evidence of work with children and parents related to the competencies. The committee makes the final decision as to whether or not to recommend the candidate to the national office for the award of the CDA Credential. In this way, the processes of training, assessment of competence, and ultimate awarding of the credential are completely separate—a real departure from conventional training and certification procedures.

Implications for other programs and research. The processes involved in the assessment and ultimate awarding of the CDA Credential are fairly complex, involving the participants in the LAT in many hours of observation and meetings. However, a number of aspects of the CDA training and credentialing process could be adopted by others without adopting the whole system.

The competencies and functional areas constituting the "standards" of CDA are both basic and reasonably universal, and can serve as guidelines for the training of preprimary personnel in a variety of cultures and settings. Competencies deemed locally inappropriate could certianly be discarded or adapted. The training system is flexible and individualized so that no single cohort of candidates must engage in all of the same exercises in the same sequence at the same time; many candidates will be able to demonstrate competence in some functional areas at the outset of their training and thus can move on to other areas for which they do need training and practice.

From the information available to date, it appears that the actual training provided to CDA candidates improves upon conventional training primarily in terms of the explicitness of its goals and objectives, and in its clear commitment to the acquisition of demonstrable skills in working with children and their families. Unfortunately, no studies of the validity of the credential have been reported as yet. Thus, while the functional areas nominated as representing essential competencies for effective teaching of young children appear to have face validity, it is not yet known whether those awarded the CDA credential and those who fail the assessment process would be judged different from each other by "blind" observers.

In addition, since the pass/fail decision to recommend the candidate for the credential award is made by the LAT, three of the four members of which are selected by the candidate, the possibility of highly biased assessment is great. (It is certainly very likely that the votes are "stacked" in the candidate's favor in advance of the assessment of competence.) In addition, the extent to which the standards applied by one LAT in one setting or community are like the standards applied by another LAT is not known. The potential for a "rubber yardstick" is indeed present. Whether universal standards for competence are important enought to forego opportunities for local input into staff quality is not a research issue, but lies rather in the realm of educational policy. The training guidelines and criteria put strong emphasis on coordinating the field work and course content in order to minimize failure. However, since the main thrust of the CDA program is on "demonstrable skills" and "observable competence in working with children," course content is programmatically in second place.

Given the generally unexplored state of the art of preprimary teacher education, elements of the CDA training and credentialing system deserve empirical study. For example, the composition of the LAT provides for genuine participation of the representatives of the local community served by the candidate and gives the candidate a role in personal assessment. What are some of the important dynamics of the process? What happens when the LAT member representing the CDA national headquarters—a specially trained representative of the national credentialing system—differs with the local judgments of the candidate's competence? How can the overall competence of the profession be upgraded or modernized to incorporate innovative practices and new ways of thinking about children if the local (and often remote) community has such a large voice in the assessment process? On the other hand, might the extent of local participation in the process facilitate dissemination of new ideas to the community in a way that formal meetings and lectures might not?

Some informal and anecdotal reports of the experiences of candidates who have progressed successfully through the CDA training and credentialing process suggest that its various elements (e.g., creating a portfolio, appointing an LAT, being observed in the classroom by the LAT members and receiving their feedback in the LAT meeting, etc.) create a type of "Hawthorne Effect." All the details involved in bringing together the assessment team, knowing that the parent/community representative will solicit parents' views, and so forth seem to emit a strong signal that the job for which one is trained and assessed is an important one, one in which the candidate as well as others have a real stake and a genuine interest. While so many people who work with young children, particularly in day care centers, feel undervalued and often depressed (cf. Whitebook, Howes, Darrah, & Friedman, 1982), the activity surrounding CDA training and credentialing may play a powerful role in improving morale and commitment. The potential side-benefits of the system should be studied with naturalistic methods and questions of the validity of the credential should be addressed with formal experimental methods; both of these types of studies should be undertaken before others are urged to adopt the rather complex and cumbersome CDA system. Research confirming validity and other positive effects would then make the CDA system a potentially valuable one, particularly in regions still in the early stages of developing training methods for preprimary teachers.

CONCLUSIONS

Information concerning the education of preprimary personnel is scattered and primarily descriptive in nature. Virtually no research concerning the relative effectiveness of alternative approaches to training and education has been found. In areas in which preservice training and education is available, approaches appear to be quite varied and to follow the general trend toward increased length as well as strengthened academic components. Research testing the relative impact of various types of content, the early versus late teaching practice, the value of training in "child observation" skills, and the application of "developmental stage" concepts to the design of preservice training would be useful. Empirical testing is also needed to address the question of the optimal proportion of preservice to in-service training, given that financial resources are limited. Preservice training seems to produce immediate effects that fade with on-the-job experience, whereas the type of in-service training represented by the advisory approach and its variants may produce positive effects in the long term.

REFERENCES

Austin, G. R. *Early childhood education: An international perspective.* New York: Academic Press, 1976.

Batten, A. Nursery nursing—Past and present (2). *Early Childhood,* 1981, *1*(5), 14–19.

Becher, R. M., & Ade, W. The relationship of field placement characteristics and students' potential field performance abilities to clinical experience performance ratings. *Journal of Teacher Education,* 1982, *33*(2), 24–33.

Bolam, R. Innovations adopted. In A. R. Thompson (Ed.), *Inservice education of teachers.* London: Commonwealth Secretariat, 1982.

Davis, M. D. *A comparison of the development of teaching sophistication and estimates of professional enhancement between eight week and sixteen week elementary student teachers at the University of Illinois.* Unpublished doctoral dissertation, University of Illinois, Urbana, IL, 1975.

*Goodnow, J., & Burns, A. Factors affecting policies in early childhood education: An Australian case. In L. G. Katz, P. J. Wagemaker, and K. Steiner (Eds.), *Current topics in early childhood education* (Vol. 5). Norwood, NJ: Ablex Publishing Corporation, in press. (ERIC Document Reproduction Service No. ED 220 178)

Grant, D. R. B. *Training teacher trainers and paraprofessional teachers.* Kingston, Jamaica: Jamaica Publishing House, 1982.

*Holt, B. *The Enabler Model of early childhood training and program development.* Unpublished manuscript, n. d. (ERIC Document Reproduction Service No. ED 214 663)

Human Development Services (United States Department of Health and Human Services). *The Child Development Associate credential.* Washington, DC: Office of Human Development Services, 1982.

Husen, T., & Postlethwaite, T. N. (Eds.). *International encyclopedia of education: Research and studies.* London: Pergammon Press, in press.

Katz, L. G. Developmental stages of preschool teachers. *Elementary School Journal,* 1972, *23* (1), 50–54.

Katz, L. G. Issues and problems in teacher education. In B. Spodek (Ed.), *Teacher education.* Washington, DC: National Association for the Education of Young Children, 1974.

Katz, L. G. Socialization of teachers for early childhood programs. In B. Spodek & H. J. Walberg (Eds.), *Early childhood education: Issues and insights.* Berkeley, CA: McCutcham Publishing Corporation, 1977.

*Katz, L. G. *Helping others learn to teach.* Urbana, IL: ERIC Clearinghouse on Elementary and Early Childhood Education, 1979. (ERIC Document Reproduction Service No. ED 164 102)

Katz, L. G., Raths, J. D., Mohanty, C., Kurachi, A., & Irving, J. Follow-up studies: Are they worth the trouble? *Journal of Teacher Education,* 1981, *32*(2), 8–14.

Klein, J. K., & Lombardi, J. Ten thousand CDA's: An event to be celebrated. *Children Today,* in press.

*Luttrell, H. D., Bane, R. K., & Mason, B. *Early elementary field-based experience: A university and public school approach.* Unpublished paper, 1981. (ERIC Document Reproduction Service No. ED 212 376)

Medley, D. M. *Teacher competency testing and the teacher educator.* Charlottesville, VA: University of Virginia Bureau of Educational Research, 1982.

National seminar on education of the teacher for the pre-school child. New Delhi, India: Indian Council of Child Welfare, 1978.

Neel, C. W. Business school curriculum design. *National Forum,* 1978, *58*(3), 277–283.

Pakjam, G. Pre-basic education. In *National seminar on education of the teacher for the pre-school child.* New Delhi, India: Indian Council of Child Welfare, 1978.

Playgroups in the Eighties. London: Pre-School Playgroups Association, in press.

Raths, J. D., & Katz, L. G. The best of intentions for the education of teachers. *Journal of Education for Teaching,* 1982, *8*(3), 276–283.

Shorter, C. A. *Early field experiences of sophomore students in two preservice teacher education programs.* Unpublished doctoral dissertation, University of Illinois, Urbana, IL, 1975.

*Singer, E. Women, children, and child-care centers. In Centre for Educational Research and Innovation (CERI), *Children and society: Issues for pre-school reforms.* Paris, France: Organisation for Economic Co-operation and Development (OECD), 1979. (ERIC Document Reproduction Service No. ED 207 679)

Vincent, N. L., & Hamby, T. M. *The Child Development Associate program: A guide to curriculum development.* Washington, DC: University Research Corporation, 1981.

Ward, E. H., and CDA Staff. The Child Development Associate Consortium's assessment system. *Young Children,* 1976, *31*(4), 244–55

Whitebook, M., Howes, C., Darrah, R., & Friedman, J. Caring for the caregivers: Staff burnout in child care. In L. G. Katz, C. H. Watkins, M. J. Spencer, and P. J. Wagemaker (Eds.), *Current topics in early childhood education* (Vol. 4). Norwood, NJ: Ablex Publishing Corporation, 1982. (ERIC Document Reproduction Service No. ED 188 764)

Woodhead, M. Preschool education in western Europe: Issues, policies, and trends. London: Longmans, 1979.

How to Obtain ERIC Documents

Within the chapters of this volume, citations that are asterisked and assigned ED numbers are indexed and abstracted in ERIC's *Resources in Education (RIE)*. Complete copies of most ERIC documents cited here are available in ERIC microfiche collections at approximately 700 libraries in the United States and other countries. For a list of ERIC collections near you, write ERIC/EECE, College of Education, University of Illinois, 805 W. Pennsylvania Ave., Urbana, IL 61801.

ERIC Documents may be ordered in either paper copy (PC), a photocopy of the original, or microfiche (MF), a transparent film card containing up to 98 pages of text. Please include ED number and specify PC or MF. Document prices given in *Resources in Education (RIE)* are subject to change. The current price schedule is provided below.

Paper Copy (per ED number): 1–25 pp., $2.15; 26–50 pp., $3.90; 51–75 pp., $5.65; 76–100 pp., $7.40. Add $1.75 for every additional 25 pp. or fraction thereof.

Microfiche (per ED number): 1–480 pp., $.97.

Prices shown do not include mailing, which must be added to all orders. First class postage (for all MF orders up to 32 MF): $.20 for 1–3 MF; $.37 for 4–8 MF; $.54 for 9–14 MF; $.71 for 15–18 MF; $.88 for 19–21 MF; $1.05 for 22–27 MF; $1.22 for 28–32 MF. UPS charges (for 33 or more MF and all PC orders): $1.55 for 1 lb; $1.93 for 2 lbs; $2.32 for 3 lbs; $2.70 for 4 lbs. (Each pound equals 75 PC pages or 75 MF.)

Send order and check to ERIC Document Reproduction Service, Computer Microfilm International, P.O. Box 190, Arlington, VA 22210.

The ERIC System and ERIC/EECE

The Educational Resources Information Center/Elementary and Early Childhood Education Clearinghouse (ERIC/EECE) is part of a system of 16 clearinghouses sponsored by the National Institute of Education to provide information about current research and developments in the field of education. The clearinghouses, each focusing on a specific area of education (such as junior colleges, teacher education, languages and linguistics), are located at universities and other institutions throughout the United States.

Each clearinghouse staff searches systematically to acquire current, significant documents relevant to education. These research studies, conference proceedings, curriculum guides, program descriptions and evaluations, and other publications are abstracted and indexed in *Resources in Education (RIE),* a monthly journal. *RIE* is available at libraries, or it may be ordered from the Superintendent of Documents, United States Government Printing Office, Washington, DC 20402. The documents themselves are reproduced on microfiche by the ERIC Document Reproduction Service for distribution to libraries and individuals.

Another ERIC publication is *Current Index to Journals in Education (CIJE),* a monthly guide to periodical literature which cites articles in more than 800 journals and magazines in the field of education. Most citations include annotations. Articles are indexed in *CIJE* by subject, author, and journal contents. *CIJE* is available at libraries or by subscription from Oryx Press, 2214 North Central at Encanto, Phoenix, AZ 85004.

The Clearinghouse on Elementary and Early Childhood Education (ERIC/EECE) publishes topical papers, bibliographies, resource lists, and newsletters for persons interested in child development, child care, and childhood education (for children from birth to age 12). The clearinghouse staff also answers individual information requests and provides computer searches of *RIE* and *CIJE* and other data bases. For more information, write ERIC/EECE, College of Education, University of Illinois, 805 W. Pennsylvania Ave., Urbana, IL 61801.

The ERIC Clearinghouses

ADULT, CAREER, AND
  VOCATIONAL EDUCATION
Ohio State University
1960 Kenny Road
Columbus, OH 43210
  (614) 486-3655

COUNSELING AND PERSONNEL
  SERVICES
The University of Michigan
School of Education Building
Room 2108, East Univ. & South
  Univ.
Ann Arbor, MI 48109
  (313) 764-9492

*ELEMENTARY AND EARLY
  CHILDHOOD EDUCATION
College of Education
University of Illinois
805 W. Pennsylvania Ave.
Urbana, IL 61801
  (217) 333-1386

EDUCATIONAL MANAGEMENT
University of Oregon
Eugene, OR 97403
  (503) 686-5043

HANDICAPPED AND GIFTED
  CHILDREN
The Council for Exceptional
  Children
1920 Association Drive
Reston, VA 22091
  (703) 620-3660

HIGHER EDUCATION
George Washington University
1 Dupont Circle N.W., Suite 630
Washington, DC 20036
  (202) 296-2597

INFORMATION RESOURCES
School of Education
Syracuse University
130 Huntington Hall
Syracuse, NY 13210
  (315) 423-3640

JUNIOR COLLEGES
University of California
  at Los Angeles
8118 Math Sciences Building
405 Hilgard Avenue
Los Angeles, CA 90024
  (213) 825-3931

LANGUAGES AND LINGUISTICS
Center for Applied Linguistics
3520 Prospect Street, N.W.
Washington, DC 20007
(202) 298-9292

READING AND
COMMUNICATION SKILLS
1111 Kenyon Road
Urbana, IL 61801
(217) 328-3870

RURAL EDUCATION AND
SMALL SCHOOLS
New Mexico State University,
Box 3AP
Las Cruces, NM 88003
(505) 646-2623

SCIENCE, MATHEMATICS,
AND ENVIRONMENTAL
EDUCATION
Ohio State University
1200 Chambers Road, Third Floor
Columbus, OH 43212
(614) 422-6717

SOCIAL STUDIES/SOCIAL
SCIENCE EDUCATION
855 Broadway
Boulder, CO 80302
(303) 492-8434

TEACHER EDUCATION
1 Dupont Circle N.W., Suite 610
Washington, DC 20036
(202) 393-2450

TESTS, MEASUREMENT AND
EVALUATION
Educational Testing Service
Princeton, NJ 08541
(609) 921-9000, Ext. 2176

URBAN EDUCATION
Teachers College, Box 40
Columbia University
New York, NY 10027
(212) 678-3437

---

* ERIC/EECE is responsible for acquiring research documents on the social, psychological, physical, educational, and cultural development of children from the prenatal period
through pre-adolescence (age 12). Theoretical and practical issues related to staff development,
administration, curriculum, and parent/community factors affecting programs for children of
this age group are also within the scope of the clearinghouse.

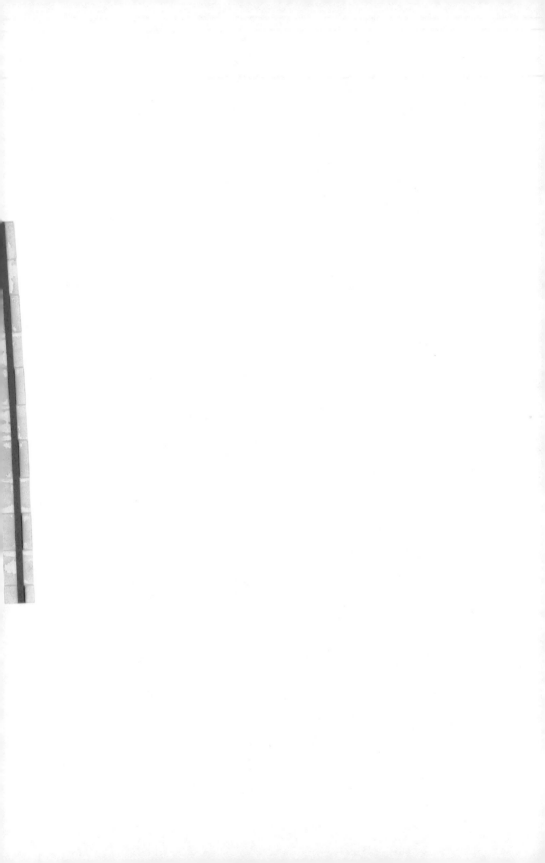